Guide
to Bible
Data

Guide to Bible Data

COMPILED BY

Andrew E. Hill

WORLD
PUBLISHING
Grand Rapids, Michigan 49418 U.S.A.

To My Parents

Contents

New Testament

Contents

Biblical Data

Preface

The present *Handbook* is intended to provide a needed supplement to standard Bible reference tools. The *Bible Lists* are the product of personal research in ancient and biblical studies during the past several years as a graduate student and sometime Bible teacher. The list format, adapted from the recent and most successful *Book of Lists,* is designed to afford convenient and rapid retrieval of vital biblical data without the verbiage that makes the customary Bible dictionary or encyclopedia valuable for other reasons. Sections I and II each consist of divisions on the Text, Chronology, and Genealogy of the Old and New Testaments respectively. These lists consolidate important biblical and extrabiblical chronological and genealogical materials, heretofore scattered throughout many different and oftentimes obscure sources, into a single handy catalog. Section III, Biblical Data, is an alphabetical arrangement of lists on a variety of subjects including prominent Bible characters, aspects of biblical culture, institutions, and natural environment, as well as metrology to name but a few.

The purpose of these *Bible Lists* is not only to furnish basic historical information to the student of the Bible as a biblical reference book but also to entertain and to encourage further individual investigation of the text. Particular effort has been made to offer an objectively balanced approach to the manifold complexities of biblical and extrabiblical chronology. In those instances where discrepancies exist in the scholarly understanding of biblical and related ancient chronology I have consciously undertaken to represent adequately the opposing viewpoints.

Although this precludes harmonization of the chronological data, it is nonetheless necessary to ensure the accurate representation of the various sources cited herein and to prevent any distortion of the very problematic nature of biblical and related ancient chronology. Likewise, the comparative chronologies have been compiled with the intention of demonstrating the wide range of dates possible for any given event within the framework of readily recognizable works of past and present biblical scholarship.

The diagrams and maps included in the book are complementary visual aids only, allowing the reader an immediate perspective on approximate geographical locations and/or distances and dimensions.

Where appropriate, the Hebrew, Aramaic, and Greek words underlying the English translation of items in Old and New Testament lists have been cited for those interested in pursuing the lexicography. Unless otherwise indicated, biblical references and English translations are based on the *New International Version* of the Bible.

Source notes are largely of an explanatory and nontechnical nature and have been deliberately limited. Bibliographic references and other resource citations identify the source or sources behind the chronological, historical, or other biblical data under consideration, or grant proper acknowledgment to the authors and/or editors and publishers of the volumes that may be cited herein.

In addition to the *Bible Lists* several blank pages have been appended to the end of the book so the reader may augment and to a degree personalize the work with his or her own lists and notations.

Finally, The Preacher says, "My son, of making many books there is no end, and much study wearies the body" (Eccles. 12:12, NIV). If this contribution to the "no end" of books helps alleviate even a fraction of the "weariness" that accompanies "much study" by supplying interesting and useful biblical information in a most accessible and readable format, while stimulating further individual Bible study, then it will have accomplished the intended purpose.

Andrew E. Hill
Ann Arbor, June, 1981

Abbreviations

Old Testament

Gen.	Genesis	Eccles.	Ecclesiastes
Exod.	Exodus	Song of Sol.	Song of Solomon
Lev.	Leviticus	Isa.	Isaiah
Num.	Numbers	Jer.	Jeremiah
Deut.	Deuteronomy	Lam.	Lamentations
Josh.	Joshua	Ezek.	Ezekiel
Judg.	Judges	Dan.	Daniel
Ruth	Ruth	Hos.	Hosea
1 Sam.	1 Samuel	Joel	Joel
2 Sam.	2 Samuel	Amos	Amos
1 Kings	1 Kings	Obad.	Obadiah
2 Kings	2 Kings	Jonah	Jonah
1 Chron.	1 Chronicles	Mic.	Micah
2 Chron.	2 Chronicles	Nah.	Nahum
Ezra	Ezra	Hab.	Habakkuk
Neh.	Nehemiah	Zeph.	Zephaniah
Esther	Esther	Hag.	Haggai
Job	Job	Zech.	Zechariah
Ps.	Psalms	Mal.	Malachi
Prov.	Proverbs		

Apocrypha

1 Esd.	1 Esdras
2 Esd.	2 Esdras
Tob.	Tobit

Jth.	Judith
Ad. Est.	Additions to Esther
Wisd. of Sol.	The Wisdom of Solomon
Ecclus.	Ecclesiasticus
Bar.	Baruch
Let. Jer.	Letter of Jeremiah
Azar.	Prayer of Azariah and the Song of the Three
Sus.	Susanna
Bel and Dragon	Bel and the Dragon
Pr. of Man.	Prayer of Manasseh
1 Macc.	1 Maccabees
2 Macc.	2 Maccabees

Pseudepigrapha

Jub.	Book of Jubilees
Arist.	Letter of Aristeas
A. & E.	Life of Adam and Eve
Mart. Isa.	Martyrdom of Isaiah
1 En.	1 Enoch
Test. XII Patr.	Testament of the Twelve Patriarchs
T. R.	Testament of Reuben
T. S.	Testament of Simeon
T. L.	Testament of Levi
T. Jud.	Testament of Judah
T. Iss.	Testament of Issachar
T. Z.	Testament of Zebulun
T. D.	Testament of Dan
T. N.	Testament of Naphtali
T. G.	Testament of Gad
T. A.	Testament of Asher
T. Jos.	Testament of Joseph
T. B.	Testament of Benjamin
Sib.	Sibylline Oracles
Ass. Mos.	Assumption of Moses
2 En.	2 Enoch (Book of the Secrets of Enoch)
2 Bar.	2 Baruch
3 Bar.	3 Baruch
4 Ez.	4 Ezra
Ps. Sol.	Psalms of Solomon
3 Macc.	3 Maccabees
4 Macc.	4 Maccabees
P. A.	Pirke Aboth
Ah.	Story of Ahikar
Zad.	Zadokite Work

New Testament

Matt.	Matthew	1 Tim.	1 Timothy
Mark	Mark	2 Tim.	2 Timothy
Luke	Luke	Titus	Titus
John	John	Philem.	Philemon
Acts	Acts	Heb.	Hebrews
Rom.	Romans	James	James
1 Cor.	1 Corinthians	1 Peter	1 Peter
2 Cor.	2 Corinthians	2 Peter	2 Peter
Gal.	Galatians	1 John	1 John
Eph.	Ephesians	2 John	2 John
Phil.	Philippians	3 John	3 John
Col.	Colossians	Jude	Jude
1 Thess.	1 Thessalonians	Rev.	Revelation
2 Thess.	2 Thessalonians		

Transliteration of Hebrew and Aramaic

א	'		ם מ	m
ב	b		ן נ	n
ג	g		ס	s
ד	d		ע	'
ה	h		ף פ	p
ו	w		ץ צ	ṣ (ts)
ז	z		ק	q
ח	ḥ (ch)		ר	r
ט	ṭ		שׂ	ś
י	y		שׁ	š (sh)
ך כ	k		ת	t
ל	l			

Transliteration of Greek

α	a	ν	n
β	b	ξ	x
γ	g	ο	o
δ	d	π	p
ε	e	ρ	r
ζ	z	σ, ς	s
η	ē	τ	t
θ	th	υ	u
ι	i	φ	ph
κ	k	χ	ch
λ	l	ψ	ps
μ	m	ω	ō

Note: Before another γ or κ or χ, γ is pronounced *ng* (e.g., αγγελος = *angelos*).

At the beginning of a word ρ is pronounced *rh* (e.g., ῥητορ = *rhētor*).

Old Testament

The Text of the Old Testament

The Books of the OT

Hebrew Order	English Order
Torah	**Law**
Genesis	Genesis
Exodus	Exodus
Leviticus	Leviticus
Numbers	Numbers
Deuteronomy	Deuteronomy
Former Prophets	**History**
Joshua	Joshua
Judges	Judges
1 Samuel	Ruth
2 Samuel	1 Samuel
1 Kings	2 Samuel
2 Kings	1 Kings
Latter Prophets	2 Kings
	1 Chronicles
Isaiah	2 Chronicles
Jeremiah	Ezra
Ezekiel	Nehemiah
Hosea	Esther

Hebrew Order	English Order
Joel	Poetry
Amos	Job
Obadiah	Psalms
Jonah	Proverbs
Micah	Ecclesiastes
Nahum	Song of Solomon
Habakkuk	
Zephaniah	Major Prophets
Haggai	Isaiah
Zechariah	Jeremiah
Malachi	Lamentations
Writings	Ezekiel
Psalms	Daniel
Job	Minor Prophets
Proverbs	
Ruth	Hosea
Song of Solomon	Joel
Ecclesiastes	Amos
Lamentations	Obadiah
Esther	Jonah
Daniel	Micah
Ezra	Nahum
Nehemiah	Habakkuk
1 Chronicles	Zephaniah
2 Chronicles	Haggai
	Zechariah
	Malachi

Authors and Dates

Book	Hebrew Title	Author	Dates Concerned
Genesis	"By way of beginning"	anonymous	creation–Joseph
Exodus	"Names"	anonymous	Moses–exodus

24

Book	Hebrew Title	Author	Dates Concerned
Leviticus	"And he called"	anonymous	Mt. Sinai-Law
Numbers	"In the wilderness"	anonymous	Mt. Sinai-Moab
Deuteronomy	"These are the words"	anonymous	Moab-Moses' death
Joshua	Joshua	anonymous	Joshua's conquest
Judges	Judges	anonymous	rule of judges
Ruth	Ruth	anonymous	rule of judges
1 Samuel	1 Samuel	anonymous	1100-1010 B.C.
2 Samuel	2 Samuel	anonymous	1010-970 B.C.
1 Kings	1 Kings	anonymous	970-853 B.C.
2 Kings	2 Kings	anonymous	853-560 B.C.
1 Chronicles	"Words of the days"	anonymous	Adam to David
2 Chronicles	"Words of the days"	anonymous	970-539 B.C.
Ezra	Ezra	anonymous	539-450 B.C.
Nehemiah	Nehemiah	Nehemiah	445-410 B.C.
Esther	Esther	anonymous	485-465 B.C.
Job	Job	anonymous	?
Psalms	"Praises"	David, Asaph, Heman, Ethan, Solomon, Moses, and others	10th cent. B.C. and later
Proverbs	Proverbs	Solomon, Agur, King Lemuel	10th cent. B.C. and later
Ecclesiastes	"The Preacher"	the preacher	?
Song of Solomon	"Song of Songs"	Solomon	970-930 B.C.
Isaiah	Isaiah	Isaiah	755-695 B.C.
Jeremiah	Jeremiah	Jeremiah	627-587 B.C.
Lamentations	"How!"	anonymous	587/86 B.C.
Ezekiel	Ezekiel	Ezekiel	593-573 B.C.
Daniel	Daniel	Daniel	605-536 B.C.
Hosea	Hosea	Hosea	755-720 B.C.
Joel	Joel	Joel	?
Amos	Amos	Amos	760-750 B.C.
Obadiah	Obadiah	Obadiah	?
Jonah	Jonah	Jonah	770-750 B.C.
Micah	Micah	Micah	745-695 B.C.
Nahum	Nahum	Nahum	630-612 B.C.

Book	Hebrew Title	Author	Dates Concerned
Habakkuk	Habakkuk	Habakkuk	?
Zephaniah	Zephaniah	Zephaniah	640–609 B.C.
Haggai	Haggai	Haggai	520 B.C.
Zechariah	Zechariah	Zechariah	520 B.C.
Malachi	Malachi	Malachi	500–450 B.C.

Chapters/Verses/Words

Book	Chapters	Verses	Words
Law			
Genesis	50	1,533	38,267
Exodus	40	1,213	32,692
Leviticus	27	859	24,546
Numbers	36	1,288	32,902
Deuteronomy	34	958	28,461
History			
Joshua	24	658	18,858
Judges	21	618	18,976
Ruth	4	85	2,578
1 Samuel	31	810	25,061
2 Samuel	24	695	20,612
1 Kings	22	816	24,524
2 Kings	25	719	23,532
1 Chronicles	29	941	20,369
2 Chronicles	36	822	26,074
Ezra	10	280	7,441
Nehemiah	13	406	10,483
Esther	10	167	5,637
Poetry			
Job	42	1,070	10,102

Figures for the chapters, verses, and words are based on the Synopsis of the Books of the Bible in the Authorized Version of 1611 (Philadelphia: National Bible Press, n.d.).

Book	Chapters	Verses	Words
Psalms	150	2,461	43,743
Proverbs	31	915	15,043
Ecclesiastes	12	222	5,584
Song of Solomon	8	117	2,661
Major Prophets			
Isaiah	66	1,292	37,044
Jeremiah	52	1,364	42,659
Lamentations	5	154	3,415
Ezekiel	48	1,273	39,407
Daniel	12	357	11,606
Minor Prophets			
Hosea	14	197	5,175
Joel	3	73	2,034
Amos	9	146	4,217
Obadiah	1	21	670
Jonah	4	48	1,321
Micah	7	105	3,153
Nahum	3	47	1,285
Habakkuk	3	56	1,476
Zephaniah	3	53	1,617
Haggai	2	38	1,131
Zechariah	14	211	6,444
Malachi	4	55	1,782
Totals	929	23,138	602,582

Source Books Cited in the OT

1. Book of the Wars of the Lord, Num. 21:14
2. Book of Jashar, Josh. 10:13; 2 Sam. 1:18
3. Book of the Annals of Solomon, 1 Kings 11:41
4. Book of the Annals of the Kings of Judah, 1 Kings 14:29; 15:7, 23; 22:45; 2 Kings 8:23; 12:19; 14:18; 15:6, 36; 16:19; 20:20; 21:17, 25
5. Book of the Annals of the Kings of Israel, 1 Kings 14:19; 15:31; 16:5, 14, 20, 27; 22:39; 2 Kings 1:18; 10:34; 13:8, 12; 14:15, 28; 15:11, 15, 21, 26, 31; 1 Chron. 9:1; 2 Chron. 20:34

6. Records of the Chronicles of King David, 1 Chron. 27:24
7. Records of Samuel the Seer, 1 Chron. 29:29
8. Records of Nathan the Prophet, 1 Chron. 29:29; 2 Chron. 9:29
9. Records of Gad the Seer, 1 Chron. 29:29
10. Prophecy of Ahijah the Shilonite, 2 Chron. 9:29
11. Visions of Iddo the Seer, 2 Chron. 9:29; 12:15; 13:22
12. Records of Shemaiah the Prophet, 2 Chron. 12:15
13. Book of the Kings of Judah and Israel, 2 Chron. 16:11; 25:26; 28:26; 32:32

    Book of the Kings of Israel and Judah, 2 Chron. 27:7; 35:27; 36:8
14. Annals of Jehu the Son of Hanani, 2 Chron. 20:34
15. Annotations on the Book of Kings, 2 Chron. 24:27
16. Events of Uzziah's reign by Isaiah the Prophet, 2 Chron. 26:22
17. Annals of the Kings of Israel, 2 Chron. 33:18
18. Records of the Seers, 2 Chron. 33:19
19. Directions of David and Solomon, 2 Chron. 35:4

OT Canon

1. The Hebrew OT contained 24 (or 22, depending upon the division used) books, equivalent to the 39 books of the Protestant OT. Samuel, Kings, the 12 Minor Prophets, Ezra-Nehemiah, and Chronicles were all considered single books.
2. This Hebrew canon, although it had been accepted for many years by the Jews, was "officially" confirmed by the Council of Jamnia in A.D. 90.
3. This canon of 24 books was recognized by Philo, Josephus, Melito, Tertullian, Origen, Eusebius, Jerome, and Augustine.
4. No book of the Apocrypha was included in the Hebrew OT.
5. Books of the Apocrypha were included in later editions of the Septuagint (LXX), the Greek translation of the Hebrew OT. The Septuagint was probably first translated in Alexandria sometime around 250 B.C.
6. The OT of Jerome's Latin Vulgate was a translation of the OT from the Septuagint, not the Hebrew OT. Naturally Jerome included the books of the Apocrypha contained in the Greek Septuagint in his Latin Bible. Interestingly enough it is clear from Jerome's other works that he did not consider the books of the Apocrypha canonical.

7. At the time of the Reformation (16th century A.D.), Luther and Calvin recognized only the Hebrew OT as canonical. Thus Protestants recognize an Old Testament canon of 39 books, with the Apocrypha considered valuable for "personal edification." The Roman Catholic Church, during the Council of Trent (1545-63), officially adopted Jerome's Vulgate as the Bible of the Church. Hence the Catholic Church recognizes an Old Testament canon of 39 books, plus the 14 books of the Apocrypha, since these books were included in Jerome's Vulgate.

Oral Law

1. The Midrash
   The earliest method used for teaching the oral law. The Midrash was a running commentary on the biblical text. This Midrash method was employed by Ezra and his associates when Ezra read the written Law to the Jews who had returned to Jerusalem from exile (cf. Neh. 8:1-8). This method of teaching was adopted by the Hebrew scribes and was the dominant teaching method of the rabbis until ca. 270 B.C.
2. The Midrash Halakah
   A Midrash exposition which yielded a legal teaching.
3. The Midrash Haggadah
   A Midrash exposition which was nonlegal, ethical, or devotional in nature.
4. The Zugoth
   A new method that rivaled the Midrash method beginning in the middle of the 3rd century B.C. Five great "pairs" of teachers promoted this method during the period between the 3rd and 1st centuries B.C. The most famous were Shammai and Hillel at the end of the 1st century B.C. The Zugoth method involved the teaching of the oral law without reference to the order of the Hebrew Scriptures. Divorced from the established sequence of the Hebrew Scriptures, the oral law could be taught by means of repetition. Thus the name "Mishnah" (from the Hebrew *šnh,* "to repeat") was attached to this oral teaching of the Law.
5. The Mishnah
   An early form of the Jewish oral law or tradition. It was gradually

compiled into written form between the 2nd century B.C. and the 2nd century A.D. This oral law became known as the "fence" or "hedge" (Hebrew, *gdr*) around the written law. The Jews developed this complex system of oral laws as a safeguard to ensure the strict adherence to the written law and thus to prevent future punishment and exile at the hands of their enemies for failure to keep God's commandments. The Pharisaic elements of Judaism were great proponents of the oral tradition.

6. The Tannaim

   A term used for the teachers of the Mishnah.

7. The Talmud

   The final form of the oral law, now written, including legal discussions, verse by verse analysis and exegesis, proverbs, prayers, fables, and Jewish folklore. Between the 3rd and 6th centuries A.D. the Mishnah, along with all its exegetical and homiletical additions, was gradually compiled into what is known as the Talmud. Two separate versions of the Talmud were produced by Jewish rabbinic schools: the Babylonian Talmud compiled by Jews in Babylonia who had not returned to Jerusalem with the other exiles; and the Palestinian Talmud edited by Jews who had returned to Palestine after the exile. The Talmud is a massive collection of Jewish law with corresponding commentary. The Babylonian Talmud came to be recognized as the authoritative source for the regulation of Jewish religious and community life.

8. The Gemara

   A term used by many as a synonym for the Talmud. Technically, the Gemara is the final collection of all the commentary, analysis, and discussion which together with the oral laws of the Mishnah comprise the Talmud.

9. The Amoraim

   Special scholars in the rabbinic schools designated to interpret, explain, discuss, and harmonize the oral teachings with the biblical text. They were active from the 3rd to 5th centuries A.D. and were largely responsible for the composition of the Talmud.

10. The Tosefta

    Additional teaching and commentary on the oral law produced by rival rabbinic schools but never incorporated into the Mishnah or Talmud. Though not included in the Mishnah or Talmud, this "additional" teaching is often referred to in discussions of the oral law.

11. The Baraitha

Another independent collection of teaching and commentary on the oral law. This, too, was "external" material; that is, it was never incorporated into the Mishnah or Talmud. Some call the Baraitha the "apocrypha" of the Mishnah.

Miscellaneous Data

1. The OT is comprised of 39 books and was written by at least 40 different authors between a period from 1400 or 1300 B.C. to about 400 or 350 B.C.

2. The OT was written in ancient Hebrew except for Gen. 31:47; Jer. 10:11; Ezra 4:8-6:18 and 7:12-26; and Dan. 2:4-7:28 which were written in Aramaic. There are approximately 9,000 separate lexical items in the OT.

3. The ancient Hebrew texts were originally consonantal. Scribal schools continued the transmission of the consonantal texts until the time of the Masoretes (ca. A.D. 500-900), who added vowel signs, or points, to insure the correct reading of the text.

4. Vowel points, punctuation, and verse divisions were introduced in the Hebrew Old Testament about A.D. 900 by the Masoretes. Chapter divisions in the Old Testament began about A.D. 1244 with Cardinal Hugh of St. Cher.

5. Literally thousands of manuscripts of the OT written in Hebrew, Greek, Latin, and other languages are in existence today. Most of these date from A.D. 900 or later. However, with the discovery of the Dead Sea Scrolls portions of the OT text dating back to 200-100 B.C. are now extant.

Old Testament Chronology

Third Dynasty of Ur

King	Date B.C.
Ur-Nammu	2113-2096
Šulgi	2095-2048
Amar-Su'en	2047-2039
Šu-Sin	2038-2030
Ibbi-Sin	2029-2006

Hammurabi Dynasty of Babylon

King	Date B.C.
Sumuabum	1894-1881
Sumulael	1880-1845
Sabium	1844-1831

Dates of Kings' reigns are approximate and are based on A. L. Oppenheim, *Ancient Mesopotamia: Portrait of a Dead Civilization* (Chicago: University of Chicago Press, 1964).

King	Date B.C.
Apil-Sin	1830-1813
Sin-Muballit	1812-1793
Hammurabi	1792-1750
Samsu-iluna	1749-1712
Abi-Ešuh	1711-1684
Ammiditana	1683-1647
Ammisaduqa	1646-1626
Samsuditana	1625-1595

Egyptian Kingdoms and Kings

Kingdom/King	Date B.C.	Years of Reign
Early Dynastic Period	3100-2686	
1st Dynasty	3100-2890	
Men/Menes		
Iti/Athothis		
Iti/Athothis		47
Iterty		
Khasty		55-60
Merpebia/Miebis		7
Irynetjer		8
Qaa		25
2nd Dynasty	2890-2686	
Hetep		
Nubnefer		
Nynetjer		45-47
Weneg/Wadjnes		19
Sened/Sethenes		

Egyptian chronologies will vary 5-10 years in the later periods and even more in the earlier periods. Dates based on I. E. S. Edwards et al., eds., *The Cambridge Ancient History,* 3rd ed., vol. 1, pt. 2; vol. 2, pts. 1 and 2 (Cambridge: Cambridge University Press, 1971, 1973, 1975).

Kingdom/King	Date B.C.	Years of Reign
Peribsen		
Aka ?		
Neferkasokar ?		8
lacuna in sources		21 ?
Khasekhemwy		17
Old Kingdom	2686-2181	
3rd Dynasty	2686-2613	
Nebka	2686-2667	19
Djoser	2667-2648	19
Djoser Teti	2648-2643	5
lacuna in sources	2643-2637	6
Huni/Nysuteh ?	2637-2613	24
4th Dynasty	2613-2495	
Sneferu	2613-2589	24
Cheops	2589-2566	23
Redjedef	2566-2558	8
Chephren	2558-2533	25 ?
Baufre ?		
Mycerinus		28 ?
Shepseskaf		4
Dedefptah ?/Thamphthis		2
5th Dynasty	2494-2341	
Userkaf	2494-2487	7
Sahure	2487-2473	14
Neferirkare Kakai	2473-2463	10
Shepseskare Isi	2463-2456	7
Neferefre	2456-2449	7 ?
Nyuserre	2449-2418	31
Menkauhor Akauhor	2418-2410	8
Djedkare Isesi	2410-2371	39
Unas	2371-2341	30

Kingdom/King	Date B.C.	Years of Reign
6th Dynasty	2341-2181	
Teti	2341-2329	12
Userkare	2329-2328	1 ?
Meryre Phiops I	2328-2279	49
Merenre Antyemsaf I	2279-2265	14
Neferkare Phiops II		94 ?
Merenre Antyemsaf II		1
Netjerykare		
Menkare ?/Nitocris		2 ?
First Intermediate Period	2181-2040	
7th Dynasty	2181-2173	
Neferkare the Younger		
Neferkare Neby		
Djedkare Shemay		
Neferkare Khendu		
Meryenhor		
Neferkamin		
Nykare		
Neferkare Tereru		
Neferkahor		
8th Dynasty	2173-2160	
Wadjkare Pepysonbe		
Neferkamin Anu		
Kakare Ibi		
Neferkare		
Neferkauhor Kapuibi		
Neferirkare		
9th Dynasty	2160-2130	
10th Dynasty	2130-2040	
Middle Kingdom	2133-1786	
11th Dynasty	2133-1991	
Mentuhotep I/Inyotef I	2133-2118	15

Kingdom/King	Date B.C.	Years of Reign
Inyotef II	2117-2069	48
Inyotef III	2068-2061	7
Nebhepetre Mentuhotep II	2060-2010	50
Sankhkare Mentuhotep III	2009-1998	11
Nebtowyre Mentuhotep IV	1997-1991	6
12th Dynasty	1991-1786	
Ammenemes I	1991-1962	29
Sesostris I (includes co-regency)	1971-1928	43
Ammenemes II (includes co-regency)	1929-1895	34
Sesostris II (includes co-regency)	1897-1878	19
Sesostris III	1878-1843	35
Ammenemes III	1842-1797	45
Ammenemes IV	1797-1790	7
Sobkneferu	1789-1786	3
Second Intermediate Period	1786-1570	
13th Dynasty	1786-1633	
14th Dynasty	1786-1603	
76 kings		184
15th Dynasty/Hyksos	1674-1567	
Mayebre Sheshi		
Meruserre Yakubher		
Seuserenre Khyan		
Auserre Apophis I		
Aqenenre Apophis II		
Asehre Khamudy (?)		
16th Dynasty/Hyksos	1684-1567	
Anather		
Semqen		
Khauserre		
Seket		
Ahetepre		

Kingdom/King	Date B.C.	Years of Reign
Sekhaenre		
Amu		
Nebkhepeshre Apophis (III) ?		
17th Dynasty	1650-1570	
New Kingdom	1570-1085	
18th Dynasty	1570-1320	
Amosis	1570-1546	24
Amenophis I	1546-1526	20
Thutmose I	1525-1512	13
Thutmose II	1512-1504	8
Hatshepsut	1504-1482	22
Thutmose III (includes co-regency)	1504-1450	54
Amenophis II	1450-1425	25
Thutmose IV	1425-1417	8
Amenophis III	1417-1379	36
Amenophis IV/Akhenaton	1379-1362	17
Semenkhkare (includes co-regency)	1364-1361	3
Tutankhamen	1361-1352	9
Ay	1352-1348	4
Haremhab	1348-1320	28
19th Dynasty	1320-1200	
Rameses I	1320-1318	2
Seti I	1318-1304	14
Rameses II	1304-1237	67
Merneptah	1236-1223	13
Amenmesses	1222-1217 ?	5
Seti II	1216-1210 ?	6
Siptah/Tewosret	1208-1200 ?	8
20th Dynasty	1200-1085	
Sethnakhte	1200-1198	2
Rameses III	1198-1166	32
Rameses IV	1166-1160	6

37

Kingdom/King	Date B.C.	Years of Reign
Rameses V	1160-1156	4
Rameses VI	1156-1148	8
Rameses VII	1148-1147	1
Rameses VIII	1147-1140	7
Rameses IX	1140-1121	19
Rameses X	1121-1113	8
Rameses XI	1113-1085	28
Late Period	1085-525	
21st Dynasty	1085-945	
Smendes	1085-1061	24
Psusennes I	1061-1015	46
Nephereheres	1015-1011	4
Amenophthis	1011-1002	9
Osochor	1002-996	6
Psinaches	996-987	9
Siamon	987-959	28
Psusennes II	959-945	14
22nd Dynasty	945-730	
Sheshonk I	945-924	21
Osorkon I	924-888	36
Takelot I	888-865	23
Osorkon II	865-836	29
Sheshonk II	836	1
Takelot II	835-811	24
Sheshonk III	811-772	39
Pemay	772-766	6
Sheshonk IV	766-730	36
23rd Dynasty/Lybians	817-730	
24th Dynasty	730-715	
25th Dynasty/Nubians	715-656	
Shabaka	715-701	14
Shabataka	701-690	11

Kingdom/King	Date B.C.	Years of Reign
Taharka	689-664	25
Tanutaman	664-656	8
26th Dynasty	664-525	
Psammetik I	664-609	55
Necho	609-594	15
Psammetik II	594-588	6
Apries/Hophra	588-568	20
Amasis	568-526	42
Psammetik III	526-525	1
Persian Period	525-332	
27th Dynasty	525-404	
28th Dynasty	404-398	
Amyrtaeus II	404-398	6
29th Dynasty	398-378	
Nepherites	398-390	8
Achoris	390-378	12
30th Dynasty	378-343	
Nectanebo I	378-361	17
Nectanebo II	359-343	16
31st Dynasty	343-332	

The Hittite Kings

	Date B.C.	
King	(CAH/Gurney)	(Ceram)
Pitkhanas of Kussara	?	?
Anittas of Kussara	?	ca. 1900
Old Kingdom		
Tudhaliyas I ?	1740-1710	1740-1710
Pu-sarrumas ?	1710-1680	1710-1680
Labarnas I	1680-1650	1680-1650
Labarnas II/Hattusilis I	1650-1620	1650-1620
Mursilis I	1620-1590	1620-1590
Hantilis I	1590-1560	1590-1560
Zidantas I	1560-1550	1560-1550
Ammunas	1550-1530	1550-1520
Huzziyas I	1530-1525	1530-1525
Telipinus	1525-1500	1525-1500
Alluwamnas	1500-1490	1500-1490
Hantilis II ?	1490-1480	1490-1480
Zidantas II ?	1480-1470	1480-1470
Huzziyas II ?	1470-1460	1470-1460
Empire		
Tudhaliyas II	1460-1440	1460-1440
Arnuwandas I	1440-1420	1440-1420
Hatusilis II	1420-1400	1420-1400
Tudhaliyas III	1400-1380	1400-1385
Suppiluliumas I	1380-1346	1375-1335
Arnuwandas II	1346-1345	1385-1375
Arnuwandas III	——	1335-1334

According to Ceram, Arnuwandas II preceded Suppiluliumas I and Arnuwandas III succeeded Suppiluliumas I. CAH/Gurney record no Arnuwandas III. In CAH/Gurney, Arnuwandas III follows Tudhaliyas; in Ceram, Arnuwandas IV follows Tudhaliyas IV.

CAH = I. E. S. Edwards et al., eds., *The Cambridge Ancient History,* 3rd ed., vol. 1, pt. 2; vol. 2, pts. 1 and 2 (Cambridge: Cambridge University Press, 1971, 1973, 1975).

Gurney = O. R. Gurney, *The Hittites,* 2nd ed. (Baltimore: Penguin, 1954).

Ceram = C. W. Ceram, *The Secret of the Hittites* (New York: Schocken, 1973).

King	Date B.C.	
	(CAH/Gurney)	(Ceram)
Mursilis II	1345-1315	1334-1306
Muwatallis	1315-1296	1306-1282
Urhi-Teshub/Mursilis III	1296-1289	1282-1275
Hattusilis III	1289-1265	1275-1250
Tudhaliyas IV	1265-1235	1250-1220
Arnuwandas III/IV	1235-1215	1220-1190
Suppiluliumas II	1215- ?	ca. 1190

Kings of Damascus

King	Date B.C.
Rezon	ca. 940-880
Ben-Hadad I	ca. 880-842
Hazael	ca. 842-806
Ben-Hadad II	ca. 806-770
Domination by Jeroboam II	ca. 770-750
Rezin	ca. 750-732
Fall of Damascus to Tiglath-Pileser III	732

Dates for Kings of Damascus based on J. Bright, *A History of Israel*, 2nd ed. (Philadelphia: Westminster, 1972).

Empires of the Ancient World

Empire	Date
Assyria	740-612 B.C.
Babylonia	612-539 B.C.
Medo-Persia	539-331 B.C.
Macedonia	330-323 B.C.
Rome	246 B.C.-A.D. 476

41

Kings of Assyria

King	Date B.C.
Enlil-naṣir II	1432-1427
Aššur-nirari II	1426-1420
Aššur-bel-nišešu	1419-1411
Aššur-rim-nišešu	1410-1403
Aššur-nadin-ahhe II	1402-1393
Eriba-Adad I	1392-1366
Aššur-uballiṭ I	1365-1330
Enlil-nirari	1329-1320
Arik-den-ili	1319-1308
Adad-nirari I	1307-1275
Shalmaneser I	1274-1245
Tukulti-Ninurta I	1244-1208
Aššur-nadin-apli	1207-1204
Aššur-nirari III	1203-1198
Enlil-kudurri-uṣur	1197-1193
Ninurta-apli-Ekur	1192-1180
Aššur-dan I	1179-1134
Aššur-reš-iši I	1133-1116
Tiglath-Pileser I	1115-1077
Ašarid-apil-Ekur	1076-1075
Aššur-bel-kala	1074-1057
Eriba-Adad II	1056-1055
Šamši-Adad IV	1054-1051
Aššurnaṣirpal I	1050-1032
Shalmaneser II	1031-1020
Aššur-nirari IV	1019-1014
Aššur-rabi II	1013-973
Aššur-reš-iši II	972-968
Tiglath-Pileser II	967-935
Aššur-dan II	934-912
Adad-nirari II	911-891
Tukulti-Ninurta II	890-884
Aššurnaṣirpal II	883-859

Dates will vary 1-5 years depending on the source. This chronology is based on A. L. Oppenheim, *Ancient Mesopotamia: Portrait of a Dead Civilization* (Chicago: University of Chicago Press, 1964).

King	Date B.C.
Shalmaneser III	858-824
Šamši-Adad V	823-811
Adad-nirari III	810-783
Shalmaneser IV	782-773
Aššur-dan III	772-755
Aššur-nirari V	754-745
Tiglath-Pileser III	744-727
Shalmaneser V	726-722
Sargon II	721-705
Sennacherib	704-681
Esarhaddon	680-669
Aššurbanipal	668-627
Aššur-etel-ilani	626-623?
Sin-šumu-lišir	623?
Sin-šar-iškun	623-612?
Aššur-uballit II	611-609?

Kings of Babylonia

King	Date B.C.
9th Dynasty of Babylon	732-626
Nabu-mukin-zeri	732-730
Tiglath-Pileser/Pulu	729-727
Shalmaneser/Ululai	726-723
Merodach-Baladan II	722-711
Sargon II	710-705
Sennacherib	705-704
Marduk-zakir-šumi II	703

Dates for the kings of the 9th Dynasty of Babylon will vary 1-2 years, depending on the source. This chronology is based on A. L. Oppenheim, *Ancient Mesopotamia: Portrait of a Dead Civilization* (Chicago: University of Chicago Press, 1964).

King	Date B.C.
Merodach-Baladan II	703
Bel-ibni	702-701
Aššur-nadin-šumi	700-695
Nergal-ušezib	694
Mušezib-Marduk	693-690
Sennacherib	689-681
Esarhaddon	680-669
Šamaš-šum-ukin	668-648
Kandalanu	647-627
interregnum	626
Chaldean Dynasty	625-539
Nabopolassar	625-605
Nebuchadnezzar II	604-562
Evil-Merodach	561-560
Neriglissar	559-556
Labaši-Marduk (3 mos.)	556
Nabonidus	555-539
Belshazzar	? -539

Kings of Medo-Persia

King	Date B.C.
Cyrus II	539-530
Cambyses II	529-522
Bardiya (6 mos.)	522
Nebuchadnezzar III (3 mos.)	522
Nebuchadnezzar IV (3 mos.)	521
Darius I	521-486

The dates for the kings of Persia are based on A. L. Oppenheim, *Ancient Mesopotamia: Portrait of a Dead Civilization* (Chicago: University of Chicago Press, 1964).

King	Date B.C.
Xerxes I	485–465
Bel-Shimanni	482
Shamash-Eriba	482
Artaxerxes I	464–424
Darius II	423–405
Artaxerxes II Mnemon	404–359
Artaxerxes III Ochus	358–338
Arses	337–336
Darius III	335–331

Ptolemies of Egypt

King	Date B.C.
Ptolemy I Soter I	323–282
Ptolemy II Philadelphus	284–246
Ptolemy III Euergetes I	246–222
Ptolemy IV Philopator	222–205
Ptolemy V Epiphanes	204–180
Ptolemy VI Philometor	180–145
Ptolemy VII Neos Philopator	145
Ptolemy VIII Euergetes II (Physcon)	145–116
Ptolemy IX Soter II (Lathyrus)	116–108
	88–80
Ptolemy X Alexander I	108–88
Ptolemy XI Alexander II	80
Ptolemy XII Auletes	80–51
Cleopatra VII	51–30

Dates for the Ptolemies are based on S. A. Cook et al., eds., *The Cambridge Ancient History,* 2nd ed., vol. 7 (Cambridge: Cambridge University Press, 1954).

Seleucids of Syria

King	Date B.C.
Seleucus I Nicator	312-280
Antiochus I Soter	280-261
Antiochus II Theos	261-247
Seleucus II Callinius	247-226
Seleucus III Soter	226-223
Antiochus III	223-187
Seleucus IV Philopator	187-175
Antiochus IV Epiphanes	175-163
Antiochus V Eupator	163-162
Demetrius I Soter	162-150
Alexander I Balas	150-145
Demetrius II Nicator	145-139, 129-125
Antiochus VI Epiphanes	145-142
Antiochus VII Sidetes	139-129
Alexander II Zabinas	128-123
Antiochus VIII Grypus	125-96
Seleucus V	125
Antiochus IX Cyzicenus	115-95
Seleucus VI Epiphanes Nicator	96-95
Antiochus X Eusebes Philopator	95-83
Antiochus XI Philadelphus	92
Philippus I Philadelphus	92-83
Demetrius III Eukairos Philopator Soter	95-88
Antiochus XII Dionysus	87-84
Tigranes of Armenia	83-69
Antiochus XIII Asiaticus	69-64
Philippus II	65-64

Dates for the Seleucids based on S. A. Cook et al., eds., *The Cambridge Ancient History*, 2nd ed., vols. 7 and 9 (Cambridge: Cambridge University Press, 1954, 1951).

The Maccabees/Hasmoneans

Ruler	Date B.C.
Judas ben Mattathias	d. 166
Eleazar	d. 161
Judas Maccabeus	d. 161
John	d. 160
Jonathan	153-42
Simon	142-34
John Hyrcanus	134-06
Aristobulus I	104-03
Alexander Jannaeus	103-76
Salome Alexandra	76-67
Aristobulus II	67-63
Hyrcanus II	63-40

Other chronologies will vary one or even two years, depending on the source. This chronology is based on R. F. Surburg, *Introduction to the Intertestamental Period* (St. Louis: Concordia, 1975).

Biblical and Extrabiblical Events 2350–550 B.C.

Event	Date B.C.
Pyramid Texts	2350-2175
Coffin Texts	2150-1700
Larsa Dynasty	2025-1763
Naplanum	2025-2005
Emişum	2004-1977
Samium	1976-1942
Zabaia	1941-1933
Gungunum	1932-1906
Abisare	1905-1895
Sumuel	1894-1866
Nur-Adad	1865-1850

Dates before 1000 B.C. are approximate. See also the several specific OT chronologies.

47

Event	Date B.C.
Sin-iddinam	1849-1843
Sin-eribam	1842-1841
Sin-iqišham	1840-1836
Ṣilli-Adad	1835
Warad-Sin	1834-1823
Rim-Sin I	1822-1763
Isin Dynasty	2017-1794
Išbi-Irra	2017-1985
Šu-ilišu	1984-1975
Iddin-Dagan	1974-1954
Išme-Dagan	1953-1935
Lipit-Ištar	1934-1924
Ur-Ninurta	1923-1896
Bur-Sin	1895-1875
Lipit-Enlil	1874-1870
Erra-imitti	1869-1862
Enlil-bani	1861-1838
Zambia	1837-1835
Iter-piša	1834-1831
Ur-dukuga	1830-1828
Sin-magir	1827-1817
Damiq-ilišu	1816-1794
Sargon I	ca. 1850
Šamši-Adad	1813-1787
Mari Age	1750-1697
Hyksos in Egypt	1700-1570
Hittites	1700-1200
Old Kingdom	1700-1400
Empire	1400-1200
Kassite Dynasty	1550-1150
Early Assyria	1700-1433
Belu-bani	1700-1691
Libaia	1690-1674
Šarma-Adad I	1673-1662
Iptar-Sin	1661-1650
Bazaia	1649-1622
Lullaia	1621-1618

Event	Date B.C.
Kidin-Ninua	1615-1602
Šarma-Adad II	1601-1599
Erišum III	1598-1586
Šamši-Adad II	1585-1580
Išme-Dagan II	1579-1564
Šamši-Adad III	1563-1548
Aššur-nirari I	1547-1522
Puzur-Aššur III	1521-1498
Enlil-naṣir I	1497-1485
Nur-ili	1484-1473
Aššur-šaduni	1473
Aššur-rabi I	1472-1453
Aššur-nadin-ahhe I	1452-1433
Mycenean Golden Age	1500-1400
Golden Age of Ugarit	1400-1300
Amarna Age	1400-1300
Hittites defeat Mitanni	ca. 1370
End of Mitannian kingdom	ca. 1328
Seti I campaigns in Palestine	1345-1315
Battle of Kadesh	1296
Merneptah in Palestine	ca. 1230
Greeks colonize Asia Minor	ca. 1200
Migration of sea peoples	ca. 1195
Aramean migration in Mesopotamia	1110-1070
Battle of Taanach	1100
Philistines invade central Palestine	1010
Solomon's temple completed	ca. 966
Division of the kingdom of Israel	930
Jehu submits to Shalmaneser III	842
Olympic Games begin	776
First Messenian War	770
Tiglath-Pileser III appoints Hoshea king	732
Nubians gain control of Egypt	725
Fall of Israel to Assyria	722
Sennacherib at Jerusalem	701
Esarhaddon conquers Egypt	670
Aššurbanipal destroys Thebes	667

Old Testament

Event	Date B.C.
Second Messenian War	ca. 650
Lydians conquer Greek Asian cities	650-550
The Draconian Laws	621
Fall of Nineveh	612
Battle of Carchemish	605
Nebuchadnezzar II raids Jerusalem	602
Nebuchadnezzar II raids Jerusalem	597
Nebuchadnezzar II sacks Jerusalem	587/86
Cyrus takes over the Median kingdom	550

Biblical and Extrabiblical Events 549–2 B.C.

Event	Date B.C.
Cyrus revolts against Astyages; Medes defeated at Pasargadae	549
Fall of Sardis	546
Cyrus enters Babylon	539
Cambyses II king of Persia	529
Destruction of Siris	527
Persians defeat Egyptians at Pelusium	525
Cambyses dies	522
Darius becomes king of Babylon	521
Carthage conquers Sardinia	520
Darius invades Egypt	517
Scythian expedition of Darius	516
Carthage makes treaty with Rome	510
Persian expedition to Naxos	499

Dates based on information from J. B. Bury et al., eds., *The Cambridge Ancient History,* 2nd ed., vols. 4–10 (Cambridge: Cambridge University Press, 1965, 1958, 1953, 1954, 1954, 1951, 1971).

Event	Date B.C.
Persian fleet defeated at Cyprus	498
Persians reconquer Cyprus	497
Persians take Miletus; Spartans defeat Argives at Sepeia	494
Battle of Marathon	490
Death of Darius; accession of Xerxes	485
Xerxes crushes revolts in Egypt and Babylonia	485
Xerxes invades Greece; battles of Thermopylae and Salamis	480
Persia loses Sestos and the Hellespont	479
Persia loses Byzantium, Bosporus, and Cyprus; formation of the League of Delos	478
Battle of Naxos	468
Battle of Eurymedon	467
Xerxes murdered; Artaxerxes I becomes king	465
Revolt in Egypt under Inaros; alliance of Athens with Argos and Thessaly	462
Age of Pericles (lasts until 428 B.C.)	461
Athenians defeat the Corinthians	458
Battles of Tanagra and Oenophyta	457
Persian army reaches Egypt under Megabyxus	456
Athenian expedition to Egypt ends in disaster	455
Athenian League moved from Delos to Athens	454
Five years' peace between Athens and Sparta; thirty years' peace between Sparta and Argos	451
Rebellion of Megabyxus in Syria; Cimon's expedition to Cyprus	450
Peace of Callias	449
Return of Ezra to Jerusalem (?); Spartan expedition to Delphi	448

Event	Date B.C.
Athenian defeat at Coronea; building of Parthenon begun	447
Return of Nehemiah to Jerusalem; The Thirty Years' Peace; Acragas defeated by Syracuse	445
Second return of Nehemiah	443
Revolt of Samos	441
First Peloponnesian invasion of Attica	431
Second Peloponnesian invasion of Attica	430
Third Peloponnesian invasion of Attica; death of Pericles	428
Fourth Peloponnesian invasion of Attica; first Athenian expedition to Sicily	427
Fifth Peloponnesian invasion of Attica; battle of Delium; death of Artaxerxes; exile of Thucydides	424
Ochus becomes king of Persia as Darius II	423
Peace of Nicias—fifty year alliance between Athens and Sparta	421
Fifty year alliance between Sparta and Argos	418
Athenians invade Sicily	415
Spartans attack Argos; siege of Syracuse; death of Lamachus	414
Athenian disaster in Sicily	413
Treaty between Persia and Sparta	412
Revolution of the 400; the government of the 5,000; destruction of the temple at Elephantine; siege of Chios	411
Democracy restored in Athens; founding of Rhodes	410
Hannibal's expedition to Sicily	409
Athenians retake Byzantium	408
Return of Alcibiades	407
Second Carthaginian expedition to Sicily; fall of Acragas; death of Sophocles and Euripides	406

Event	Date B.C.
Siege of Athens; peace between Carthage and Syracuse	405
Death of Darius II; Arsaces becomes king as Artaxerxes II; end of the Peloponnesian War; thirty tyrants in Athens; death of Alcibiades	404
Fall of the thirty tyrants; restoration of democracy in Athens	403
Cyrus gathers his army at Sardis; battle of Cunaxa	401
Sparta declares war on Tissaphernes; Tissaphernes besieges Cyme	400
Death of Agis, king of Sparta; death of Socrates	399
Nepherites crowned king of Egypt; Dionysius takes Motya	398
Defeat of Syracusan fleet; return of Ezra to Jerusalem	397
Revolt of Rhodes from Sparta	396
Outbreak of Corinthian War	395
Battles of Cnidus, Nemea, and Coronea	394
Achoris becomes king of Egypt; Spartans defeated at Lechaeum; Dionysius besieges Rhegium; Gauls sack Rome; Spartan fleet captures Samos and Cnidus	390
Cyprus revolts against Persia in alliance with Athens and King Achoris of Egypt	389
Dionysius captures Rhegium	387
The King's Peace	386
Artaxerxes at war with Egypt (until 383 B.C.)	385
Birth of Aristotle	384
Revolt of Tyre; second war of Dionysius with Carthage	383
Evagoras' fleet defeated by the Persians	381
Peace between Evagoras and the Persians	380
Dionysius takes Croton; liberation of Thebes	379

Event	Date B.C.
Battle of Cronium; alliance between Athens and Thebes; death of Achoris, accession of Nectanebo I	378
Athenian victory over Sparta at Naxos	376
Death of Evagoras; peace between Athens and Sparta	374
Peace of Callias	371
Assassination of Jason	370
Third war of Dionysius with Carthage	368
The Tearless Battle; death of Dionysius, Dionysius II succeeds; peace between Syracuse and Carthage	367
Ariobarzanes and other satraps revolt against Persia; alliance between Athens and Arcadia; Corinthians make peace with Thebes; exile of Dion	366
Dionysius II assists Sparta against Thebes	365
Battle of Cynoscephalae	364
Battle of Mantinea	362
Death of Nectanebo I	361
Death of Ariobarzanes; Sestos besieged by Cotys	360
Accession of Nectanebo II in Egypt	359
Death of Artaxerxes II, accession of Artaxerxes III	359
Return of Dion to Syracuse	357
Dion besieges Ortygia; Philip captures Pydna, Potidaea, and Amphipolis; Alexander born	356
Phocians seize Delphi	355
Battle of Neon; Dion murdered; Callippus a tyrant at Syracuse	354
Artabazus helped by Thebes; Philip takes Methone	353
Philip takes Pherae and Pagasae	352

Event	Date B.C.
Nysaeus a tyrant at Syracuse	351
Artaxerxes helps Thebes; Phocion helps Persians in Cyprus	350
Philip takes Chalcidice	348
Dionysius II expels Nysaeus and recovers Syracuse; death of Plato	347
Peace of Philocrates	346
Revolt of Tennes, king of Sidon	345
Artaxerxes captures Sidon; Philip reorganizes Thessaly; battle of Adranum	344
Persian reconquest of Egypt	343
Philip in Thrace	342
Formation of Euboean League; battle of Crimisus	341
Philip besieges Byzantium; war declared by Athens	340
Thracian expedition of Philip	339
Battle of Mandonium; Artaxerxes murdered; Arses becomes king; battle of Chaeronea	337
Arses murdered; Darius III becomes king; assassination of Philip; accession of Alexander	335
Alexander in Thrace; Thebes destroyed	335
Alexander starts his Persian campaign; battle of Granicus; sieges of Miletus and Halicarnassus	334
Conquest of Lycia, West Pisidia, and Cilicia; battle of Issus	333
Capture of Tyre; conquest of Egypt	332
Battle of Megalopolis; Alexandria founded; Alexander occupies Babylon, Susa, and Persepolis	331
Alexander at Ecbatana; death of Darius	331
Alexander conquers Bactria and Sogdiana	328

Event	Date B.C.
Alexander invades India	327
Conquest of Malli	326
Alexander in Gedrosia	325
Mutiny of Macedonians at Opis	324
Alexander at Babylon; death of Alexander; Perdiccas rules Asia; outbreak of Lamian War	323
Battle of Crannon; death of Aristotle	322
Death of Perdiccas in Egypt; Antipater becomes regent of Alexander's empire	321
Death of Antipater; Syria annexed by Ptolemy	319
Eumenes captures Babylon	318
Eumenes defeated at Gabiene; Athenians make terms with Cassander	317
Cassander captures Pydna, rebuilds Thebes	316
Antigonus occupies Syria	315
Antigonus captures Tyre; Antigonus proclaims freedom for Greek cities	314
Ptolemy crushes a revolt in Cyprus	313
Ptolemy defeats Demetrius at Gaza; Seleucus establishes himself in Babylon; Carthaginian invasion of Sicily	312
Antigonus ravages Babylonia; Agathocles invades Africa; Ptolemy takes Cyprus	310
Ptolemy makes peace with Cassander	308
Agathocles defeated; four years' war between Demetrius and Cassander	307
Antigonus defeated in Egypt; peace between Syracuse and Carthage	306

Event	Date B.C.
Demetrius besieges Rhodes; Cassander defeated at Elatea	305
Antigonus makes peace with Rhodes	304
Demetrius reforms Corinthian League	303
Battle of Ipsus; death of Antigonus; Corinthian League breaks up	301
Partition of Antigonus' kingdom; founding of Antioch; Celtic conquest of South Gaul	300
Alliance of Seleucus and Demetrius	299
Death of Cassander and his son Philip IV	297
Ptolemy acquires Cyprus, Seleucus, Ionia, and Cilicia; Lachares seizes power in Athens; Roman victory at Sentinum	295
Demetrius Poliocetes takes Athens and becomes king of Macedonia	294
Antiochus I joint king of Asia	292
Demetrius takes Thebes	291
Ptolemy acquires Tyre and Sidon; Demetrius invades Asia; the Hortensian Laws	287
Demetrius surrenders to Seleucus	285
Death of Ptolemy I; Ptolemy II becomes king in Egypt; death of Demetrius; his son Antigonus rules in Macedonia	282
Death of Lysimachus; Antigonus takes Athens	281
Death of Seleucus; Antiochus I rules in Syria; Ptolemy Keraunos becomes king of Macedonia	280
Treaty between Antigonus and Antiochus; Gauls invade Macedonia; Romans defeated at Asculum	279
Gauls invade Asia; Roman treaty with Carthage	278
First Syrian War; Antiochus I defeats Ptolemy II	276
Antiochus I defeats Gauls	275
Egyptian conquests in Asia Minor	274

Event	Date B.C.
End of First Syrian War	272
Death of Arsinoe II; Antigonus annexes Euboea	270
Coalition of Athens, Sparta, and Egypt against Antigonus	267
Chromonidean War begins; battle of Corinth; death of Areus II of Sparta; Hiero declared king of Syracuse	265
First Punic War begins	264
Death of Acrotatus of Sparta	263
Death of Antiochus I; accession of Antiochus II; Antigonus takes Athens; warfare in Sicily; capture of Agrigentum	262
Peace between Ptolemy II and Antigonus	261
Second Syrian War begins	260
Antiochus II retakes Ephesus	259
Battle of Cos; Regulus lands in Africa and defeats Carthaginians	256
Antigonus secures the Island League; Regulus' army defeated; Roman fleet wrecked off Pachynus	255
Death of Antiochus II; accession of Seleucus II; death of Alexander of Corinth; Hamilcar Barca invades Sicily	247
Death of Ptolemy II; accession of Ptolemy III; Antigonus recovers Corinth; Third Syrian War begins	246
Aratus becomes general of Achaian League	245
Agis IV becomes king of Sparta	244
Aratus takes Corinth	243
Peace between Ptolemy III and Seleucus II; death of Eumenes I and accession of Attalus I; death of Agis IV; Rome occupies Sicily	241
War of the Brothers, Seleucus II and Antiochus Hierax (240-36)	240
Death of Antigonus Gonatas; accession of Demetrius II	239

Event	Date B.C.
War of Demetrius with the League begins	238
Cleomenes III becomes king of Sparta	237
Battle of Cleonae; Carthaginian conquests in Spain	235
Battle of Phylacia	233
War of Attalus I with Antiochus Hierax	230
Death of Demetrius II; Antigonus Doson becomes king of Macedonia; death of Hamilcar; First Illyrian War	229
Athens regains independence; Cleomenic War; founding of New Carthage	228
Revolution at Sparta	227
Death of Seleucus II; accession of Seleucus III; Ebro Treaty between Rome and Hasdrubal of Spain	226
Invading Gauls routed at Telamon	225
Antigonus takes Argos	224
Death of Seleucus III; accession of Antiochus III; Achaeus recovers Seleucid Asia Minor (223-20)	223
Antigonus takes Sparta; battle of Clastidium	222
Death of Ptolemy III; accession of Ptolemy IV; death of Antigonus Doson; accession of Philip V; death of Hasdrubal; Hannibal becomes general in Spain	222
Fourth Syrian War begins; death of Cleomenes; War of the Allies begins	220
Second Illyrian War; Hannibal takes Saguntum	219
War declared between Rome and Carthage; Philip V sacks Thermum	218
Peace of Naupactus; Hannibal crosses the Alps	217
Death of Hiero; Hannibal in South Italy; alliance between Syracuse and Carthage	215

Event	Date B.C.
Philip's second Illyrian campaign	214
Death of Aratus; siege of Syracuse begins	213
Antiochus recovers Armenia	212
Hannibal marches on Rome; fall of Capua and Syracuse	211
Antiochus in Media; fall of Agrigentum	210
Antiochus in Parthyene; Attalus in Pergamum	209
Antiochus in Bactria; Attalus returns to Asia; death of Marcellus; Hasdrubal leaves Spain for Italy	208
Philip raids Aetolia; Spartans defeated at Mantinea; Hasdrubal defeated at Metaurus	207
Antiochus makes peace with Bactria; Nabis king of Sparta	206
Scipio lands in Sicily and recaptures Locri; death of Ptolemy Philopator	205
Cretan War begins	204
Hannibal recalled to Africa	203
Antiochus and Philip form a coalition against Egypt; Antiochus invades South Syria; victory of Scipio at Zama	202
Antiochus takes Gaza; Philip in Asia Minor	201
Philip returns from Asia Minor	200
Antiochus takes Sidon	199
Antiochus reduces all of South Syria; Cato in Sardinia	198
Antiochus invades Asia Minor, occupies Ephesus; defeat of Philip at Cynoscephalae; peace between Rome and Macedonia	197
Antiochus reaches Thrace; final defeat of Insubres; Hannibal begins democratic reforms at Carthage	196
Peace between Antiochus and Egypt; Hannibal joins Antiochus at Ephesus; Cato sent to quell revolts in Spain	195

Event	Date B.C.
Marriage of Ptolemy V and Cleopatra; Lusitani at war with Rome	194
Breach between Rome and Antiochus; Masinissa raids Carthage	193
Antiochus's fleet defeated off Corycus; Spartans forced to join the Achaian League; Rome declares war on Antiochus	192
Antiochus defeated at Thermopylae and flees to Ephesus	191
Antiochus's fleets defeated at Side and Myonnesus	190
Antiochus defeated at Magnesia, peace talks at Sardis; Sparta secedes from the Achaian League; peace between Rome and Aetolia	189
Treaty of Apamea	188
Death of Antiochus; accession of Seleucus IV; second Roman evacuation of Greece	187
Cato the Elder becomes a censor	184
War between Pontus and Pergamum; the Messenians revolt against the Achaians; death of Scipio Africanus	183
Death of Hannibal; Masinissa raids Carthage	182
Death of Ptolemy V; accession of Ptolemy Philometor; expedition of Philip to the Balkans; Romans advance north in Spain	181
End of war between Pontus and Pergamum	180
Death of Philip; accession of Perseus; Gracchus ends war in Spain	179
Latins expelled from Rome	177
Death of Seleucus IV; accession of Antiochus IV Epiphanes	175
Roman mission in Greece	172
War between Rome and Perseus	171
War between Syria and Egypt; Philippus marches into Macedonia; Lex Voconia	169
Aemilius Paullus defeats Perseus at Pydna	168

61

Event	Date B.C.
Attempts to hellenize the Jews; Macedonia and Illyria divided into protectorates; 1,000 Achaians deported to Italy (including Polybius)	167
Maccabean revolt in Palestine; Book of Daniel possibly written	166
Hasmonean revolt	165
Rededication of the temple at Jerusalem	164
Death of Antiochus Epiphanes	163
Lex Fannia	161
Defeat and death of Judas Maccabeus; death of Eumenes II of Pergamum, accession of Attalus II	160
Judea becomes an independent priestly state; Roman campaigns in Dalmatia	157
Rome at war with Lusitania (154–38)	154
Romans defeated in war with the Celtiberians (153–51)	153
Alexander Balas, rival of Demetrius, recognizes Jonathan as high priest	152
Carthage declares war on Masinissa	151
Death of Demetrius, Alexander Balas becomes king, and a client of Egypt; Carthaginians defeated	150
Rome intervenes on behalf of Carthage	149
War between Rome and the Achaians, Corinth sacked; Romans defeated at Carthage, Carthage sacked	146
Egyptian intervention in Syria; death of Ptolemy Philometor and Alexander Balas	145
Numantine War	143
Tryphon king of Syria; independence for the Jews	142
Defeat and capture of Demetrius by Parthians; death of Attalus II of Pergamum, accession of Attalus III	139

Event	Date B.C.
Death of Tryphon	138
First Sicilian Slave War	135
Death of Simon; John Hyrcanus becomes high priest; Syrian power restored in Judea	134
Death of Attalus III of Pergamum; death of Gracchus	133
Victory of P. Rupilius in Slave War	132
Civil war in Egypt; Cleopatra II sole ruler	131
Death of Antiochus Sidetes of Syria in war with Parthia; decline of Seleucid power	130
Ptolemy Physcon restored to Alexandria	129
Mithridates II of Parthia consolidates his kingdom; war in Gaul against Arverni and Allobroges	124
Rome begins to colonize Africa	123
Assassination of Mithridates V of Pontus; Rome defeats Arverni and Allobroges	121
Reconciliation of Ptolemy Physcon and Cleopatra II; order restored in Egypt	118
Death of Hiempsal	117
Death of Ptolemy Physcon; Cyrene separated from Egypt under Ptolemy Apion; rise of Jugurtha	116
Mithridates VI seizes power in Pontus	115
War declared on Jugurtha	112
Peace with Jugurtha	111
War reopened in Africa	110
Capture of Jugurtha	106
Second Sicilian Slave War	104
Jannaeus Alexander priest-king of Judea	103

Event	Date B.C.
Marius defeats Teutoni	102
Mithridates Eupator occupies Galatia; Marius and Catulus defeat Cimbri	101
Mithridates occupies Cappadocia; end of Second Sicilian Slave War; riots in Rome; Marius restores order	100
Marius puts down revolts in Spain	98
Ptolemy Apion dies; Cyrene bequeathed to Rome	96
Mithridates ordered out of Cappadocia by Rome; Cappadocia placed under Ariobarzanes; Tigranes becomes king of Armenia	95
Death of Nicomedes II of Bithynia	94
Tigranes drives Ariobarzanes out of Cappadocia	93
Sulla restores Ariobarzanes	92
Assassination of Drusus; outbreak of Social War; massacre of Romans at Asculum	91
Mithridates overruns Asia Minor and orders massacre of Romans and Italians; siege of Rhodes; Sulla occupies Rome; Athens joins Mithridates	88
Cinna and Marius in power; massacre in Rome; Sulla lands in Greece	87
Fall of Athens	86
Kingdom of Nabat extends to Damascus	85
Cinna assassinated	84
Murena begins war on Mithridates; Sulla lands in Italy; civil war in Italy; Sulla victorious	83
Murena driven out of Cappadocia; Pompey puts down enemies of Sulla in Sicily	82
Sulla dictator in Rome; Pompey in Africa	81

Event	Date B.C.
Ptolemy X Alexander II, king of Egypt, is assassinated; Ptolemy Auletes seizes throne	80
Sulla lays down dictatorship	79
Death of Sulla	78
Pompey crushes revolts in Spain	77
Death of Jannaeus Alexander; Salome Alexandra becomes queen of Judea	76
Death of Nicomedes III of Bithynia; kingdom bequeathed to Rome	75
Mithridates declares war on Rome and invades Bithynia	74
Rise of Spartacus	73
Perperna defeated and colonization begins in Spain; Lucullus defeats Bessi and Dardani	72
Mithridates routed by Lucullus; Crassus crushes Spartacus's army; Pompey returns from Spain	71
First consulship of Crassus and Pompey	70
Lucullus invades Armenia	69
Death of Salome Alexandra, civil war in Judea; victory of Mithridates at Zela	67
Phraates III of Parthia attacks Tigranes; final defeat of Mithridates	66
Pompey campaigns against the Iberi and Albani	65
Pompey in Syria; end of the Seleucid monarchy	64
Death of Mithridates; fall of Jerusalem and end of Hasmonean power	63
Pompey makes Hyrcanus high priest in Judea; Bithynia, Cilicia, and Syria become Roman provinces; Crete annexed; birth of Octavian	62
Caesar governor of Spain	61

Event	Date B.C.
Ptolemy Auletes king of Egypt; Caesar consul in Rome	59
Ptolemy driven out of Alexandria; Cyprus annexed	58
Civil war in Parthia between Mithridates III and Orodes II; Caesar defeats Belgae and Nervii; Crassus in Normandy; rioting in Rome between Clodius and Milo	57
Caesar campaigns against Veneti and Morini	56
First Roman expedition to Britain	55
A. Gabinius of Syria restores Ptolemy; Mithridates III executed by Orodes II; Caesar's second expedition to Britain	54
Parthians defeat Crassus; unrest in Gaul	53
Death of Ptolemy Auletes; Ptolemy XII and Cleopatra VII rulers of Egypt; Parthian invasion of Syria	51
Caesar organizes Gaul	50
Cleopatra and Ptolemy XII at war; Caesar defeats Pompeian army in Spain; civil war in Rome; Pompey leaves for Africa; Caesar declared dictator	49
Pompey assassinated in Egypt; Caesar arrives and fights the Alexandrine War; Ptolemy XII dies; Caesar makes Cleopatra and Ptolemy XIII rulers in Egypt	48
Caesar leaves Egypt; he settles affairs in Syria and Asia Minor; Antony maintains order in Rome	47
Caesar in Spain; suicide of Cato the Younger	46
Caesar returns from Spain	45
Caesar assassinated	44
Triumvirate of Antony, Octavius, and Lepidus rules in Rome	43
Suicide of Cassius and M. Brutus; birth of Tiberius	42
Antony meets Cleopatra at Tarsus, visits Alexandria	41

Event	Date B.C.
Parthian invasion of Syria; Herod made king of Judea by Roman Senate; L. Antonius surrenders Perusia to Octavian	40
Agrippa campaigns in Gaul	39
Capture of Jerusalem by Herod; Antony marries Cleopatra in Antioch	37
Lepidus ceases to be triumvir	36
Sextus Pompeius is killed in Asia by Titius	35
Octavian in Dalmatia; Antony invades Armenia	34
Death of Bocchus	33
Antony and Cleopatra in Ephesus; Octavia divorced by Antony	32
Antony and Cleopatra in Greece; battle of Actium	31
Suicide of Antony; Phraates captures Media; Octavian enters Alexandria; Crassus in the Balkans; suicide of Cleopatra	30
Octavian's triple triumph	29
Imperial authority given to Octavian, now called Augustus; Augustus in Gaul and Spain (27-25)	27
Suicide of C. Gallus	26
Annexation of Galatia; marriage of Julia and Marcellus	25
Agrippa made vice-regent of the East; Augustus resigns the consulship; death of Marcellus	23
Augustus in Greece and Asia (22-19)	22
Marriage of Agrippa and Julia	21
Tiberius enters Armenia and makes Tigranes king; rebuilding of temple in Jerusalem begins; Agrippa quells revolts in Gaul and Spain	20
Agrippa sent to the East; Augustus in Gaul (16-13)	16
Agrippa visits Jerusalem	15

Event	Date B.C.
Tiberius becomes consul; death of Lepidus	13
Augustus becomes pontifex maximus; death of Agrippa; Drusus campaigns in Germany (12-9)	12
Marriage of Tiberius and Julia	11
Death of Drusus; Herod invades Nabatea	9
Census taken	8
Rome divided into 14 regions	7
Tiberius retires to Rhodes; death of Tigranes II; revolt in Armenia	6
Birth of Christ (5/4); Augustus's 12th consulship; C. Caesar introduced to public life	5
Death of Herod; execution of Antipater	4
Parthian King Phraates assassinated, accession of Phraataces; Augustus's 13th consulship; L. Caesar introduced to public life; Julia exiled	2

Comparative Chronology of the Patriarchs

Traditional Dating Based on an Early Date Exodus

Event	Date B.C.
Abraham born	2166
Abraham enters Canaan	2091
Ishmael born	2080
Isaac born	2066
Sarah dies	2030
Isaac marries Rebekah	2026
Jacob and Esau born	2006
Abraham dies	1991
Joseph born	1915
Joseph sold into slavery	1898

Event	Date B.C.
Isaac dies	1886
Joseph exalted	1885
Jacob enters Egypt	1876
Jacob dies	1859
Joseph dies	1805
Israel made slaves in Egypt	1730
Moses born	1527
Joshua born	1500
Moses flees to Midian	1487
Moses returns to Egypt	1447
Exodus	1446
Desert wanderings	1446–1406
Crossing of Jordan into Canaan	1406
Death of Joshua	1390
Elders rule Israel	1390–1375
Judges rule Israel	1375–1050
Saul reigns as king of Israel	1050–1010

Dating Based on a Late Date Exodus

Event	Date B.C.
Patriarchs	2000–1700
Jacob's family enters Egypt	1700–1660
Exodus	1290
Israel's entrance into Canaan	1260/1250
Judges rule Israel	1200–1020
Saul reigns as king of Israel	1020–1000

Chronology of the Exodus

The Early Date

1. Suggested Early Dates:

Date B.C.	Reigning Pharaoh
1446	Amenophis II, 1450–25
1440	Amenophis II, 1450–25
1437	Amenophis II, 1450–25

2. Arguments For the Early Date:

   a. 1 Kings 6:1 indicates the exodus occurred 480 years prior to the 4th year of King Solomon's reign. Solomon's 4th year is variously dated at 966/960/957, making the date of the exodus 1446/1440/1437 B.C.

   b. According to Judg. 11:26 Israel had occupied Canaan for a span of 300 years before the judgeship of Jephthah. Jephthah's judgeship is dated between 1100 and 1050 B.C. This dates Joshua's conquest between 1400 and 1350 B.C. Adding the 40 years Israel spent in the desert the exodus is dated between 1440 and 1390 B.C.

   c. Moses lived in exile in Midian for 40 years (Acts 7:3; cf. Exod. 2:23) while the pharaoh of the oppression was still alive. The only pharaohs who ruled 40 years or longer were Thutmose III (1504–1450 B.C.) and Rameses II (1290–1224 B.C.).

   d. The Merneptah Stela (ca. 1220 B.C.) indicates Israel was already an established nation at this time.

   e. The Amarna tablets (ca. 1400 B.C.) speak of a period of chaos caused by the "Habiru," likely identified as the Hebrews.

   f. The early date allows for the length of time assigned to the period of the judges (at least 250 years). The late date allows for only a 180 year time span for the period of the judges.

   g. The Dream Stela of Thutmose IV indicates he was not the legal heir to the throne (i.e., the legal heir would have died in the 10th plague).

   h. Archaeological evidence from Jericho, Hazor, etc. supports a 15th century B.C. date for the exodus.

   i. Exodus 12:40 dates the entrance of Jacob into Egypt during the reign of Sesostris/Senusert III (1878-43), rather than during the Hyksos period (1674-1567).

The Late Date

1. Suggested Late Dates:

Date B.C.	Reigning Pharaoh
1350	Tutankhamen, 1361-52
1290	Rameses II, 1304-1237
1280	Rameses II, 1304-1237
1275	Rameses II, 1304-1237
1225	Rameses II, 1304-1237

2. Arguments For the Late Date:

   a. The 480 years of 1 Kings 6:1 is a symbolic figure for 12 generations. Since a generation is about 25 years, the actual figure should be 300 years, placing the exodus around 1266/1260 B.C.

   b. The 300 year figure cited by Jephthah is merely an exaggerated generalization, since he had no access to historical records.

   c. The 40 years Moses spent with the Midianites is not a chronological figure, but a symbolic figure indicating a "long" period of time.

   d. The Merneptah Stela (ca. 1220 B.C.) indicates Israel was in the land of Palestine by this date. The name Israel does not occur in any other historical records or documents before 1220 B.C. This would be unlikely had Israel begun occupation of the land 200 years earlier, in 1400 B.C.

   e. The "Habiru" of the Amarna tablets cannot be identified with the Hebrews. The "Habiru" were a diverse people, native Canaanites. They are attested from the 18th to the 12th centuries B.C.

   f. With the overlapping of judgeships and the use of symbolic numbers (i.e., 40 years) the period of the judges need not span more than 150 years.

71

g. That Thutmose IV was not the legal heir to the Egyptian throne in no way proves the legal heir died in the 10th plague.

h. Archaeological evidence from Lachish, Jericho, Bethel, Hazor, Debir, etc. supports a 13th century B.C. date for the Exodus.

i. The 430 years of Exod. 12:40 from the late date for the exodus places Jacob's entrance into Egypt during the Hyksos period (1730-1570 B.C.). This period of foreign domination in Egypt is a more likely time period for Israel's entrance into Egypt.

j. The civilizations of Edom, Ammon, and Moab were not in existence in the 15th century B.C., thus it would have been impossible for Israel to have had contact with these nations if the exodus occurred in the 15th century B.C. Since Israel did indeed have contact with these nations, the exodus must be dated to the 13th century B.C.

k. The OT does not mention the Palestinian invasions of Seti I or Rameses II, likely because Israel was not yet in the land of Palestine.

l. The Israelites were building Pithom and Raamses (Exod. 1:11), cities of the delta region. The city of Raamses was founded by Seti I (1318-1304 B.C.) and completed by Rameses II (1304-1237 B.C.).

m. Thutmose III was not noted as a great builder.

Israel's Desert Itinerary (Num. 33:1–49)

1. Rameses to
2. Succoth to
3. Etham to
4. Pi Hahiroth (near Migdol) to
5. Marah to
6. Elim to
7. the sea (Sea of Reeds) opposite Baal-Zephon to
8. Desert of Sin to
9. Dophkah to
10. Alush to
11. Rephidim to
12. Desert of Sinai to
13. Kibroth Hattaavah to
14. Hazeroth to
15. Rithmah to

16. Rimmon Perez to
17. Libnah to
18. Rissah to
19. Kehelathah to
20. Mt. Shepher to
21. Haradah to
22. Makheloth to
23. Tahath to
24. Terah to
25. Mithcah to
26. Hashmonah to
27. Moseroth to
28. Bene Jaakan to
29. Hor Haggidgad to
30. Jotbathah to
31. Abronah to
32. Ezion Geber to
33. Kadesh to
34. Mt. Hor to
35. Zalmonah to
36. Punon to
37. Oboth to
38. Iyim (Iye Abarim) to
39. Dibon Gad to
40. Almon Diblathaim to
41. Mountains of Abarim to
42. Plains of Moab across from Jericho

The Route of the Exodus: Northern Route
(distances are approximate)

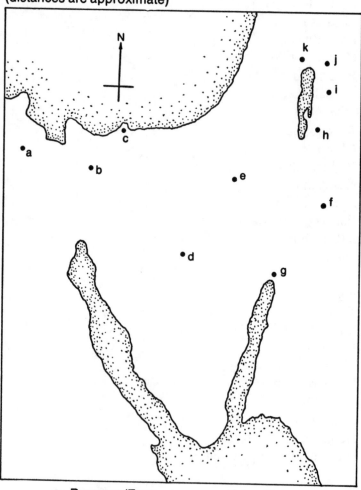

a. Rameses/Zoan
b. Migdol
c. Baal-Zephon
d. Mt. Sinai
e. Kadesh Barnea
f. Mt. Hor

g. Ezion Geber
h. Iyim
i. Dibon
j. Heshbon
k. Jericho

The Route of the Exodus: Southern Route
(distances are approximate)

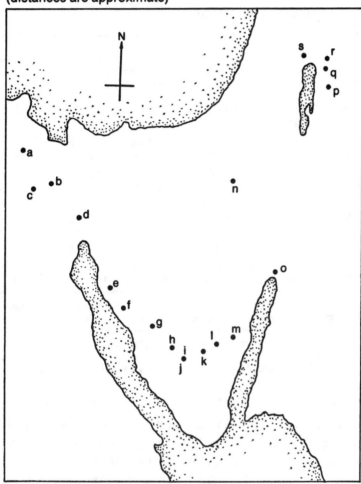

a. Rameses or Zoan
b. Succoth
c. Pithom
d. Baal-Zephon
e. Marah
f. Elim
g. Dophkah
h. Alush
i. Rephidim
j. Mt. Sinai

k. Taberah
l. Kibroth Hattavah
m. Hazeroth
n. Kadesh Barnea
o. Ezion Geber
p. Dibon
q. Jahaz
r. Heshbon
s. Jericho

Comparative Chronology of the Judges

Based on an Early Date Exodus

Judge	Years of Judgeship	Reference	Date B.C.		
			J. H. Walton	L. J. Wood	J. B. Payne
Othniel	40	3:9-11	1377-1337	1367-1327	1374-1334
Ehud	80	3:15-30	1319-1240	1309-1229	1316-1236
Shamgar	10	3:31	1260-1250	1250-1240	
Deborah	40	4:4-5:31	1240-1200	1209-1169	1216-1176
Gideon	40	6:7-8:35	1193-1153	1162-1122	1169-1129
Tola	23	10:1-2	1150-1127	1119-1096	1120-1097
Jair	22	10:3-5	1127-1105	1119-1096	1120-1097
Jephthah	6	11:1-12:7	1087-1081	1078-1072	1085-1079
Ibzan	7	12:8-10	1081-1073	1078-1050	
Elon	10	12:11-12	1073-1063	1078-1050	
Abdon	8	12:13-15	1063-1056	1078-1050	
Samson	20	13:2-16:31	1076-1056	1075-1055	1090-1070

W. F. Albright, *The Biblical Period from Abraham to Ezra,* rev. ed. (New York: Harper Torchbook, 1963); J. Bright, *A History of Israel,* 2nd ed. (Philadelphia: Westminster, 1972); K. A. Kitchen, *Ancient Orient and Old Testament* (Downers Grove, IL: Inter-Varsity, 1966); J. B. Payne, "Chronology" in *Zondervan Pictorial Encyclopedia of the Bible,* ed. M. C. Tenney, vol. 1 (Grand Rapids: Zondervan, 1975); J. H. Walton, *Chronological Charts of the Old Testament* (Grand Rapids: Zondervan, 1978); L. J. Wood, *A Survey of Israel's History* (Grand Rapids: Zondervan, 1970).

Based on a Late Date Exodus

Scholars adhering to a late date for the exodus date the period of the judges between 1220 and 1050 B.C. (e.g., K. A. Kitchen) or 1200 and 1020 B.C. (e.g., W. F. Albright and J. Bright). Since the judges are considered to have had overlapping judgeships and some of the dates are viewed as symbolic no exact chronology for the 12 judges is possible.

Chronological Outline of the Book of Judges

Event	Scripture Reference
Joshua dies at age 110	2:8
Cushan-Rishathaim, king of Aram Naharaim, oppresses Israel for 8 years	3:8
Othniel defeated Cushan-Rishathaim and Israel had peace for 40 years	3:11
Eglon, king of Moab, oppressed Israel for 18 years	3:14
Ehud delivers Israel from Moabite oppression and Israel has peace for 80 years	3:30
Jabin, king of Canaan, oppressed Israel for 20 years	4:3
Deborah defeats the Canaanites and Israel has peace for 40 years	5:3
The Midianites oppress Israel for 7 years	6:1
Gideon delivers Israel from the Midianites and the land has peace for 40 years	8:28
Abimelek rules in Shechem for 3 years	9:22
Tola judges Israel for 23 years	10:2
Jair judges Israel for 22 years	10:3
The Philistines and Ammonites oppress Israel for 18 years	10:8
Jephthah defeats the Ammonites and judges Israel for 6 years	12:7
Ibzan judges Israel for 7 years	12:9
Elon judges Israel for 10 years	12:11
Abdon judges Israel for 8 years	12:14
The Philistines oppress Israel for 40 years	13:1
Samson delivers Israel from Philistine oppression and judges the land for 20 years	15:20

Comparative Chronology of the Kings of the United Monarchy

King	Date B.C.	
	K. A. Kitchen/T. C. Mitchell	J. Bright
Saul	1050/45-1011/10	1020-1000
Ishbosheth	1011/10-1009/08	1000-998
David	1011/10-971/70	1000-961
Solomon	971/70-931/30	961-922

On the chronology of the kings of the United Monarchy, Israel and Judah, see also E. R. Thiele, *A Chronology of the Hebrew Kings* (Grand Rapids: Zondervan, 1977); J. Bright, *A History of Israel*, 2nd ed. (Philadelphia: Westminster, 1972); K. A. Kitchen and T. C. Mitchell, "OT Chronology" in *The New Bible Dictionary*, ed. J. D. Douglas, rev. ed. (Grand Rapids: Eerdmans, 1965).

Comparative Chronology of the Kings of Israel

King	Date B.C.	
	K. A. Kitchen/T. C. Mitchell	J. Bright
Jeroboam I	931/30-910/09	922-901
Nadab	910/09-909/08	901-900
Baasha	909/08-886/85	900-877
Elah	886/85-885/84	877-876
Zimri	885/84	876
Tibni	885/84-880	876-871
Omri	885/84-874/73	876-869
Ahab	874/73-853	869-850
Ahaziah	853-852	850-849
Joram	852-841	849-842
Jehu	841-814/13	842-815
Jehoahaz	814/13-798	815-801

Other chronologies will vary 1-3 years from these two basic chronologies.

J. Bright, *A History of Israel*, 2nd ed. (Philadelphia: Westminster, 1972); K. A. Kitchen and T. C. Mitchell, "OT Chronology" in *The New Bible Dictionary*, ed. J. D. Douglas, rev. ed. (Grand Rapids: Eerdmans, 1965).

	Date B.C.	
King	K. A. Kitchen/T. C. Mitchell	J. Bright
Jehoash	798-782/81	801-786
Jeroboam II	*793/782/81-753	786-746
Zechariah	753-752	746-745
Shallum	752	745
Menahem	752-742/41	745-738
Pekahiah	742/41-740/39	738-737
Pekah	*752/740/39-732/31	737-732
Hoshea	732/31-723/22	732-724
Fall of Samaria	722	722/21

*Indicates the date of coregency.

Comparative Chronology of the Kings of Judah

	Date B.C.	
King	K. A. Kitchen/T. C. Mitchell	J. Bright
Rehoboam	931/30-913	922-915
Abijah	913-911/10	915-913
Asa	911/10-870/69	913-873
Jehoshaphat	*873/72/870/69-848	873-849
Jehoram	853/848-841	849-842
Ahaziah	841	842
Athaliah	841-835	842-837
Joash	835-796	837-800
Amaziah	796-767	800-783
Azariah (Uzziah)	*791/90/767-740/39	783-742
Jotham	*750/740/39-732/31	*750/42-735

*Indicates the date of coregency.

Other chronologies will vary 1-3 years from these two basic chronologies.

J. Bright, A History of Israel, 2nd ed. (Philadelphia: Westminster, 1972); K. A. Kitchen and T. C. Mitchell, "OT Chronology" in The New Bible Dictionary, ed. J. D. Douglas, rev. ed. (Grand Rapids: Eerdmans, 1965).

King	Date B.C.	
	K. A. Kitchen/T. C. Mitchell	J. Bright
Ahaz	*744/43/732/31-716/15	735-715
Hezekiah	*729/716/15-687/86	715-687/86
Manasseh	*696/95/687/86-642/41	687/86-642
Amon	642/41-640/39	642-640
Josiah	640/39-609	640-609
Jehoahaz	609	609
Jehoiakim	609-597	609-598
Jehoiachin	597	598/97
Zedekiah	597-587	597-587
Fall of Jerusalem	587-586	587

The Prophets of Israel and Judah

Prophet	King
Samuel	Saul
Nathan	David
Gad	David
Ahijah	Solomon, Jeroboam I
Iddo	Solomon, Rehoboam, Abijah
Shemaiah	Rehoboam
Azariah	Asa
Hanani	Asa
Jehu	Jehoshaphat, Baasha
Jahaziel	Jehoshaphat
Elijah	Ahab, Ahaziah, Jehoram
Micaiah	Ahab
Eliezer	Jehoshaphat
Zechariah	Joash
Elisha	Ahaziah, Jehoram, Jehu, Jehoahaz, Jehoash
Isaiah	Uzziah, Jotham, Ahaz, Hezekiah
Hosea	Uzziah, Jotham, Ahaz, Hezekiah, Jeroboam II
Amos	Uzziah, Jeroboam II

Prophet	King
Micah	Jotham, Ahaz, Hezekiah
Jonah	Jeroboam II
Oded	Pekah
Huldah	Josiah
Zephaniah	Josiah
Jeremiah	Josiah, Jehoahaz, Jehoiakim, Jehoiachin, Zedekiah
Uriah	Jehoiakim
Ezekiel	none named
Daniel	Jehoiakim, Nebuchadnezzar of Babylon, Belshazzar, Darius the Mede, Cyrus of Persia
Haggai	Darius of Persia
Zechariah	Darius of Persia
Obadiah	none named
Joel	none named
Nahum	none named
Habakkuk	none named
Malachi	none named

Old Testament Genealogy

Generations from Adam to Noah (Gen. 5:1–32)

Adam
Seth
Enosh
Kenan
Mahalalel
Jared
Enoch
Methuselah
Lamech
Noah

Generations from Shem to Abram (Gen. 11:10–26)

Shem
Arphaxad
Shelah
Eber
Peleg
Reu
Serug
Nahor
Terah
Abram/Nahor/Haran

The Table of Nations (Gen. 10:1-32)

Noah		
Japheth	Ham	Shem
Gomer	Cush	Elam
Ashkenaz	Seba	Asshur
Riphath	Havilah	Arphaxad
Togarmah	Sabtah	Shelah
Magog	Raamah	Eber
Madai	Sheba	Peleg
Javan	Dedan	Joktan
Elishah	Sabtecah	Almodad
Tarshish	Nimrod	Sheleph
Kittim	Mizraim	Hazarmaveth
Rodanim	Ludites	Jerah
Tubal	Anamites	Hadoram
Meshech	Lehabites	Uzal
Tiras	Naphtuhites	Diklah
	Pathrusites	Obal
	Casluhites	Abimael
	Philistines	Sheba
	Caphtorites	Ophir
	Put	Havilah
	Canaan	Jobab
	Sidon	Lud
	Hittites	Aram
	Jebusites	Uz
	Amorites	Hul
	Girgashites	Gether
	Hivites	Meshech
	Arkites	
	Sinites	
	Arvadites	
	Zemarites	
	Hamathites	

The Patriarchal Family Tree

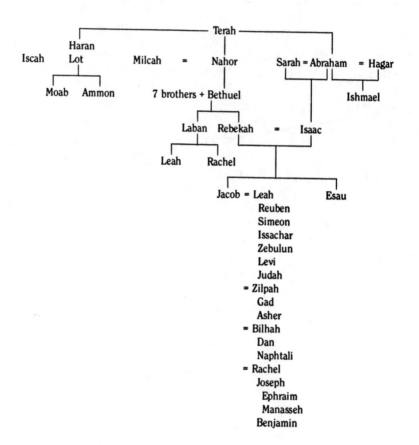

The Family of Abraham (Gen. 11:24–32; 16:15; 19:30–38; 21:1–5; 22:20–24; 25:1–4)

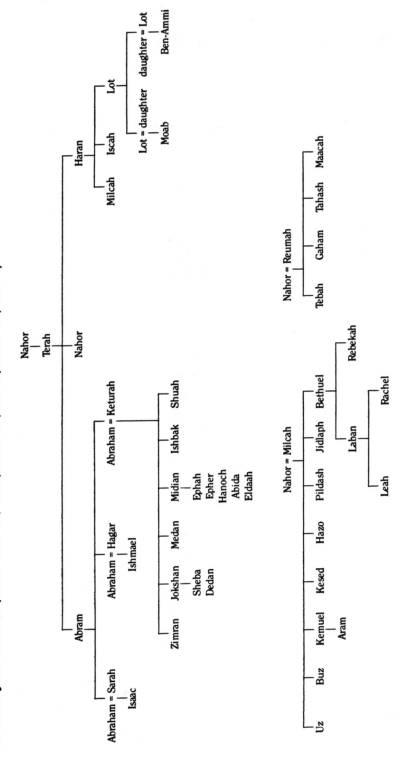

The Family of Ishmael (Gen. 25:12–18)

Abraham = Hagar

Ishmael

Nebaioth
Basemath
Kedar
Adbeel
Mibsam
Mishma
Dumah
Massa
Hadad
Tema
Jetur
Naphish
Kedemah

The Family of Esau (Gen. 36:1-14)

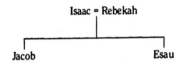

Isaac = Rebekah

Jacob   Esau

Esau = Adah	Esau = Oholibamah	Esau = Basemath
Eliphaz	Jeush	Reuel
Teman	Jalam	Nahath
Omar	Korah	Zerah
Zepho		Shammah
Gatam		Mizzah
Kenaz		
Amalek		

The Family of Jacob (Israel) (Gen. 46:8–27)

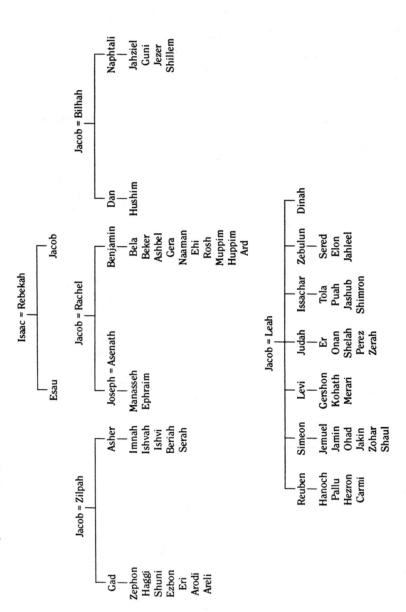

Isaac = Rebekah

Esau

Jacob

Jacob = Zilpah

Gad
Zephon
Haggi
Shuni
Ezbon
Eri
Arodi
Areli

Asher
Imnah
Ishvah
Ishvi
Beriah
Serah

Jacob = Rachel

Joseph = Asenath
Manasseh
Ephraim

Benjamin
Bela
Beker
Ashbel
Gera
Naaman
Ehi
Rosh
Muppim
Huppim
Ard

Jacob = Bilhah

Dan
Hushim

Naphtali
Jahziel
Guni
Jezer
Shillem

Jacob = Leah

Reuben
Hanoch
Pallu
Hezron
Carmi

Simeon
Jemuel
Jamin
Ohad
Jakin
Zohar
Shaul

Levi
Gershon
Kohath
Merari

Judah
Er
Onan
Shelah
Perez
Zerah

Issachar
Tola
Puah
Jashub
Shimron

Zebulun
Sered
Elon
Jahleel

Dinah

The Family of Levi, Aaron, and Moses (Exod. 2:21–22; 6:14–27; 15:20–21; 18:2–3; Num. 3:17–20; 1 Chron. 6:1–30, 50–53)

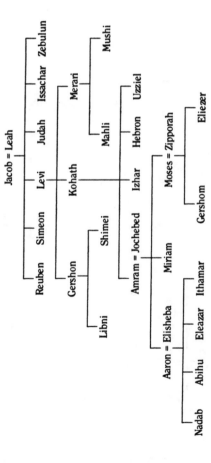

The Family of Saul (1 Chron. 9:35–44)

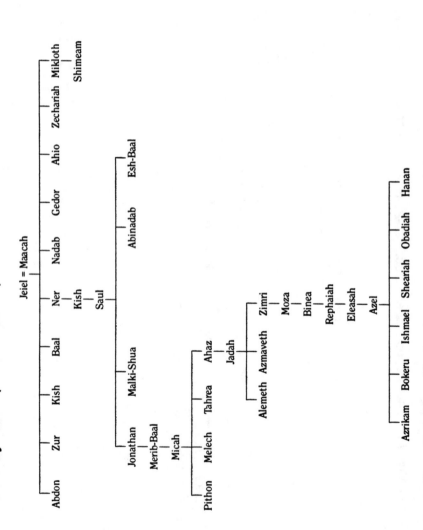

The Family of David

Ruth 4:18–21

1 Chron. 2:3–17

Perez
Hezron
Ram
Amminadab
Nahshon
Salmon
Boaz
Obed
Jesse
David

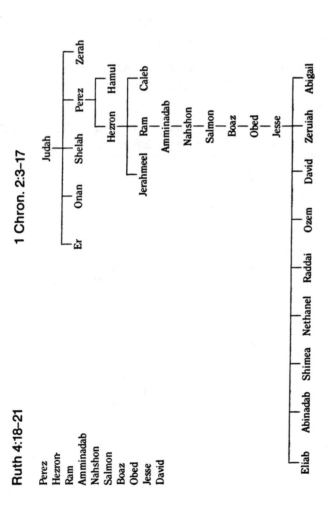

David's Wives and Sons

Wives	Sons
Michal, 1 Sam. 18:27	
Abigail, 1 Sam. 25:42	Daniel, 1 Chron. 3:1
Ahinoam, 1 Sam. 25:43	Amnon, 1 Chron. 3:1
Maacah, 1 Chron. 3:2	Absalom, 1 Chron. 3:2
Haggith, 1 Chron. 3:3	Adonijah, 1 Chron. 3:2
Abital, 1 Chron. 3:3	Shephatiah, 1 Chron. 3:3
Eglah, 1 Chron. 3:3	Ithream, 1 Chron. 3:3
Bathsheba, 1 Chron. 3:5	Shammua, Shobab, Nathan, Solomon, 2 Sam. 5:14, 1 Chron. 3:5
Others	Ibhar, Elishua, Elpelet, Nogah, Nepheg, Japhia, Elishama, Beeliada (Eliada), Eliphelet, 2 Sam. 5:14, 1 Chron. 3:6-8, 1 Chron. 14:4-7

David's Sons

Born at Hebron

2 Sam. 3:2-5	1 Chron. 3:1-4
Amnon	Amnon
Kileab	Daniel
Absalom	Absalom
Adonijah	Adonijah
Shephatiah	Shephatiah
Ithream	Ithream

Born at Jerusalem

2 Sam. 5:14–16	1 Chron. 3:5–9	1 Chron. 14:4–7
Shammua	Shammua	Shammua
Shobab	Shobab	Shobab
Nathan	Nathan	Nathan
Solomon	Solomon	Solomon
Ibhar	Ibhar	Ibhar
Elishua	Elishua	Elishua
—	Eliphelet	Elpelet
—	Nogah	Nogah
Nepheg	Nepheg	Nepheg
Japhia	Japhia	Japhia
Elishama	Elishama	Elishama
Eliada	Eliada	Beeliada
Eliphelet	Eliphelet	Eliphelet

Genealogy of Ezra and the Aaronic Priesthood

1 Chron. 6:3–15	Ezra 7:1–6
Aaron	Aaron
Eleazar	Eleazar
Phinehas	Phinehas
Abishua	Abishua
Bukki	Bukki
Uzzi	Uzzi
Zerahiah	Zerahiah
Meraioth	Meraioth
Amariah	Azariah
Ahitub	Amariah
Zadok	Ahitub
Ahimaaz	Zadok
Azariah	Shallum
Johanan	Hilkiah

Names in Ezra are reversed from the listed order.

1 Chron. 6:3–15	Ezra 7:1–6
Azariah	Azariah
Amariah	Seraiah
Ahitub	Ezra
Zadok	
Shallum	
Hilkiah	
Azariah	
Seraiah	
Jehozadak	

The Family of the Maccabeans/Hasmoneans

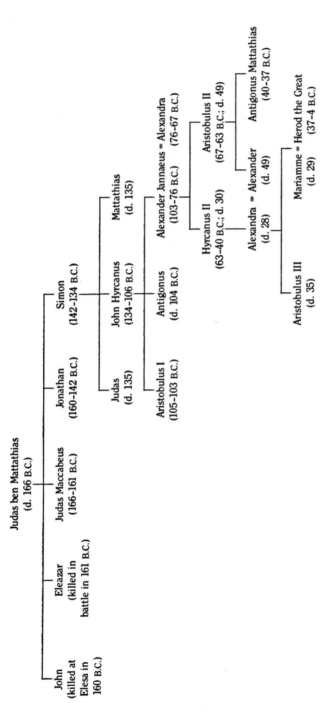

New Testament

The Text of the New Testament

The Books of the NT with Authors and Dates

Book	Author	Cosenders	Amanuensis	Date	Destination	Written From
Matthew	Matthew?			70–85	?	Antioch?
Mark	John Mark			50–70	?	Rome?
Luke	Luke			ca. 60	Theophilus	Caesarea/Rome?
John	John the Apostle?			80–95	?	?
Acts	Luke			63/64	Theophilus	Rome?
Romans	Paul		Tertius	57/58	Rome	Corinth
1 Corinthians	Paul	Sosthenes		53–55	Corinth	Ephesus
2 Corinthians	Paul	Timothy		56/57	Corinth	Macedonia
Galatians	Paul			48/49	Galatia	Jerusalem?
Ephesians	Paul			61/62	Ephesus	Rome
Philippians	Paul	Timothy		61–62	Philippi	Rome
Colossians	Paul	Timothy		61/62	Colosse/Laodicea	Rome
1 Thessalonians	Paul	Silas/Timothy		50	Thessalonica	Corinth
2 Thessalonians	Paul	Silas/Timothy		51/52	Thessalonica	Corinth
1 Timothy	Paul			60–64	Timothy/Ephesus	Macedonia?
2 Timothy	Paul			64–67	Timothy	Rome
Titus	Paul			60–64	Titus/Crete	Rome
Philemon	Paul	Timothy		61/62	Philemon/Colosse	Rome
Hebrews	?			60–70	?	?
James	James, Jesus' brother?			45–50	Diaspora	Jerusalem?
1 Peter	Peter		Silas	58–68	Asia Minor	Rome?
2 Peter	Peter?		John Mark?	65–68	Asia Minor	Rome
1 John	John the Apostle?			80–90	Asia Minor?	?
2 John	John the Apostle?			80–90	?	?
3 John	John the Apostle?			80–90	Gaius	?
Jude	Jude, Jesus' brother			60–68	?	?
Revelation	John the Apostle?			89–96	Asia Minor	Patmos

Dates for NT books are based on the arguments found in F. F. Bruce, *Paul: Apostle of the Heart Set Free* (Grand Rapids: Eerdmans, 1977); and D. Guthrie, *New Testament Introduction*, 3rd ed. (Downers Grove, IL: Inter-Varsity, 1970).

Chapters/Verses/Words

Book	Chapters	Verses	Words
Gospels			
Matthew	28	1,071	23,684
Mark	16	678	15,171
Luke	24	1,151	25,944
John	21	879	19,099
History			
Acts	28	1,007	24,250
Pauline Letters			
Romans	16	433	9,447
1 Corinthians	16	437	9,489
2 Corinthians	13	257	6,092
Galatians	6	149	3,098
Ephesians	6	155	3,039
Philippians	4	104	2,002
Colossians	4	95	1,998
1 Thessalonians	5	89	1,857
2 Thessalonians	3	47	1,042
1 Timothy	6	113	2,269
2 Timothy	4	83	1,703
Titus	3	46	921
Philemon	1	25	445
General or Catholic Letters			
Hebrews	13	303	6,913
James	5	108	2,309
1 Peter	5	105	2,482
2 Peter	3	61	1,559
1 John	5	105	2,523
2 John	1	13	303

Figures for the chapters, verses, and words are based on the Synopsis of the Books of the Bible in the Authorized Version of 1611 (Philadelphia: National Bible Press, n.d.).

Book	Chapters	Verses	Words
3 John	1	14	299
Jude	1	25	613
Apocalypse			
Revelation	22	404	1,200
Totals	260	7,957	169,751

The 10 OT Books Most Frequently Cited in the NT

Book	No. of Quotations or Allusions
1. Isaiah	419
2. Psalms	414
3. Exodus	240
4. Genesis	238
5. Deuteronomy	196
6. Ezekiel	141
7. Daniel	133
8. Jeremiah	125
9. Leviticus	107
10. Numbers	73

The 10 OT Verses Most Frequently Cited in the NT

Verse	No. of Quotations or Allusions	References
1. Psalm 110:1	18	Matt. 22:44; 26:64; Mark 12:36; 14:62; 16:19; Luke 20:42–43; 22:69; Acts 2:34–35; Rom. 8:34; 1 Cor. 15:25; Eph. 1:20; Col. 3:1; Heb. 1:3, 13; 8:1; 10:12, 13; 12:2

Verse	No. of Quotations or Allusions	References
2. Daniel 12:1	13	Matt. 24:21; Mark 13:19; Phil. 4:3; Jude 9; Rev. 3:5; 7:14; 12:7; 13:8; 16:18; 17:8; 20:12; 21:27
3. Isaiah 6:1	12	John 12:41; Rev. 4:2, 9, 10; 5:1, 7, 13; 6:16; 7:10, 15; 19:4; 21:5
4. Ezekiel 1:26-28	12	Rev. 4:2, 3, 9, 10; 5:1, 7, 13; 6:16; 7:10, 15; 19:4; 21:5
5. 2 Chronicles 18:18 Psalm 47:8 1 Kings 22:19	11	Rev. 4:2, 9, 10; 5:1, 7, 13; 6:16; 7:10, 15; 19:4; 21:5
6. Psalm 2:7	10	Matt. 3:17; 17:5; Mark 1:11; 9:7; Luke 3:22; 9:35; John 1:49; Acts 13:33; Heb. 1:5; 5:5
7. Isaiah 53:7	10	Matt. 26:63; 27:12, 14; Mark 14:60-61; 15:4-5; 1 Cor. 5:7; 1 Peter 2:23; Rev. 5:6, 12; 13:8
8. Amos 3:13 (LXX)	10	Rev. 1:8; 4:8, 13; 11:17; 15:3; 16:7, 14; 19:6, 15; 21:22
9. Amos 4:13 (LXX)	10	2 Cor. 6:18; Rev. 1:8; 4:8; 11:17; 15:3; 16:7, 14; 19:6, 15; 21:22
10. Leviticus 19:18	10	Matt. 5:43; 19:19; 22:39; Mark 12:31, 33; Luke 10:27; Rom. 12:19; 13:9; Gal. 5:14; James 2:8

The Percentage of the OT in the NT

Book	Percentage	# of OT Quotations or Allusions	
Matthew	31	310 of	1,071 verses
Mark	19	131	678
Luke	28	328	1,151

Figures based on information in the indexes of K. Aland et al., eds., *The Greek New Testament* (New York: United Bible Societies, 1968).

Book	Percentage	# of OT Quotations or Allusions	
John	14	129 of	890 verses
Acts	23	231	1,006
Romans	35	153	433
1 Corinthians	26	115	437
2 Corinthians	22	57	257
Galatians	19	28	149
Ephesians	30	46	155
Philippians	14	15	104
Colossians	10	9	95
1 Thessalonians	18	16	89
2 Thessalonians	34	16	47
1 Timothy	19	22	113
2 Timothy	14	12	83
Titus	15	7	46
Philemon	0	0	25
Hebrews	69	210	303
James	47	51	108
1 Peter	69	72	105
2 Peter	23	14	61
1 John	10	10	105
2 John	8	1	13
3 John	7	1	14
Jude	68	17	25
Revelation	150	605	404
Totals	32%	2,559 of 7,964 verses	

Extrabiblical Writers Quoted or Alluded to in the NT

Aratus

A Greek writer, poet, and Stoic philosopher of Soli in Cilicia. Born 315 B.C., died 240/239 B.C. Paul refers to his:
Phaenomena (5) in Acts 17:28

Cleanthes

A Greek writer and Stoic philosopher, the son of Phanias of Assos. Born 331 B.C., died 232 B.C. He was a disciple of Zeno. Paul refers to his:
Hymn to Zeus in Acts 17:28

Epimenides
A religious teacher and wonder worker of Crete during the 7th or 6th centuries B.C. Legend says he lived to be 299 years old, and that he had a miraculous sleep of 57 years. His writings exist only in fragments. Paul refers to his:
de Oraculis in Titus 1:12

Menander
An Athenian poet and playwright. Born 342/41 B.C., died 293/89 B.C. He was a leading writer of the "New Comedy" in Greece. Paul refers to his:
Thais (218) in 1 Cor. 15:33

The NT Canon

1. Marcion's Canon

    Luke
    Romans
    1 Corinthians
    2 Corinthians
    Galatians
    Ephesians
    Philippians
    Colossians
    1 Thessalonians
    2 Thessalonians
    Philemon

2. Irenaeus' Canon

    Matthew
    Mark
    Luke
    John
    Acts
    Romans
    1 & 2 Corinthians
    Galatians
    Ephesians

Philippians
Colossians
1 & 2 Thessalonians
1 & 2 Timothy
Titus
Philemon
1 Peter
1 John
Revelation

3. Muratorian Canon

Matthew
Mark
Luke
John
Acts
Romans
1 & 2 Corinthians
Galatians
Ephesians
Philippians
Colossians
1 & 2 Thessalonians
1 & 2 Timothy
Titus
Philemon
2 of John's Epistles ?
Jude
Revelation
Apocalypse of Peter

4. Origen's Canon

Origen recognized the same canonical books as Irenaeus. Origen lists the following books as "disputed":

Hebrews
2 Peter
2 & 3 John

James
Jude
Epistle of Barnabas
Shepherd of Hermas
Didache
Gospel of the Hebrews

5. Eusebius' Canon

Eusebius cites the following books as "disputed":

James
Jude
2 Peter
2 & 3 John

6. Syriac Canon

The original Syriac canon excluded:

James
1 & 2 Peter
1 & 2 & 3 John
Jude
Revelation

The first revision added:

1 Peter
1 John
James

The second revision added the remaining "disputed" books:

2 Peter
2 & 3 John
Jude
Revelation

7. Athanasius' Canon

In A.D. 367 Athanasius listed those books he believed to be "divine" in an Easter letter to his congregation. His canon includes the 27 books recognized as "canonical" today:

Matthew
Mark
Luke
John
Acts
Romans
1 & 2 Corinthians
Galatians
Ephesians
Philippians
Colossians
1 & 2 Thessalonians
1 & 2 Timothy
Titus
Philemon
Hebrews
James
1 & 2 Peter
1 & 2 & 3 John
Jude
Revelation

8. Jerome's Canon

Jerome listed the same 27 books as Athanasius.

9. Augustine's Canon

Augustine listed the same 27 books as Athanasius.

10. Synod of Hippo

In A.D. 393 the Synod of Hippo confirmed the 27 books recognized by Athanasius, Jerome, and Augustine as the NT canon.

11. Luther's Canon

Martin Luther separated four NT books from the rest and included them at the end of his canon as "lesser" books:

Hebrews
James
Jude
Revelation

Extrabiblical Historians

1. Appianus of Alexandria (ca. A.D. 160)

   An imperial governor who wrote a Roman history, in 24 volumes, complete through his own day. Most of his work (*Roman History*) is now lost.

2. Eusebius of Caesarea (ca. A.D. 263-340)

   A theologian, scholar, and church historian. Under Diocletian he suffered imprisonment and exile. He became bishop of Caesarea in A.D. 313. His writings include: *The Martyrs of Palestine, The Life of Constantine, Ecclesiastical History, Praeparatio Evangelica* (Preparation for the Gospel), *Chronicle,* and *Theophania.*

3. Hegesippus (2nd century A.D.)

   A Jewish-Christian apologist and historian whose works exist only in fragments in Eusebius and others.

4. Herodianus (3rd century A.D.)

   A Syrian official who wrote an eight-volume *Historiae* under Septimius Severus. His work covers the time span from the death of Aurelius to A.D. 238.

5. Herodotus (ca. 484-425 B.C.)

   Ancient Greek traveler and historian, often called the "father of history." Herodotus was born in Halicarnassus and later settled in Thurii in southern Italy. His work, *The Histories,* covers the period from the rise of the Persian Empire to the invasion of Xerxes and the war between the Greeks and the Persians (479 B.C.).

6. Josephus, Flavius (A.D. 37-97)

   A Jewish historian and apologist. He served as the Jewish emissary to Rome (64) and later was taken prisoner during the Jewish War by Vespasian (67). He was pensioned by the Romans and spent the rest of his life in Rome writing. His works include: *Antiquities of the Jews, Bellum Judaicum (The Jewish War), Contra Apionem (Against Apion),* and *Vita (Life).*

7. Livy (Titus Livius, 59 B.C.-A.D. 17)

   Roman historian born in Padua in northern Italy. In 9 B.C. he published his *History of Rome* in 142 books. The history is a chronicle of the Roman Empire from the founding of the city of

Rome (753 B.C.) to the death of Nero Claudius Drusus Germanicus (9 B.C.). Livy's *History of Rome* remains the primary source for Roman history.

8. Manetho (3rd century B.C.)

   A priest of On and an Egyptian theologian and historian. His writings exist only as fragments in Josephus, Eusebius, and others.

9. Nicolaus of Damascus (late first century B.C.)

   A Greek historian whose works are known only in fragments.

10. Pausanias (2nd century A.D.)

    A Greek historian, traveler, and geographer. His work *Journey Through Greece* was an ancient "travel-guide" and is a valuable source for historical information on the topography, monuments, and cults of ancient Greece.

11. Philo of Alexandria (20 B.C.-A.D. 50)

    A Hellenistic Jewish philosopher and scholar. Philo tried to correlate the OT with Greek philosophy by means of allegorical interpretation. He was a voluminous writer and his works include: *On the Sacrifices of Abel and Cain; On Abraham; On the Migrations of Abraham; On Joseph; On the Life of Moses; Questions on the Exodus;* and *On the Decalogue.*

12. Polybius (ca. 203-120 B.C.)

    A Greek historian born in Megalopolis. He was one of the 1,000 nobles sent from Achaia to Rome after the conquest of Macedonia (168 B.C.). He spent the latter part of his life writing his *Universal History.* The work covers the period from 266-146 B.C. Only 5 of the 40 volumes are preserved.

13. Sallust (Sallustius Crispus, ca. 86-35 B.C.)

    Sallust joined Julius Caesar during the civil war (49-45 B.C.) and later Caesar made him governor of Numidia. He retired to Rome and took up history writing. His works include: *The Catiline War, The Jugurthine War,* and *Histories.*

14. Strabo (ca. 64 B.C.-A.D. 24)

    A Greek geographer and historian born in Amasya in Pontus. His *Geography* is a detailed description of the world as known to the ancients.

15. Suetonius Tranquillus (ca. A.D. 69-140)

     A Roman historian and biographer. He was private secretary to the emperor Hadrian from 119-121 and had access to the imperial Roman archives. His writings include: *The Twelve Caesars,* a collection of biographies of twelve Roman rulers from Julius Caesar to Domitian; and *Concerning Illustrious Men,* a collection of biographies of Roman writers.

16. Tacitus, Cornelius (ca. A.D. 58-120)

     A Latin historian probably born in Rome and known to have held the offices of quaestor, praetor, and consul. Only about half of the writings of Tacitus have been preserved. They include: *Agricola, Germania, Historiae,* and *Annals.*

17. Thucydides (ca. 460-400 B.C.)

     A Greek historian born in Athens. Thucydides is known for his scientific method; his careful analytic style became the model for later historians. His great work was *The History of the Peloponnesian War* and covers the period from 431-404 B.C., of which he was a contemporary.

18. Xenophon (ca. 430-355 B.C.)

     A Greek soldier and historian and a disciple of Socrates. *Anabasis* is Xenophon's account of the Persian expedition and the march of the 10,000. His other writings include: *Cyropaedia* (a biography of Cyrus the Great), *Hellenica* (a continuation of Thucydides' *History of the Peloponnesian War* covering the period from 411-363 B.C.), and *Memorabilia* (recollections of Socrates).

For more complete biographical and bibliographical information see N. G. L. Hammond and H. H. Scullard, eds., *The Oxford Classical Dictionary,* 2nd ed. (Oxford: Clarendon Press, 1970).

Miscellaneous Data

1. The NT was written by at least 9 different authors during the period A.D. 40 to A.D. 100.
2. The NT was written in Koiné Greek. It contains approximately 5,450 lexical items. Of these 5,450 words, 3,600 occur 4 times or less, and approximately 1,686 occur only once in the NT. There are 1,100 words that occur 10 times or more.

3. Chapter divisions began in the 4th century A.D. with the Codex Vaticanus. Verse divisions first appeared in 1551 in the 4th edition of the NT printed by Stephanus (Robert Estienne).

4. New Testament manuscripts date to as early as A.D. 120-150 (*p* 52). These manuscripts include:

Greek MSS:
    78 papyri
    224 uncials (LITERARY STYLE, ALL CAPITAL LETTERS)
    30 uncial fragments
    2,650 minuscules (nonliterary style, all lower case letters)
    2,000 lectionaries (Scripture passages arranged in units for reading in the church)

Latin MSS: 8,000
MSS in other languages: 1,000

5. Hand copying of manuscripts through the centuries produced many errors and variants in the New Testament text. There are literally thousands of variants in the NT, and they result from a number of factors related to the transmission of the text. These include:

a. errors of sight:

1) wrong division of words
2) confusion of one letter for another
3) homoioteleuton (skipping from one similar ending to another)
4) haplography (writing a letter or word once when it should be written twice)
5) dittography (writing a letter or word twice when it should be written only once)
6) metathesis (changing the order of letters or words)

b. errors of writing
c. errors of hearing (if the scribe was copying a manuscript being dictated to him)
d. errors of memory
e. errors of judgment
f. intentional changes in the text

1) grammatical changes due to a different understanding of syntax, grammar, etc.

2) liturgical changes
3) harmonization of parallel passages
4) conflation (combining of two or more variants into one reading)
5) correction of an earlier MS error
6) correction or elimination of apparent discrepancies
7) changes for doctrinal purposes

New Testament Chronology

Biblical and Extrabiblical Events: 10 B.C. to A.D. 140

Event	Date B.C.
Herod's inauguration of Caesarea	10
Death of Drusus; Herod invades Nabatea	9
Census of Caesar Augustus; Polemo captured and executed by his queen Dynamis; Death of Horace	8
The city of Rome is divided into 14 regions	7
Tiberius retires to Rhodes for 5 years; Paphlagonia added to Galatia; Death of Tigranes II; Armenia revolts	6
12th consulship of Augustus; birth of Jesus	5
Execution of Antipater; death of Herod the Great	4
13th consulship of Augustus; exile of Julia	2

Event	Date A.D.
Return of Tiberius from Rhodes; death of L. Caesar	2
Tiberius adopted by Augustus; Tiberius invades Germany; death of C. Caesar	4

Dates based on S. A. Cook et al., eds., *The Cambridge Ancient History,* 2nd ed., vols. 10 and 11 (Cambridge: Cambridge University Press, 1971, 1965).

Event	Date A.D.
Assessment of Judea by Quirinius; procurators begin to rule in Judea and Samaria	6
Jesus at temple when 12; banishment of Ovid	8
Lex Papia Poppaea; revolt crushed in Dalmatia	9
Aspurgus in control of Bosporan kingdom	10/11
Death of Augustus, accession of Tiberius	14
Suicide of Drusus Libo	16
Triumph of Germanicus in Germany; earthquake in Asia Minor; death of Livy	17
Germanicus in Asia Minor and Syria; consulship of Tiberius III and Germanicus; Joseph Caiaphas becomes high priest of the Jews; death of Ovid	18
Death of Germanicus	19
Trial and suicide of Cn. Piso	20
Consulship of Tiberius IV and Drusus; Tiberius retires to Campania	21
Death of Drusus; Ptolemy succeeds Juba as king of Mauretania	23
Suicide of Cremutius Cordus	25
Pontius Pilate appointed procurator of Judea	26
Tiberius withdraws to Capreae	27
Titius Sabinus executed; death of Julia	28
Death of Livia; banishment of Agrippina and Nero (widow and son of Germanicus); John the Baptist begins his ministry	29
Jesus begins his public ministry	29/30
Suicide of Nero	30
Consulship of Tiberius V and Sejanus	31
Death of Agrippina; financial crisis in Rome; crucifixion of Christ	33

Event	Date A.D.
Death of Herod Philip the tetrarch	34
Pontius Pilate sent to Rome for misadministration	36
Death of Tiberius, accession of Gaius Caligula and consulship with Claudius; Herod Agrippa I given a kingdom in Syria; birth of Flavius Josephus	37
Polemo II made king in Pontus; Cotys made king in Armenia Minor; death and deification of Drusilla	38
Gaius leaves Rome for Germany	39
Gaius returns to Rome	40
Gaius assassinated, Claudius made emperor; Seneca exiled to Corsica, recalled in 49; Herod Agrippa I made king of Judea and Samaria	41
Lycia made an imperial province	43
Claudius is victorious in Britain; Achaea and Macedonia transferred to the Senate; death of Herod Agrippa I, Judea made a province	44
Thrace is made a province	45
Marriage of Claudius and Agrippina the Younger	48
Domitius/Nero is adopted by Claudius; Herod Agrippa II rules Chalcis after the death of Herod III	50
Consulship of Vespasian	51
Gallio proconsul of Achaia	51/52
Felix made procurator in Judea	52
Marriage of Nero and Octavia	53
Claudius poisoned by Agrippina, accession of Nero	54
Zealot terrorism in Palestine	54-66
Revolt of the Egyptian (Acts 21:38); consulship of Nero and L. Antistius Vetus; Britannicus poisoned	55

Event	Date A.D.
Nero orders the participation of senators and knights in the games; revolt of Hyrcania	57
Corbulo captures and sacks Artaxata	58
Agrippina murdered; Nero introduces Greek games in Rome; Corbulo takes Tigranocerta	59
Puteoli made a Roman colony; Corbulo made governor of Syria; Festus succeeds Felix as procurator of Judea	60
Revolt of Iceni; Galilee and Perea added to the kingdom of Herod Agrippa II	61
Death of Burrus; Fall of Seneca; Nero divorces Octavia and marries Poppaea; Octavia banished and murdered	62
Fire in Rome, Nero persecutes Christians, Paul martyred(?); Pontus incorporated with the province of Galatia; Gessius Florus becomes procurator of Judea	64
Conspiracy of Piso; death of Poppaea; death of Seneca	65
Nero marries Statilia Messallina; Nero executes Scribonius Rufus and Scribonius Proculus; death of Petronius; riots in Caesarea and Jerusalem, Jewish War 66-73	66
Nero begins work on canal of Corinth; Corbulo ordered to commit suicide; Vespasian made legate in Judea; Josephus surrenders to Vespasian; military action taken against the Samaritans	67
Vespasian attacks Jerusalem; death of Nero, accession of Galba; suicide of Vindex	68
Death of Galba, accession of Otho; suicide of Otho, accession of Vitellius; death of Vitellius, accession of Vespasian; Hordeonius Flaccus murdered	69
Vespasian arrives at Rome; Titus captures and sacks Jerusalem; decree against astrologers	70
Astrologers and philosophers banished from Rome	71

Event	Date A.D.
Jewish revolts in Egypt and Cyrene; Antiochus IV deposed; Armenia Minor added to Cappadocia	72
Censorship of Vespasian and Titus; Roman operations in Upper Germany; Greece made a senatorial province	73
Herod Agrippa II and Bernice move to Rome; invasion of Media and Armenia by the Alani	75
Agricola becomes governor in Britain	77
Conspiracy of A. Caecina Alienus and Eprius Marcellus	78
Death of Vespasian, accession of Titus; eruption of Mt· Vesuvius; death of the Elder Pliny; publication of Josephus's *Jewish War,* 75–79	79
Burning of Rome; dedication of Colosseum	80
Death of Titus, accession of Domitian; arch of Titus dedicated	81
Romans conquer Southwest Germany, 83–85	83
Recall of Agricola	85
Inauguration of the Capitoline Games	86
1st Dacian War	86–87
Revolt in Mainz	88
2nd Dacian War	89
3rd Dacian War; palaces on the Palatine completed	92
Death of Agricola; trial of Baebius Massa	93
Persecution of senators and philosophers; publication of Josephus's *Antiquities*	93–94
Persecution of Jews and Christians	94–95
Philosophers expelled from Italy; birth of Arrian	95
Domitian assassinated, accession of Nerva	96
Lex Agraria	97

Event	Date A.D.
Death of Nerva, accession of Trajan	98
Trajan arrives in Rome	99
Trajan begins his campaign against Dacia	101
Suicide of Decebalus; annexation of Arabia	106
Pliny the Younger made governor in Bithynia	111
Persecution of Christians in Bithynia; death of Pliny the Younger; Trajan leaves Rome for war in Parthia	113
Persecution of Christians in Syria; annexation of Armenia and Mesopotamia	114
2nd Jewish War	115-117
Jewish revolt in Cyrene	115
Jewish revolts in Egypt and Cyprus	116
Death of Trajan, accession of Hadrian	117
Consulship of Antoninus	120
Hadrian's 1st tour of the provinces	121-126
Hadrian visits Britain; 2nd Moorish revolt	122
Death of Plutarch	126
Hadrian's 2nd tour of the provinces	129-134
Birth of Galen	129
Hadrian founds Antinoopolis	130
Bar-Kochba rebellion crushed, Jerusalem razed, Jews dispersed	132-135
Invasion of Parthia by the Alani; Antoninus proconsul of Asia	134
Aelia Capitolina built on Jerusalem site; Syria-Palestine re-organized	135
Death of Hadrian, accession of Antoninus Pius	138

NT Events

Event	Date B.C.
Census of Caesar Augustus	8
Birth of Jesus; visit of the Magi	5
Death of Herod the Great; Herod Archelaus ethnarch of Judea to A.D. 6; Herod Philip tetrarch of Iturea to A.D. 34; Herod Antipas tetrarch of Galilee to A.D. 39	4

Event	Date A.D.
Assessment of Judea by Quirinius, governor of Syria from 6-11; Annas high priest of the Jews, 6-15; procurators begin to rule Judea	6
Jesus at the temple when twelve	8
Josephus Caiaphas high priest of the Jews, 18-37	18
Pontius Pilate becomes procurator of Judea, 26-36	26
John the Baptist begins his ministry	29
Baptism of Jesus and commencement of his public ministry	29/30
Christ's 1st Passover	30
Christ's 2nd Passover	31
Death of John the Baptist	31?
Christ's 3rd Passover	32
Christ's crucifixion at Passover	33
Christ's ascension, 40 days after his resurrection	33
Pentecost, 50 days after Christ's resurrection	33
Martyrdom of Stephen; conversion of Saul	35

NT chronology adapted from F. F. Bruce, *Paul: Apostle of the Heart Set Free* (Grand Rapids: Eerdmans, 1977), and W. H. Hoehner, *Chronological Aspects of the Life of Christ* (Grand Rapids: Zondervan, 1977).

Event	Date A.D.
1st visit of Saul to Jerusalem	38
Herod Agrippa I made king of Judea, 41-44	41
James, the son of Zebedee martyred	42
Revolt of Theudas	45?
Famine under Claudius, Paul's 2nd visit to Jerusalem	46
Paul's 1st missionary journey	47-48
Council of Jerusalem, Paul's 3rd visit to Jerusalem	49
Claudius expels Jews from Rome	50?
Paul's 2nd missionary journey	49/50-52/53
Zealot disturbances in Palestine; Paul in Corinth	50-52
Gallio proconsul in Corinth	51-52
Antonius Felix becomes procurator of Judea	52
Paul's 3rd missionary journey	53/54-57/58
Paul in Ephesus	53/54-55/56
Revolt of the Egyptian (Acts 21:38)	55?
Paul arrested in Jerusalem	57/58
Paul imprisoned in Caesarea	57/58-59/60
Paul taken to Rome	59/60
Paul imprisoned in Rome	60-62
Porcius Festus becomes procurator of Judea	60
Martyrdom of James, the brother of Jesus	62
Paul travels in Macedonia, Spain(?)	62-64
Great fire in Rome	64
Persecution of Christians by Nero	64-68
Martyrdom of Peter and Paul	65?

Event	Date A.D.
The Jewish War	66-73
Titus takes Jerusalem, the temple is destroyed	70
Masada falls	73
Persecution of Christians under Domitian; John exiled to Patmos(?)	81-96
John returns to Ephesus(?)	96
Death of John the Apostle	100?

Christ's Life and Ministry

Event	Reference	Date B.C.
Birth of Christ	Luke 2:1-7	
Jesus circumcised and named 8 days after birth	Luke 2:21	
Jesus presented in the temple 40 days after birth	Luke 2:22	
Simeon and Anna see Jesus	Luke 2:25, 36	5
The Magi visit Jesus	Matt. 2:1-12	
Joseph and Mary take Jesus to Egypt	Matt. 2:13-15	
Herod has all male children age 2 and under killed	Matt. 2:16-18	4?
Herod the Great dies		4
Joseph and Mary return from Egypt with Jesus and take up residence in Nazareth	Matt. 2:21-23	4/3

Scholars postulate Jesus and his disciples operated on a Galilean calendar, whereby Passover was celebrated on Thursday Nisan 14, and that Jerusalem Jews operated on a Judean calendar whereby Passover was celebrated on Friday Nisan 15. In this way Jesus could eat the Passover Meal on Thursday and die as the Passover Lamb on Friday. See H. W. Hoehner, *Chronological Aspects of the Life of Christ* (Grand Rapids: Zondervan, 1977).

Event	Reference	Date A.D.
Jesus, age 12, at the temple questioning the teachers during Passover	Luke 2:41-52	8
John the Baptist begins his ministry as Jesus' forerunner	Luke 3:1-3	
John baptizes Jesus	Mark 1:9-11	
Jesus is tempted 40 days in the desert	Mark 1:12-13	29
Jesus' 1st Passover	John 2:13	30
John the Baptist killed	Matt. 14:1-12	31?
Jesus at "the feast of the Jews"	John 5:1	30/31?
Jesus' 2nd or 3rd Passover	John 6:4	31/32?
Jesus at the Feast of Tabernacles (Sept.)	John 7:2, 10	31/32?
Jesus at the Feast of the Dedication (Dec.)	John 10:22-39	31/32?
Jesus' final week	John 12:1-20:28	
Jesus arrives in Bethany 6 days before the Passover (a Saturday), has dinner with Simon the Leper, Lazarus, Mary, and Martha	John 12:1-11; cf. Mark 14:1-9	
Triumphal entry into Jerusalem and cleansing of the temple and cursing of fig tree (a Sunday)	Matt. 21:1-22	
Jesus returns to Jerusalem the next day (a Monday)	Mark 11:27	
Mary of Bethany anoints Jesus on Tuesday, 2 days before the Passover	Matt. 26:1-13	
Jesus eats the Passover meal with his disciples, is betrayed by Judas Iscariot and arrested in the Garden of Gethsemane on Thursday evening	Luke 22:7-53	
Jesus is tried before the Sanhedrin at daybreak on Friday	Luke 22:66-71	
Jesus goes to Pilate, to Herod, and back to Pilate on Friday morning	Luke 23:6-12	
Jesus is crucified at 9:00 a.m. on Friday	Mark 15:25	
Darkness for 3 hours (12:00-3:00 p.m.)	Mark 15:33	32/33?

Event	Reference	Date A.D.
Jesus dies at 3:00 p.m. on Friday	Luke 24:44-46	
The temple curtain is torn in two	Matt. 27:51	
An earthquake occurs	Matt. 27:51	
Many saints are resurrected	Matt. 27:52	
Jesus is buried toward evening	Matt. 27:57-61	
The tomb is sealed on Saturday	Matt. 27:62-66	
Jesus is raised from the dead on Sunday at dawn	Matt. 28:1-2	
Jesus appears to Mary Magdalene	John 20:11-18	
Jesus appears to other women	Matt. 28:9-10	
Jesus appears to Simon Peter	Luke 24:33-35	
Jesus appears to 2 disciples on the road to Emmaus	Luke 24:13-32	
Jesus appears to 10 disciples Sunday evening	John 20:19-23	
Jesus appears to 11 disciples one week later	John 20:26-28	
Jesus appears to 7 disciples in Galilee	John 21:1-25	
Jesus appears to the apostles and more than 500 disciples in Galilee	Matt. 28:16-20, 1 Cor. 15:6	
Jesus appears to James, his brother	1 Cor. 15:7	
Jesus ascends 40 days after his resurrection	Acts 1:3-9	
Pentecost occurs 50 days after Jesus' resurrection	Acts 2:1-13	32/33?

Comparative Chronology of Christ

Event	Date B.C.
Birth	Anderson, 4
	Eusebius, 2
	Hastings, Dec./5
	Hoehner, Winter 5/4
	IDB, 6-4
	ISBE, 6
	Ogg, 8/7
	Reicke, 5/4
	S-H, 6/5
	Scroggie, 5
	ZPEB, 6/5

Event	Date A.D.
Baptism	Anderson, 28
	Eusebius, 29
	Hastings, 27
	Hoehner, 29
	IDB, 27/28

R. Anderson, *The Coming Prince*, reprint ed. (Grand Rapids: Kregel, 1957); Eusebius of Caesarea, *Ecclesiastical History*, trans. C. F. Cruse, reprint ed. (Grand Rapids: Baker, 1955); J. Hastings, *Dictionary of the Bible* (Edinburgh: T. and T. Clark, 1900), 5 vols.; G. A. Buttrick et al., eds., *The Interpreter's Dictionary of the Bible* (Nashville: Abingdon, 1962), 4 vols. plus *Supplement* (1976), hereafter cited as *IDB*; G. W. Bromiley et al., eds., *The International Standard Bible Encyclopedia*, rev. ed. (Grand Rapids: Eerdmans, 1979), vol. 1, hereafter cited as *ISBE*; G. Ogg, *The Chronology of the Public Ministry of Jesus* (Cambridge, 1940); B. Reicke, *The New Testament Era*, trans. D. E. Green (Philadelphia: Fortress, 1968); S. M. Jackson et al., eds., *The New Schaff-Herzog Encyclopedia of Religious Knowledge*, reprint ed. (Grand Rapids: Baker, 1977), 12 vols. plus index and extension (2 vols.), hereafter cited as *S-H*; W. G. Scroggie, *The Unfolding Drama of Redemption*, reprint ed. (Grand Rapids: Zondervan, 1970); M. C. Tenney et al., eds., *The Zondervan Pictorial Encyclopedia of the Bible* (Grand Rapids: Zondervan, 1975), 5 vols., hereafter cited as *ZPEB*.

Event	Date A.D.
	ISBE, 28
	Ogg, 29
	Reicke, 28/29
	S-H, 26
	Scroggie, 27
	ZPEB, Fall 26
Crucifixion	Anderson, Nisan 13/32
	Eusebius, 33
	Hastings, Nisan 14/29
	Hoehner, April 3/33
	IDB, 30
	ISBE, 30
	Ogg, 33
	Reicke, 33
	S-H, 30
	Scroggie, 30
	ZPEB, 29/30

Paul's Ministry

Event	Date A.D.
Death of Christ	33
Saul persecutes the church	33-35
Conversion of Saul	35
1st Jerusalem visit	38
Famine collection taken to Jerusalem	46
1st missionary journey	46-48
Galatians written	48/49
Jerusalem Council	49
2nd missionary journey	49-52
Paul in Corinth	50-52

Chronology of Paul's ministry adapted from F. F. Bruce, *Paul: Apostle of the Heart Set Free* (Grand Rapids: Eerdmans, 1977).

Event	Date A.D.
1 Thessalonians written	50
2 Thessalonians written	51
3rd missionary journey	53-57
Paul in Ephesus	53-55
1 Corinthians written	55
Paul in Macedonia and Achaia	55-57
2 Corinthians written	56
Romans written	57
Paul arrested in Jerusalem	57
Imprisonment at Caesarea	57-59
Journey to Rome	59-60
Imprisonment at Rome	60-62/3
Captivity letters written	60-62/3
Paul released and in Macedonia or Spain(?)	63?
2nd imprisonment at Rome	63-64?
Pastoral letters written	63-64?
Paul's death	64/65?

Comparative Chronology of Paul

Event	Date A.D.
Conversion	Alford, 37
	Bengel, 31

H. Alford, *Greek New Testament*, 3rd ed. (London: Rivingtons, 1941); J. A. Bengel, *Gnomon of the New Testament*, trans. C. T. Lewis (Philadelphia: Perkinpine & Higgins, 1860), 2 vols.; F. F. Bruce, *Paul: Apostle of the Heart Set Free* (Grand Rapids: Eerdmans, 1977); W. J. Conybeare and J. S. Howson, *The Life and Epistles of St. Paul*, reprint ed. (Grand Rapids: Eerdmans, 1976); J. Hastings, *Dictionary of the Bible* (Edinburgh: T. and T. Clark, 1900), 5 vols.; G. W. Bromiley et al., eds., *The International Standard Bible Encyclopedia*, rev. ed. (Grand Rapids: Eerdmans, 1979), vol. 1, hereafter cited as *ISBE*; K. Lake and F. J. F. Jackson, *The Acts of the Apostles*, reprint ed. (Grand Rapids: Baker, 1979), 5 vols.; H. A. W. Meyer, *Commentary on the New Testament*, rev. ed., trans. P. J. Gloag (New York: Funk & Wagnalls, 1883), 11 vols.; G. Ogg, *The Chronology of the Life of Paul* (London, 1968); W. M. Ramsay, *St. Paul the Traveller and the Roman Citizen*,

Event	Date A.D.
	Bruce, 33
	C & H, 39/40
	Hastings, 34/35
	ISBE, 36
	Lake, 32
	Meyer, 35
	Ogg, 34/35
	Ramsay, 31
	Scroggie, 37
	ZPEB, 34
Famine visit to Jerusalem	Alford, 44
	Bengel, 41–44
	Bruce, 46
	C & H, 45
	Hastings, 45/46
	ISBE, 44–48
	Lake, 46
	Meyer, 44
	Ogg, 45/46
	Ramsay, 45
	Scroggie, 45
	ZPEB, 45
1st missionary journey	Alford, 45
	Bengel, 45–46
	Bruce, 47–48
	C & H, 45–50
	Hastings, 47–48
	ISBE, 47–48
	Lake, 46–47
	Meyer, 45–51
	Ogg, 46–47
	Ramsay, 47–49

3rd ed. (New York: Putnam, 1898); W. G. Scroggie, *The Unfolding Drama of Redemption*, reprint ed. (Grand Rapids: Zondervan, 1970); M. C. Tenney et al., eds., *The Zondervan Pictorial Encyclopedia of the Bible* (Grand Rapids: Zondervan, 1975), 5 vols., hereafter cited as *ZPEB*.

Event	Date A.D.
	Scroggie, 47–49
	ZPEB, 46–48
Council of Jerusalem	Alford, 50
	Bengel, 47
	Bruce, 49
	C & H, 50/51
	Hastings, 49/50
	ISBE, 49
	Lake, 46
	Meyer, 52
	Ogg, 48
	Ramsay, 50
	Scroggie, 50
	ZPEB, 49
2nd missionary journey	Alford, 51–54
	Bengel, 47–49
	Bruce, 49–52
	C & H, 51–54
	Hastings, 51–54
	ISBE, 49–51
	Lake, 49–51
	Meyer, 52–55
	Ogg, 48–51
	Ramsay, 50–53
	Scroggie, 50–53
	ZPEB, 49–52
3rd missionary journey	Alford, 54–58
	Bengel, 49–53
	Bruce, 52–57
	C & H, 54–58
	Hastings, 54–57
	ISBE, 51–54
	Lake, 52–55
	Meyer, 55–59
	Ogg, 54–59

Event	Date A.D.
	Ramsay, 53–57
	Scroggie, 54–58
	ZPEB, 53–57
Arrest in Jerusalem and imprisonment in Caesarea	
	Alford, 58–60
	Bengel, 53–55
	Bruce, 57–59
	C & H, 58–60
	Hastings, 58–60
	ISBE, 58–61
	Lake, 55–57
	Meyer, 59–62
	Ogg, 59–61
	Ramsay, 57–59
	Scroggie, 58–60
	ZPEB, 57–60
Arrival in Rome and Roman imprisonment	
	Alford, 61–63
	Bengel, 56–58
	Bruce, 60–62
	C & H, 61–63
	Hastings, 60–62
	ISBE, 57–59
	Lake, 57–59
	Meyer, 62–64
	Ogg, 62–64
	Ramsay, 60–62
	Scroggie, 61–63
	ZPEB, 61–63
Martyrdom	
	Alford, ?
	Bengel, ?
	Bruce, 65?
	C & H, 68
	Hastings, 65–67?

Event	Date A.D.
	ISBE, 67
	Lake, ?
	Meyer, ?
	Ogg, ?
	Ramsay, 65
	Scroggie, 67/68
	ZPEB, 67

The Corinthian Chronology

Event	Reference
Paul visits Corinth on his second missionary journey	Acts 18:1-18
Apollos is in Corinth	Acts 19:1
Paul sends a letter (now lost) to Corinth	1 Cor. 5:9
Paul receives news in Ephesus from Chloe's household regarding factions in the Corinthian church.	
Stephanas, Fortunatus, and Achaicus bring a letter from Corinth to Paul in Ephesus	1 Cor. 16:17
Paul writes 1 Corinthians from Ephesus	
Timothy is sent to Corinth, probably before Paul finishes his letter; but he stays only briefly and apparently is unsuccessful in his mission	1 Cor. 4:17; cf. 16:10ff.
Paul makes a second "painful" visit to Corinth from Ephesus	2 Cor. 2:1; 13:2
Paul writes a "harsh" letter (now lost) to Corinth from Ephesus	2 Cor. 2:3-4
Paul writes 2 Corinthians from Macedonia	
Paul makes a third visit to the Corinthian church	2 Cor. 12:14; 13:1

Governmental Officials Named in the NT

Name	Reference
1. Blastus the chamberlain (*koitōnos*) of Herod Agrippa	Acts 12:20
2. The Caesar (*kaisar*) a. Caesar Augustus, 27 B.C.–A.D. 14 b. Caesar Tiberius, A.D. 14–37	Luke 2:1 Matt. 22:17–21; Mark 12:14–17; Luke 3:1; Luke 20:22–25; 23:2; John 19:12–15
c. Caesar Claudius, A.D. 41–54 d. Caesar Nero (not named in NT), A.D. 54–68	Acts 11:28; 17:7; 18:2 Acts 25:8–21; 26:32; 27:24; 28:19
3. Candace queen (*basilissa*) of Ethiopia	Acts 8:27
4. Claudius Lysias the commander (*chiliarchos*) of the Roman garrison in Jerusalem	Acts 23:26
5. Cuza the manager (*epitropos*) of Herod Antipas' household	Luke 8:3
6. Erastus the city treasurer (*oikonomos*) of Corinth	Rom. 16:23
7. Ethiopian eunuch the ruler (*dunastēs*) of the treasury (*gaza*) for Candace	Acts 8:27
8. Felix, Antonius ruler (*hēgemōn*, Roman procurator) of Judea from A.D. 52–60	Acts 23:24–24:27
9. Festus, Porcius successor to Felix as procurator of Judea from A.D. 60–62?	Acts 24:27–25:27

Name	Reference
10. Gallio proconsul (*anthupatos*) of Achaia from A.D. 51-52 or 52-53	Acts 18:12-17
11. Herods	
a. Herod the Great king (*basileus*) of Israel from 40/37 to 4 B.C.	Matt. 2:1-12; Luke 1:5
b. Herod Archelaus followed his father Herod the Great as ruler of Judea (without the title of king) from 4 B.C.-A.D. 6	Matt. 2:22
c. Herod Philip tetrarch (*tetraarchēs*) of Batanea and Trachonitis until his death in A.D. 34	Matt. 14:3; Mark 6:17; Luke 3:1, 19
d. Herod Antipas tetrarch (*tetraarchēs*) of Galilee and Perea until A.D. 39	Matt. 14:1-6; Mark 6: 14-22; Luke 3:1, 19; 9: 7-9; 13:31; 23:7-15
e. Herod Agrippa I succeeded Herod Philip as tetrarch of Batanea and Trachonitis and Syria from A.D. 37-41 and reigned as king of the Judean area from A.D. 41-44	Acts 12:1-21
f. Herod Agrippa II son of Herod Agrippa, the last of the Herodian dynasty ruled as king (*basileus*) in the Judean area from A.D. 60/61? to 100?, from A.D. 53 to 60/61 he was tetrarch of the area governed formerly by Herod Philip and Herod Agrippa	Acts 25:13-26; 26:1-32
12. Lysanias tetrarch (*tetraarchēs*) of Abilene when John the Baptist began his ministry (A.D. 28 or 29), exact dates of his rule are unknown	Luke 3:1
13. Pilate, Pontius ruler (*hēgemōn*, Roman procurator) of Judea from A.D. 26-36	Matt. 27:2-65; Mark 15: 1-44; Luke 3:1; 13:1; 23: 1-52; John 18:29-38; 19: 1-38; Acts 3:13; 4:27; 13:28; 1 Tim. 6:13

Name	Reference
14. Publius the "chief official" (*tō prōtō*) of Crete	Acts 28:7
15. Quirinius ruler (*hēgemōn*) of Syria for several years beginning in A.D. 6; scholars postulate an early governorship of Quirinius in Syria to reconcile the census information with the birth of Christ; this earlier rule is dated anywhere between 8 and 2 B.C.	Luke 2:2
16. Sergius Paulus proconsul (*anthupatos*) of Cyprus, dates unknown	Acts 13:7
17. Tertullus an orator or lawyer (*rhētor*)	Acts 24:1-9

The Herods

1. Herod the Great, king of Judea from 40/37-4 B.C.

Herod was born in ca. 73 B.C., the son of Antipater and Kypros. He was appointed procurator of Judea in 47 B.C. by Julius Caesar. Advised by Antony and Octavian, the Roman Senate made Herod "king of the Jews" in 40 B.C. (some sources say 37 B.C.). Herod ruled in Judea until his death in 4 B.C. Herod was married ten times: Doris, Mariamme I, Mariamme II, Malthace, Cleopatra, Pallas, Phaedra, Elpis, to a daughter of Salome, to a niece. Herod was a prolific builder and his greatest accomplishment was the reconstruction of the temple of Jerusalem. Herod was an Edomite and for the most part was despised by the Jews. Jesus was born shortly before Herod's death (Matt. 2:1).

2. Herod Archelaus, ruled Judea from 4 B.C.-A.D. 6

Also called Herod the Ethnarch, he was Herod the Great's elder son by his Samaritan wife Malthace. He ruled Judea in his father's place

134

without the title of king. He had the worst reputation of all Herod's sons (cf. Matt. 2:22).

3. Herod Philip, tetrarch of Batanea and Trachonitis until A.D. 34

Herod Philip was the son of Herod the Great and his fifth wife, Cleopatra. He married Salome, the daughter of Herodias who danced before Herod Antipas (Mark 6:22). There is some confusion in regard to the marriages of Herod Philip. The NT (Mark 6:17) indicates Herod Philip was married to Herodias, who left him to marry his half-brother, Herod Antipas. Other sources (mainly Josephus) record only one marriage of Herod Philip, that to Salome, the daughter of Herodias. It seems the first marriage of Herodias was to Herod II (Philip), the half-brother of Herod Antipas, and the son of Herod the Great and his third wife, Mariamme II. Herod Philip died without an heir in A.D. 34. His tetrarchy was made part of Syria, then assigned to Herod Agrippa I in A.D. 37.

4. Herod Antipas, tetrarch of Galilee and Perea until A.D. 39

The younger son of Herod the Great by Malthace and the younger brother of Herod Archelaus. He married a daughter of Aretas IV, king of Nabatea, but divorced her to marry Herodias, the wife of his half-brother Philip (cf. Luke 3:19-20). He imprisoned and executed John the Baptist (Mark 6:14-28). Pilate sent Jesus to him for judgment, which he refused (Luke 23:7-12). He built the city of Tiberias on the Sea of Galilee. He was the most able of all Herod's sons but he was deposed from his tetrarchy in A.D. 39 and spent the remainder of his life in exile.

5. Herod Agrippa I, tetrarch of Batanea and Trachonitis beginning in A.D. 37; Galilee and Perea were included in his tetrarchy in A.D. 39; from A.D. 41-44 he was king of Judea, Batanea, Trachonitis, Perea, and Galilee

The son of Aristobulus (the son of Herod the Great by Mariamme I) and Bernice. Herod, king of Chalcis, was his brother and Herodias was his sister. Caligula granted him the tetrarchy of Herod Philip in A.D. 37. In A.D. 39 the tetrarchy of Herod Antipas was added to his kingdom. In A.D. 41 Claudius added Judea and Samaria to

Agrippa's kingdom and granted him the title of king. Agrippa persecuted the early church and had James, the brother of John, executed (Acts 12:1-4). Herod Agrippa died in A.D. 44 at the age of 54 (cf. Acts 12:19-23). Herod Agrippa left three daughters: Bernice, who married Marcus, Herod of Chalcis, and Polemon, king of Cilicia, and lived with her brother Herod Agrippa II (cf. Acts 25:13); Drusilla, who married King Azizus and later became the third wife of the procurator Antonius Felix (Acts 24:24); Mariamme; and one son Herod Agrippa II. Since Agrippa II was a minor, the kingdom of Agrippa I was reduced to a providence and was ruled by procurators.

6. Herod Agrippa II, king of Chalcis from A.D. 50-53, ruler of territory in Batanea and Trachonitis from A.D. 53-56, and later (56 or 61?) made king of Galilee, Perea, and part of Judea by Nero.

Only seventeen when his father, Agrippa I, died, Agrippa II was a minor and unable to take over his father's throne. He succeeded his uncle (and brother-in-law) as king of Chalcis and later received larger territories in Batanea and Trachonitis. Nero made him king over Galilee, Perea, Batanea, Trachonitis, and part of Judea in A.D. 56/61(?). Agrippa's armies participated in the assault on Jerusalem during the Jewish War. After the Jewish War Agrippa had additional territories added to his kingdom. He and Bernice moved to Rome in A.D. 75. He corresponded with Josephus when Josephus was writing *The Jewish War.* Agrippa died in A.D. 100, ending the Herodian dynasty. He heard Paul's case at Festus' request (Acts 25:26).

7. Bernice, born A.D. 28, died ?

The sister of Herod Agrippa II and the daughter of Agrippa I and Kypros. She married Marcus, the son of Alexander. Later she married Herod III, king of Chalcis (her uncle). When Herod III died in A.D. 48 she lived, apparently incestuously, with her brother Agrippa II. She married Polemo(n) the king of Cilicia, but left him after a brief stay and returned to Agrippa II. She was with Agrippa II when he heard Paul's case at the request of Festus (Acts 25:13, 23). She moved to Rome in A.D. 75 with Agrippa II and subsequently became the mistress of Vespasian and Titus. Later she was "banished" by Titus.

8. Drusilla, born A.D. 38, died ?

The daughter of Agrippa I and Kypros, and the sister of Bernice and Agrippa II. She married Azizus, king of Emesa, ca. A.D. 53. Later she became the third wife of Antonius Felix, procurator of Judea from A.D. 52-60. She had one son by Felix, Antonius Agrippa, who died in the eruption of Mt. Vesuvius in A.D. 79.

9. Herodias

The daughter of Aristobulus and Bernice. In the Gospels Herodias is recorded as the wife of Herod Philip and mistress of Herod Antipas (Matt. 14:3-6; Mark 6:17-23; Luke 3:19). According to Josephus Herodias was married first to Herod II (Philip), the son of Herod the Great by his third wife, Mariamme II. Later, according to Josephus, she married Herod Antipas. Josephus records only one marriage of Herod Philip, that to Salome, the daughter of Herodias.

10. Salome, the daughter of Herodias

Known only as the daughter of Herodias in the Gospels (Matt. 14:6; Mark 6:22), she was the daughter of Herod II (Philip) and Herodias. Her dancing on the birthday of her step-father resulted in the beheading of John the Baptist (Mark 6:14-29). She was married to Herod Philip and Aristobulus II.

The Jewish High Priests from 200 B.C. to the Reign of Herod the Great

1. Simon the Righteous, ?
2. Onias II, ?-175 B.C.
3. Jason/Jesus, 175-172 B.C.
4. Menelaus, 172-162 B.C.

Dates for the High Priests before Herod the Great are based on E. Schürer, *A History of the Jewish People in the Time of Jesus Christ,* trans. S. Taylor and P. Christie, 2nd ed. (Edinburgh: T. and T. Clark, 1885-90), 5 vols.

5. Alcimus/Jacim, 162-159 B.C.
6. Jonathan, 152-142 B.C.
7. Simon, 142-135 B.C.
8. John Hyrcanus I, 134-104 B.C.
9. Aristobulus I, 104-103 B.C.
10. Alexander Jannaeus, 103-76 B.C.
11. Hyrcanus II, 76-67 B.C.
12. Aristobulus II, 67-63 B.C.
13. Hyrcanus II, 63-40 B.C.
14. Antigonus, 40-37 B.C.

The Jewish High Priests from Herod the Great to the Destruction of Jerusalem

High Priest	Appointed by
1. Ananel, 37-36 B.C., 34 B.C. ?	Herod the Great
2. Aristobulus III, 35 B.C.	
3. Jesus, son of Phiabi, ?-22 B.C.	
4. Simon, son of Boethus, 22-5 B.C.	
5. Matthias, son of Theophilus, 5-4 B.C.	
6. Joseph, son of Elam, 5 B.C.	
7. Joezer, son of Boethus, 4 B.C.	
8. Eleazar, son of Boethus, 4 B.C.-?	Herod Archelaus
9. Jesus, son of Sie, ?-A.D. 6	
10. Annas, A.D. 6-15	Quirinius
11. Ishmael, son of Phiabi I, A.D. 15-16	Valerius Gratus
12. Eleazar, son of Annas, A.D. 16-17	
13. Simon, son of Kamithos, A.D. 17-18	
14. Joseph Caiaphas, A.D. 18-37	
15. Jonathan, son of Annas, A.D. 37	Vitellius
16. Theophilus, son of Annas, A.D. 37-41	

Dates for the High Priests after Herod the Great are based on E. Schürer, *A History of the Jewish People in the Time of Jesus Christ*, trans. S. Taylor and P. Christie, 2nd ed. (Edinburgh: T. and T. Clark, 1885), 5 vols.

High Priest	Appointed by
17. Simon Kantheras, son of Boethus, A.D. 41-?	Herod Agrippa I
18. Matthias, son of Annas, ?	
19. Elionaius, son of Kantheras, ?	
20. Joseph, son of Kami, ?	Herod of Chalcis
21. Ananias, son of Nebedaius, A.D. 47-55 ?	
22. Ishmael, son of Phiabi III, A.D. 55-61 ?	Herod Agrippa II
23. Joseph Qabi, son of Simon, A.D. 61-62	
24. Ananus, son of Ananus, A.D. 62	
25. Jesus, son of Damnaius, A.D. 62-65	
26. Joshua, son of Gamaliel, A.D. 63-65	
27. Matthias, son of Theophilus, A.D. 65-67	
28. Phinnias, son of Samuel, A.D. 67-70	the people

Roman Procurators of Judea and Palestine

1. Ethnarch Archelaus, 4 B.C.-A.D. 6
2. Coponius, A.D. 6-9
3. M. Ambivius, A.D. 9-12
4. Annius Rufus, A.D. 12-15
5. Valerius Gratus, A.D. 15-26
6. Pontius Pilate, A.D. 26-36
7. Marcellus, A.D. 36-37
8. Marullus, A.D. 37 ?
9. Herennius Capito, A.D. 37-41
10. Cuspius Fadus, A.D. 44-46
11. Tiberius Julius Alexander, A.D. 46-48

No procurator ruled in Judea during A.D. 41-44. Herod Agrippa ruled as king in Galilee, Perea, Iturea, Trachonitis, Samaria, and Judea from A.D. 41 until his death in A.D. 44 (cf. Acts 12:20-23). Procurators ruled Judea from A.D. 6-41 and 44-66. The term "procurator" was used as a title for the ruler of a Roman province of the third class, like Judea. The NT word, *hēgemōn*, is usually translated "governor." In the Roman system of administration the term "procurator" also indicated a financial officer of a province. Four procurators are named in the NT: Quirinius (Luke 2:2), Pilate (Matt. 27:2), Felix (Acts 23:24), and Festus (Acts 24:27).

Dates for Procurators of Judea and Palestine based on B. Reicke, *The New Testament Era*, trans. P. E. Green (Philadelphia: Fortress, 1968).

New Testament

12. Ventidius Cumanus, A.D. 48-52
13. Antonius Felix, A.D. 52-60
14. Porcius Festus, A.D. 60-62 ?
15. Clodius Albinus, A.D. 62-64
16. Gessius Florus, A.D. 64-66

Roman Legates in Palestine

1. Vespasian, A.D. 67-69
2. Titus, A.D. 70
3. Sextus Vettulenus Cerealis, A.D. 70
4. Lucilius Bassus, A.D. 71
5. L. Flavius Silva, A.D. 72-80 ?
6. M. Salvidenus, A.D. 80-85
7. Cn. Pompeius Longinus, A.D. 86-?
8. Atticus, ca. A.D. 107
9. Pompeius Falco, ca. A.D. 107-114
10. Tiberianus, ca. A.D. 114-117
11. Lusius Quietus, ca. A.D. 117-?
12. Tineius Rufus, A.D. 132-135
13. Julius Severus, A.D. 135

Dates for the Roman legates in Palestine are based on E. Schürer, *A History of the Jewish People in the Time of Jesus Christ,* trans. J. Macpherson (Edinburgh: T. and T. Clark, 1885-90), 5 vols.

Roman Legates in Syria

1. Aulus Gabinius, 57-55 B.C.
2. Marcus Licinius Crassus, 54-53 B.C.
3. Sextus Caesar, 47-46 B.C.
4. Caecelius Bassus, 46 B.C.
5. Gaius Cassius Longinus I, 44-42 B.C.
6. Decidius Saxa, 41-40 B.C.
7. Ventidius, 39-38 B.C.
8. Gaius Sosius, 38-37 B.C.
9. Marcus Tullius Cicero, ?

Historical sources are incomplete and often conflicting, making exact dating impossible.

10. Varro, to 23 B.C.
11. Marcus Agrippa, 23-13 B.C.
12. Gaius Sentius Saturninus, 9-6 B.C.
13. Publius Quinctilius Varus, 6-3 B.C.
14. Publius Sulpicius Quirinius, 3-2 B.C. ?
15. Gaius Caesar, 1 B.C.-A.D. 4
16. Marcus Lollius, ?
17. Lucius Marcius Censorinus, ?
18. Lucius Volusius Saturninus, ?
19. Publius Sulpicius Quirinius, A.D. 6-11
20. Quintus Caecilius Metellus Creticus Silanus, ?
21. Cnaeus Calpurnius Piso, A.D. 17-19
22. Cnaeus Sentius Saturninus, A.D. 19-20
23. Aelius Lamia, A.D. 20-?
24. Lucius Pomponius Flaccus, A.D. ?-33 or A.D. 32-35
25. Lucius Vitellius, A.D. 35-39 or 37-39
26. Publius Petronius, A.D. 39-42
27. Gaius Vivius Marsus, A.D. 42-45
28. Gaius Cassius Longinus II, A.D. 45-49
29. Gaius Ummidius Quadratus, ?
30. Domitius Corbulo/Gaius Itius, colegates, A.D. 60-63
31. Cestius Gallus, A.D. 63-66
32. Gaius Licinius Mucianus, A.D. 67-69

The Twelve Caesars

Caesar	Birth/Death	Reign
1. Julius Caesar	102/100-44 B.C.	Dictator 49-44 B.C.
2. Augustus	63 B.C.-A.D. 14	Emperor 27 B.C.-A.D. 14
3. Tiberius	42 B.C.-A.D. 37	A.D. 14-37
4. Gaius Caligula	A.D. 12-41	A.D. 37-41
5. Claudius	10 B.C.-A.D. 54	A.D. 41-54
6. Nero	A.D. 37-68	A.D. 54-68
7. Galba	3 B.C.-A.D. 69	A.D. 6/68-1/69

Dates for the Twelve Caesars based on J. Gavorse, ed., *Suetonius: The Lives of the Twelve Caesars* (New York, 1937).

141

Caesar	Birth/Death	Reign
8. Otho	A.D. 32-69	Emperor A.D. 1/15-4/16 69
9. Vitellius	A.D. 15-69	A.D. 1/2-12/22 69
10. Vespasian	A.D. 9-79	A.D. 69-79
11. Titus	A.D. 39/41-81	A.D. 79-81
12. Domitian	A.D. 51-96	A.D. 81-96

Later Roman Emperors

1. Marcus Cocceius Nerva, A.D. 96-98
2. Marcus Ulpius Traianus Trajan, A.D. 98-117
3. Publius Aelius Hadrian, A.D. 117-138
4. Antonius Pius, A.D. 138-161
5. Marcus Aurelius, A.D. 161-180
   Lucius Aurelius Verus, coemperor, A.D. 161-169
6. Lucius Aelius Aurelius Commodus, A.D. 180-192
7. Publius Helvius Pertinax, A.D. 192-193
8. Didius Severus Julianus, A.D. 193
9. Lucius Septimius Severus, A.D. 193-211
10. Caracalla, coemperor, A.D. 196-198; A.D. 211-217
11. Marcinus, A.D. 217-218
12. Heliogabalus, A.D. 218-222
13. Alexander Severus, A.D. 222-235
14. Maximus Thrax, A.D. 235-249
15. Gaius Messius Quintus Decius, A.D. 249-251
16. C. Vibius Afinius Trebonianus Gallus, A.D. 251-253
    Hostilianus, coemperor, A.D. 251
17. Marcus Aemilius Aemilianus, A.D. 253
18. Publius Licinius Valerianus, A.D. 253-260
    Gallienius, coemperor, A.D. 253-260
19. Macrianus, A.D. 260-261
    Quietus, coemperor, A.D. 260-261
20. Gallienius, A.D. 261-268

Dates for the Later Roman Emperors are based on S. A. Cook et al., eds., *The Cambridge Ancient History*, 2nd ed., vols. 11 and 12 (Cambridge: Cambridge University Press, 1965, 1956).

21. Marcus Aurelius Claudius II, A.D. 268-270
22. Quintillus, A.D. 270
23. Aurelian, A.D. 270-275
24. Tacitus, A.D. 275-276
25. Florian, A.D. 276
26. Probus, A.D. 276-282
27. Carus, A.D. 282-283
28. Carinus (West), A.D. 283-285
    Numerian (East), A.D. 283-284
29. Diocletian, A.D. 284-305
    Maximian, coemperor, A.D. 286-305
    Constantius (Caesar of West), A.D. 293-306
    Galerius (Caesar of East), A.D. 293-311
30. Constantine, A.D. 306-337
31. Constantine II, A.D. 337-340

Genealogy of Christ

Matthew (1:1-17)

Abraham	Solomon	Jeconiah
Isaac	Rehoboam	Shealtiel
Jacob	Abijah	Zerubbabel
Judah	Asa	Abiud
Perez	Jehoshaphat	Eliakim
Hezron	Joram	Azor
Ram	Uzziah	Zadok
Amminadab	Jotham	Akim
Nahshon	Ahaz	Eliud
Salmon	Hezekiah	Eleazar
Boaz	Manasseh	Matthan
Obed	Amon	Jacob
Jesse	Josiah	Joseph
David	Jeconiah	Jesus

Luke (3:23–38)

Jesus	Elmadam	Judah
Joseph	Er	Jacob
Heli	Joshua	Isaac
Matthat	Eliezer	Abraham
Levi	Jorim	Terah
Melki	Matthat	Nahor
Jannai	Levi	Serug
Joseph	Simeon	Reu
Mattathias	Judah	Peleg
Amos	Joseph	Eber
Nahum	Jonam	Shelah
Esli	Eliakim	Cainan
Naggai	Melea	Arphaxad
Maath	Menna	Shem
Mattathias	Mattatha	Noah
Semein	Nathan	Lamech
Josech	David	Methuselah
Joda	Jesse	Enoch
Joanan	Obed	Jared
Rhesa	Boaz	Mahalaleel
Zerubbabel	Salmon	Cainan
Shealtiel	Nahshon	Enos
Neri	Amminadab	Seth
Melki	Ram	Adam
Addi	Hezron	God
Cosam	Perez	

The Family of Herod

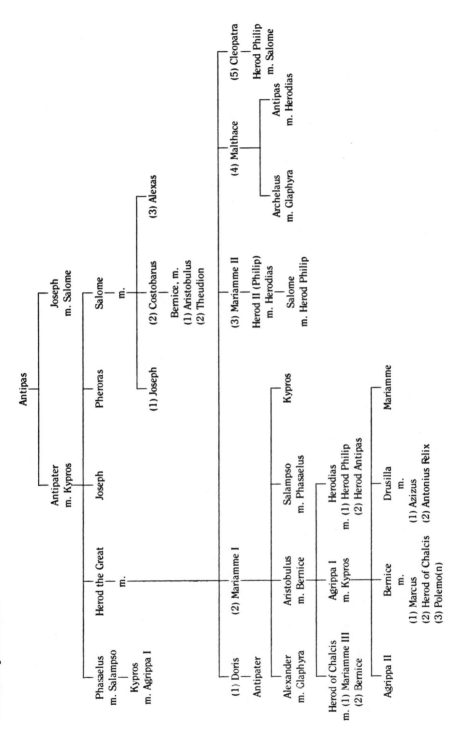

Biblical Data

Acrostics in the Old Testament

An acrostic is a poem in which the first letters of consecutive lines or stanzas form an alphabet, a word, or a phrase. The OT contains 14 acrostic poems in which consecutive lines or stanzas begin with the 22 characters of the Hebrew alphabet. Unfortunately this literary device cannot be fully appreciated in English translations of the OT, although the acrostics are often indicated in the margins or in footnotes. The NT contains no acrostics. However, the early church used ΙΧΘΥΣ ("fish") as an acrostic for *Iēsous Christos Theou Huios Sōtēr*, that is, Jesus Christ God's Son Savior.

OT Acrostics

1. Psalms 9 and 10.
2. Psalm 25
3. Psalm 34
4. Psalm 37
5. Psalm 111
6. Psalm 112
7. Psalm 119
8. Psalm 145
9. Proverbs 31:10-31
10. Lamentations 1
11. Lamentations 2
12. Lamentations 3
13. Lamentations 4
14. Nahum 1:2-10 (a partial acrostic)

Apostles in the New Testament

A distinction is made between "disciple" (*mathētēs*, "follower" or "pupil") and "apostle" (*apostolos*, "delegate, envoy, one commissioned") in the NT. This distinction is clearly seen in Matt. 10:1-5. Acts 1:15-26 lists two qualifications for an apostle: (1) someone who had accompanied the disciples during the course of Jesus' public ministry, (2) someone who was a witness of Christ's resurrection.

Those called "apostle" in the NT

1. Simon Peter, Matt. 10:2
2. Andrew, Matt. 10:2
3. James, the son of Zebedee, Matt. 10:2
4. John, the son of Zebedee, Matt. 10:2
5. Philip, Matt. 10:3
6. Bartholomew, Matt. 10:3
7. Thomas (Didymus), Matt. 10:3
8. Matthew (Levi), Matt. 10:3
9. James, the son of Alphaeus, Matt. 10:3
10. Lebbaeus (Thaddaeus, or Judas, the son of James), Matt. 10:3
11. Simon the Zealot, Matt. 10:4
12. Judas Iscariot, Matt. 10:4
13. Matthias, Acts 1:26
14. Saul, called Paul, Rom. 1:1
15. Barnabas, Acts 14:4

16. Silas (Silvanus), 1 Thess. 2:7
17. Jesus Christ, the Apostle, Heb. 3:1
18. James, the Lord's brother, Gal. 1:19[1]
19. Andronicus and Junias, kinsmen of Paul, Rom. 16:7[2]
20. Cleopas and his unnamed companion, Luke 24:18[3]

---

1. The "except" (*ei mē*) in Galatians 1:19 can be understood in an "inclusive" sense, that is, James is one of the apostles; or in an "exclusive" sense, meaning Paul saw no apostles, "only" James, the Lord's brother.

2. The Greek preposition *en* can mean "in, with, by, among," etc. These two men are either notable "among" the apostles, meaning they are apostles themselves; or they are notable "with" the apostles, in the sense they are not apostles but have been recognized in some special way by the apostles.

3. Technically, the antecedent of (*duo ex autōn*) is "the apostles" (Luke 24:10). Therefore, it is possible to consider these two apostles. It is more likely they were disciples close to the Eleven (cf. Luke 24:33).

Archaeological Periods of Palestine

Prehistoric Eras	Date B.C.
Early Stone Age	down to 9000
Middle Stone Age	9000-7000
Late Stone Age	7000-3600
Copper Stone Age	3600-3200

Historical Eras	Date B.C.
Mesolithic (Natufian)	8000-6000
Pre-pottery Neolithic	6000-5000
Pottery Neolithic	5000-4000
Chalcolithic	4000-3200
Esdraelon	3200-3000
Early Bronze Age (EB)	3000-2100
EB I	3000-2800
EB II	2800-2600
EB III	2600-2300

The above dates are commonly recognized archaeological eras of Palestine. Other charts may vary by a century or two in some periods. This dating framework is based on C. F. Pfeiffer, ed., *The Biblical World* (Grand Rapids: Baker, 1966).

Historical Eras	Date B.C.
EB IV or III B	2300–2100
Middle Bronze Age (MB)	2100–1550
MB I or EB-MB	2100–1900
MB II A	1900–1700
MB II B	1700–1600
MB II C	1600–1550
Late Bronze Age (LB)	1550–1200
LB I	1550–1400
LB II A	1400–1300
LB II B	1300–1200
Iron Age I or Early Iron (EI)	1200– 900
I A	1200–1150
I B	1150–1025
I C	1025– 950
I D	950– 900
Iron Age II or Middle Iron (MI)	900– 600
II A	900– 800
II B	800– 700
II C	700– 600
Iron Age III, Late Iron or Persian	600– 300
Hellenistic	300– 63
Roman	63 B.C.–A.D. 323
Byzantine	A.D. 323–636
Islamic	A.D. 636–present

Calendars

Babylonian Calendar (with probable etymologies)

Nisanu, the first month
Aiaru, procession month
Simanu, time of brickmaking
Duzu, month of Tammuz, the god of fertility
Abu, month of torches
Ululu, month of purification
Tashritu, month of beginnings
Arahsamnu, eighth month
Kislimu, ?
Tebetu, month of plunging (into water)
Shabatu, month of rain
Addaru, month of threshing

Jewish Calendar (with corresponding seasons)

Nisan, barley harvest, Neh. 2:1; Esther 3:7; 2 Macc. 11:30, 33
Iyyar, general harvest, 1 Kings 6:1
Sivan, wheat harvest, vine tending, Esther 8:9
Tammuz, first grapes, no reference
Ab, grapes, olives and figs, no reference
Elul, vintage, Neh. 6:15; 1 Macc. 14:27
Tishri, plowing, 1 Kings 8:2

Marhesvan, grain planting, 1 Kings 6:38
Kislev, Neh. 1:1; Zech. 7:1; 1 Macc. 1:54
Tebeth, rainy season, Esther 2:16
Shebat, winter figs, Zech. 1:7; 1 Macc. 16:14
Adar, pulling flax, almonds bud, Ezra 6:15; Esther 3:7; 1 Macc. 7:43
Adar Sheni, intercalary month

Since the Jewish calendar was based on the lunar month (29.5 days) the lunar year (354.25 days) fell short of the solar year (365.25 days). Therefore an intercalary month was inserted every two or three years to make adjustments for the lunar calendar's shortage of days. Although not directly stated this concept is implied in Num. 9:11; 2 Chron. 30:2-3, and 1 Kings 12:32-33.

Macedonian Calendar

Dios
Apellaios
Audynaios
Peritios
Dystros
Xanthikos
Artemisios
Daisios
Panemos
Loos
Gorpiaios
Hyperberetaios

Equivalents of the Julian Calendar

Julian Calendar	Babylonian–Jewish Calendar
Mar./Apr.	Nisan, preexilic Hebrew name *'Abib,* Exod. 12:2
Apr./May	Iyyar, preexilic Hebrew name *Ziu,* 1 Kings 6:1
May/June	Sivan
June/July	Tammuz
July/Aug.	Ab
Aug./Sept.	Elul
Sept./Oct.	Tishri, preexilic Hebrew name *'Etanim,* 1 Kings 8:2

Julian Calendar	Babylonian–Jewish Calendar
Oct./Nov.	Marhesvan, preexilic Hebrew name *Bul*, 1 Kings 6:38
Nov./Dec.	Kislev
Dec./Jan.	Tebeth
Jan./Feb.	Shebat
Feb./Mar.	Adar

Jewish Calendar: Festivals

Month	Dates	Festival
Nisan	1	New moon (Num. 10:10)
	10	Selection of Passover lamb (Exod. 12:3)
	14	Passover lamb killed (Exod. 12:6), Passover begins (Num. 28:16)
	15	First day of unleavened bread (Num. 28:17)
	16	Firstfruits (Lev. 23:10)
	21	End of Passover and unleavened bread (Lev. 23:6)
Iyyar	1	New moon (Num. 1:18)
Sivan	1	New moon
	6	Pentecost (50 days after firstfruits) Feast of weeks (Lev. 23:15-21)
Tammuz	1	New moon
Ab	1	New moon
	9	Day of Mourning for destruction of Temple
Elul	1	New moon

Jewish years are counted according to the World Era, beginning with the creation of man (estimated to be the year 3761 B.C.). Thus Israel became a nation again in the Jewish year 5709 (A.D. 1948). Rather than counting time from the birth of Christ, Jewish people indicate the years before Christ as B.C.E. (Before the Common Era); and the years following Christ's birth as C.E. (The Common Era). On ancient calendars see J. Finegan, *Handbook of Biblical Chronology* (Princeton: Princeton University Press, 1964). Also, see below "Holy Days and Feasts."

156

Month	Dates	Festival
Tishri	1	New moon, New Year, Feast of Trumpets (Lev. 23:24; Num. 29:1-2)
	10	Day of Atonement (Lev. 23:26ff.)
		The Fast (cf. Acts 27:9)
	15-21	Feast of Tabernacles (Lev. 23:33ff.)
Marhesvan	1	New moon
Kislev	1	New moon
	25	Feast of dedication of the temple (1 Macc. 4:52ff.)
		Hanukkah or feast of lights, an eight-day festival
Tebeth	1	New moon
Shebat	1	New moon
Adar	1	New moon
	14-15	Feast of Purim (Esther 9:21)

Cities

Ancient Capital Cities

Nation	Capital City
Judah	Jerusalem
Israel	Tirzah, Samaria
Moab	Kir-Moab
Ammon	Rabbath-Ammon
Syria	Damascus
Edom	Bozrah, Sela/Petra
Egypt	Memphis, Thebes/No-Amon, Lisht
Assyria	Nineveh
Babylonia	Babylon
Hittite Kingdom	Kushshar, Hattusas
Persia	Susa, Persepolis, Ecbatana
Greece	Athens
Italy	Rome

Cities of Decapolis

1. Scythopolis
2. Hippos
3. Gadara
4. Pella
5. Philadelphia
6. Gerasa
7. Dion
8. Canatha
9. Damascus
10. Raphana

Cities of Decapolis

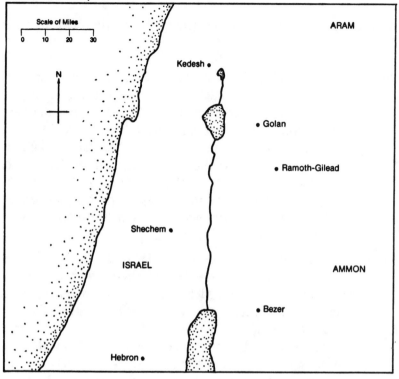

The Cities of Galatia

Two theories have been proposed regarding the location of the Galatian churches

North   This view argues Paul established churches in northern Asia Minor and the letter of Galatians is written to these churches. The supporting texts given for a Pauline mission in northern Asia Minor are Acts 16:6 and 28:23. Those holding to the North-Galatian view contend Paul uses "Galatia" in an ethnic and geographical sense, thus denoting the ancient kingdom of Galatia bordered on the west by Phrygia, on the north by Bithynia and Pontus, on the east by Cappadocia, and on the south by Lycaonia. The major cities of North Galatia were Tavium, Pessinus, and Ancyra.

South   This view asserts Paul uses "Galatia" in the Roman political sense, thus ascribing to Galatia all the territory it included after the old ethnic kingdom became a Roman province with the death of Amyntas in 25 B.C. Along with the ethnic territory of old Galatia the Roman province of Galatia included parts of Pontus, Phrygia, Lycaonia, Pisidia, Paphlagonia, and Isauria. According to the South-Galatian view the cities of Galatia are the cities of Antioch (Pisidia), Lystra, Derbe, and Iconium. These cities were evangelized by Paul on his first missionary journey (Acts 13-14).

Because of the work of Sir William Ramsay the South-Galatian view is held by the majority of scholars today. If Paul was ever in North Galatia it was only briefly, and he founded no churches there. The geographical term "Galatia" also occurs in 1 Cor. 16:1; 2 Tim. 4:10; and 1 Peter 1:1.

Levitical Cities (Joshua 20–21)

The Cities of Levi

Since the members of the tribe of Levi received no inheritance they were given, by lot, 48 cities and surrounding land (Josh. 21:3; Num. 18:20ff.; 35:1-8; Deut. 12:12ff.):

1) Levites, sons of Aaron, 13 cities, Josh. 21:4
2) Gershon, 1st son of Levi, 13 cities, Josh. 21:6
3) Kohath, 2nd son of Levi, 10 cities, Josh. 21:5
4) Merari, 3rd son of Levi, 12 cities, Josh. 21:7

The Cities of Refuge

Six of the Levitical cities became cities of refuge. These cities of refuge were without parallel in the ancient Near East. The cities of refuge were:

1) Kedesh in Galilee, Josh. 20:7
2) Shechem in Ephraim, Josh. 20:7
3) Hebron in Judah, Josh. 20:7

These three cities were on the western side of the Jordan River.

4) Bezer (Bozrah) of Reuben (near Heshbon), Josh. 20:8
5) Ramoth-Gilead of Gad, Josh. 20:8
6) Golan in Bashan of Manasseh, Josh. 20:8

These three cities were on the eastern side of the Jordan River.

The Purpose of the Cities

1. The city was for those who had committed accidental manslaughter.
2. The city was a refuge from the "avenger of blood," that is, the victim's nearest male relative who was obligated to avenge the death of his kin.
3. The refugee was to declare his case to the elders at the city gate.
4. If the refugee left the city before the death of the high priest, the avenger of blood had the right to try to take his life and avenge the victim's death.
5. No bribe or ransom was to be given to free the refugee.

Other References to the Cities of Refuge:

1. Num. 18:20-32; 35:1-34
2. Deut. 4:41-43; 12:12-32; 19:1-13

The Cities of Refuge

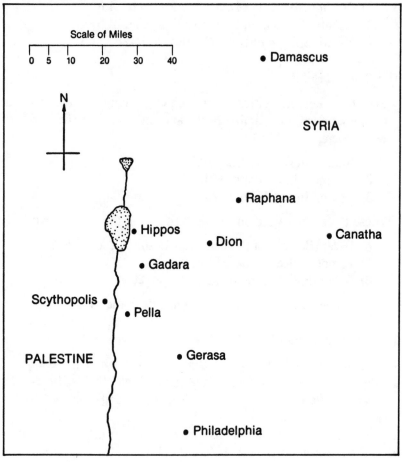

Coinage

Coinage appears to have been in use in the ancient world as early as the 7th century B.C. Before, and no doubt continuing after that, precious metals and perishable and imperishable goods were exchanged in a barter system. Precious metals were weighed at each exchange and some of the names for weights were adopted as coin names. Coins from three sources circulated in Palestine in NT times: official imperial money (Roman); provincial money minted at Antioch and Tyre (Greek); and Jewish money, possibly minted at Caesarea. Money was coined in brass, bronze, silver, and gold. The most frequently mentioned coins in the NT are the Greek *tetradrachma* and the Roman *denarius,* a day's wages for the common laborer.

Jewish	Greek	Roman	Approximate U.S. Equivalent
1 lepton		½ quadrans	⅛ cent
2 leptons		1 quadrans	¼ cent
		4 quadrantes = 1 as	1 cent
	1 drachma	16 asses = 1 denarius	16 cents
1 shekel	1 stater or (tetradrachma)	4 denarii	64 cents
	25 drachmai	1 aureus	4 dollars
30 shekels	1 mina	100 denarii	16 dollars
	1 talent (60 minas)	240 aurei	960 dollars

The figures for U.S. monetary equivalents are based on the now somewhat dated approximations of J. D. Douglas, ed., *The New Bible Dictionary* (Grand Rapids: Eerdmans, 1965).

Cosmetics in the OT

1. balsam oil (*bśm*), Song of Sol. 5:13
2. mirror ? (*glyn*), Isa. 3:23
3. eye paint (*khl*), Ezek. 23:40
4. oil of myrrh (*mr*), Esther 2:12
5. aromatic herbs (*mrqh*), Song of Sol. 5:13
6. ointment jar (*mrqhh*), Job 41:23
7. blended perfumes (*mrqhym*), 2 Chron. 16:14
8. mixture of ointments (*mrqht*), Exod. 30:25
9. perfume bottles ? (*npš*), Isa. 3:20
10. anoint with oil (*swk*), 2 Sam. 14:2
11. eye paint (*pwk*), 2 Kings 9:30
12. cassia oil (*qdh*), Ezek. 27:19
13. spiced wine (*rqh*), Song of Sol. 8:2
14. ointment-mixer, perfumer (*rqh*), 1 Sam. 8:13
15. ointment, perfume (*rqh*), Isa. 57:9
16. to mix ointment (*rqh*), Eccles. 10:1
17. oil, perfumed oil (*šmn*), Isa. 25:6; Amos 6:6
18. massage with ointments (*tmrq*), Esther 2:3, 9, 12; Prov. 20:30

The English translation of these alphabetized Hebrew words is based on W. L. Holladay, *A Concise Hebrew and Aramaic Lexicon of the Old Testament* (Grand Rapids: Eerdmans, 1971). The several standard modern English versions of the Bible render these terms in a slightly different manner.

Crafts, Trades, and Other Aspects of Life in Bible Times

1. ambassador, messenger (*ml'k, ṣyr, presbeuō*), 2 Chron. 35:21; Isa. 18:2; 2 Cor. 5:20
2. apostle (*apostolos*), Matt. 10:1-5
3. apothecary, ointment-mixer, perfume-maker (*rqḥ*), Neh. 3:8
4. archer (*mwrh, rb*), 1 Sam. 31:3; Jer. 50:29
5. armorbearer (*nwś' kly*), Judg. 9:54
6. astrologer, conjurer, enchanter (*'šp*), Dan. 1:20
7. athlete (implied in Paul's allusion to the "runner" (*trechō*) and the "boxer" (*pukteuō*) in 1 Cor. 9:24-26)
8. baker (*'wph*), Gen. 40:5
9. barber (*glb*), Ezek. 5:1
10. bishop, overseer (*episkopos*), Phil. 1:1
11. blacksmith, carpenter, gem cutter (*ḥrš*), Exod. 28:11; 2 Kings 12:12; 1 Sam. 13:19
12. builders (*bwny, oikodomos*), 1 Kings 5:18; Acts 4:11
13. buyer, merchant (*qwnh*), Isa. 24:2
14. captain, leader, official (*śr, chiliarchos*), 1 Sam. 17:18; Mark 6:21
15. captives, prisoner (*šwbym, desmios*), Isa. 14:2; Mark 15:6
16. carpenter (*ḥršy 's*), 2 Sam. 5:11
17. caulkers, shipwrights (*mḥzyqy bdqk*), Ezek. 27:9

The English translations of the Hebrew and Greek terms contained in the list are based on F. W. Gingrich, *Shorter Lexicon of the Greek New Testament* (Chicago: University of Chicago Press, 1965); and W. L. Holladay, *A Concise Hebrew and Aramaic Lexicon of the Old Testament* (Grand Rapids: Eerdmans, 1971).

18. centurion (*hekatontarchēs, kenturiōn*), Luke 7:6; Mark 15:39
19. charmer, enchanter, medium (*ḥwbr, mlḥsym*), Deut. 18:11; Ps. 58:5
20. chief, ruler, minor king (*nśy', rwʾš, prōtos*), Ezek. 10:11; Gen. 23:6; Matt. 20:27
21. chief musician, music director (*mnṣḥ*), Ps. 4:1
22. Christian (*christianos*), Acts 11:26
23. citizen (*politēs*), Acts 21:39
24. concubine (*plgš*), Gen. 22:24
25. cook (*ṭbḥ*), 1 Sam. 9:23
26. coppersmith, blacksmith, metalworker (*chalkeus*), 2 Tim. 4:14
27. counselor (*y'ṣ, bouleutēs*), 2 Sam. 15:12; Luke 23:50
28. craftsman (*ḥwrš, tektōn*), 1 Kings 7:14; Matt. 13:55
29. creditor (*nwšh, daneistēs*), Isa. 24:2; Luke 7:41
30. cupbearer, butler (*mšqh*), Gen. 40:21
31. dancer (*mḥwl*), Jer. 31:4
32. deacon (*diakonos*), 1 Tim. 3:8
33. deaconess (*diakonos*), Rom. 16:1
34. debtor (*ḥwb, chreopheiletēs*), Ezek. 18:7; Luke 7:41
35. disciple (*lmwd, mathetēs*), Isa. 50:4; Luke 6:40
36. diviner, soothsayer (*qwśm*), Deut. 18:10
37. drawers of water (*šw'b*), Josh. 9:21
38. dreamer, foreteller (*ḥwlm*), Deut. 13:1
39. drunkard (*methusos*), 1 Cor. 5:11
40. elder (*zqn, presbuteros*), Exod. 19:7; Luke 7:3
41. embalmers (*ḥrwp'ym lḥnwt*), Gen. 50:2
42. enchanter (*mnḥš*), Deut. 18:10
43. eunuch (*śryś, eunochos*), 2 Kings 20:18; Acts 8:27
44. evangelist (*euangelistes*), Eph. 4:11
45. executioner (*spekoulatōr*), Mark 6:27
46. exorcist (*exorkistēs*), Acts 19:13
47. expert, skilled craftsman (*ḥkm, gnostēs*), Isa. 40:20; Ezek. 27:9; Acts 26:3
48. farmer, husbandman (*'kr, geōrgos*), Isa. 61:5; Matt. 21:33
49. father (*'b, patēr*), Jer. 3:4; Matt. 10:21
50. fishers (*dyg, halieus*), Isa. 19:8; Matt. 4:18
51. foot soldier (*rgly*), 1 Kings 20:29
52. fowler (*yqwš*), Jer. 5:26
53. friend (*r', philos*), Gen. 38:12; John 15:15

54. fruit tender, fruit picker (*bwls šqmym*), Amos 7:14
55. fuller, bleacher, washerman (*kwbs, gnapheus*), Isa. 36:2; Mark 9:3
56. gardener (*kēpouros*), John 20:15
57. gleaner (*mlqt*), Isa. 17:5
58. governor (*phh, hēgemōn*), 1 Kings 10:15; Luke 21:12
59. grape-gatherer (*bwṣr*), Jer. 6:9
60. gravedigger (*hmqbrym*), Ezek. 39:15
61. grinder, miller (*alēthō*), Matt. 24:41
62. guard, doorkeeper, watchman (*ṭbḥ, šwmr, phulax*), 2 Kings 25:8, 10, 18; Acts 5:23
63. guide, leader, commander (*qṣyn*), Prov. 6:7
64. handmaid, maidservant (*šphh*), Gen. 16:1
65. harpist (*kitharōdos*), Rev. 14:2
66. harvesters, reapers (*qwṣr*), Ruth 2:3
67. herald (*krwz*), Dan. 3:4
68. hireling, hired laborer, day worker (*škyr, misthōtos*), Lev. 19:13; John 10:12
69. horseman, cavalryman (*rwkb, hippeus*), Ezek. 23:6, 12; Acts 23:23
70. hunter (*ṣyd*), Jer. 16:16
71. innkeeper (*pandocheus*), Luke 10:35
72. interpreter, spokesman (*mlyṣ*), Gen. 42:23
73. interpreter (of dreams) (*pwtr*), Gen. 40:8
74. interpreter (of tongues) (*diermeneia*), 1 Cor. 14:28
75. jailor (*desmophulax*), Acts 16:23
76. judge (*šwpṭ, kritēs*), Num. 25:5; Luke 18:6
77. king (*mlk, basileus*), 2 Sam. 3:21; Acts 12:1
78. laborer, worker (*ergatēs*), Matt. 10:10
79. lawyer, jurist (*nomikos*), Titus 3:13
80. lawyer, teacher of the law (*nomodidaskalos*), Luke 5:17
81. leader, prince, chief priests (*ngyd*), 2 Chron. 11:11; 19:11
82. lender (*mlwh*), Prov. 22:7; or borrower (*lwh*), Prov. 22:7
83. magician, soothsayer (*hrṭwm*), Gen. 41:8
84. magistrate, official (*archōn*), Rom. 13:3
85. magus, wiseman (*magos*), Matt. 2:7
86. maidservant, female slave (*'mh*), Gen. 20:17
87. manservant, male slave (*'bd*), Gen. 12:16
88. mason, stonecutter, quarryman (*hwṣb*), 2 Kings 12:12
89. masterbuilder (*architektōn*), 1 Cor. 3:10

90. merchant (*swḥr, emporos*), Gen. 23:16; Matt. 13:45
91. messenger (*ml'k, angelos*), Isa. 23:2; Luke 7:24
92. metal worker, silversmith (*ḥwrs, ṣwrp*), Judg. 17:4; 1 Sam. 13:19
93. midwife (*myldt*), Exod. 1:15
94. minister (*mšrt, diakonos*), Exod. 24:13; Matt. 20:26
95. money changer (*kollubistēs, kermatistēs*), Matt. 21:12; John 2:14
96. mother (*'m, mētēr*), Gen. 2:24; Matt. 1:18
97. mourner (*'bl*), Job 29:25
98. murderer (*rwṣh, anthrōpoktonos, phoneus*), Num. 35:16; John 8:44; Matt. 22:7
99. musician (*mousikos*), Rev. 18:22
100. necromancer (*dwrš hmtym*), Deut. 18:11
101. officer, foreman (*šwṭr*), Exod. 5:6
102. overseer, supervisor, captain (*mpqdym, pqdn*), 2 Kings 12:11; Jer. 37:13
103. parents (*goneus*), Mark 13:12
104. pastor (of a church) (*poimēn*), Eph. 4:11
105. peacemaker (*eirēnopois*), Matt. 5:9
106. pharisee (*pharisaios*), Matt. 23:26
107. philosopher (*philosophos*), Acts 17:18
108. physician, doctor, healer (*rwp', iatros*), Gen. 50:2; Mark 5:26
109. piper, flute player (*aulētēs*), Rev. 18:22
110. plasterer (*śyd*), Deut. 27:2, 4
111. policeman, constable, officer (*praktōr*), Luke 12:58
112. poor man (*'bywn, ptōchos*), Deut. 15:4; Luke 14:13
113. porter, doorkeeper (*šw'r, thurōros*), 2 Kings 7:10; Mark 13:34
114. potter (*ywṣr, kerameus*), 1 Chron. 4:23; Rom. 9:21
115. preacher (*qwhlt, kērux*), Eccles. 1:1; 2 Peter 2:5
116. priest (*kwhn, hiereus, archiereus*), Lev. 21:9; Matt. 8:4; John 18:19
117. prince (*srn, archon*), 1 Sam. 2:8; Matt. 20:25
118. princess, lady (*śrh*), Judg. 5:29
119. proconsul (*anthupatos*), Acts 13:7
120. procurator, guardian (*epitropos*), Gal. 4:2
121. prophet (*nby', prophētēs*), 1 Kings 22:7; Matt. 14:5
122. prophetess (*nby'h, prophētis*), Exod. 15:20; Luke 2:36
123. prostitute, harlot (*zwnh, pornē*), 1 Kings 3:16; Luke 15:30
124. psalmist (*zmyr*), 2 Sam. 23:1
125. quacks, worthless physicians (*rwp'y 'll*), Job 13:4

126. queen (*mlkh, basilissa*), 1 Kings 10:1; Matt. 12:42
127. reader (*qr', anagnōsis*), Dan. 5:7; 1 Tim. 4:13
128. reaper (*qwṣr, theristēs*), 2 Kings 4:18; Matt. 13:30
129. recorder (*mzkyr*), 2 Sam. 8:16
130. refiner (of metals) (*mṭhr*), Mal. 3:3
131. retailer, huckster, peddler (*kapēlos*), 2 Cor. 2:17
132. ringleader (*prōtostatēs*), Acts 24:5
133. robber (*pryṣ, lēstēs*), Jer. 7:11; Mark 11:17
134. rowers, oarsmen (*šṭym*), Ezek. 27:26
135. sadducee (*saddoukaios*), Acts 5:17
136. sailor (*mlḥ*), Jonah 1:5
137. satrap ('*ḥšwrpn*), Esther 3:12
138. scholar (*mbyn*), 1 Chron. 25:8
139. scribe, secretary, clerk (*swpr, grammateus*), Jer. 36:26; Acts 19:35
140. seer, diviner (*m'wnn*), Deut. 18:10
141. servant, helper (*hupēretēs*), Acts 13:5
142. servant, maidservant (*špḥh*), Gen. 16:1
143. shepherd (*rw'h, poimēn*), Gen. 4:2; Luke 2:8
144. silversmith (*argurokopos*), Acts 19:24
145. singer (*šr*), 2 Sam. 19:36; Ps. 68:25
146. slave, servant ('*bd, doulos*), Gen. 12:16; 1 Cor. 7:21
147. slinger (*ql'*), 2 Kings 3:25
148. sluggard, unemployed, lazy man ('*ṣl, argos*), Prov. 6:6; Matt. 20:3
149. smith, artisan (*msgr*), 2 Kings 24:14
150. snake charmer (*hlšn*), Eccles. 10:11
151. soldier, military man (*ḥyl, stratiotēs*), Exod. 14:4; Matt. 8:9
152. soothsayer, enchanter (*ḥrš*), Isa. 3:3
153. sorcerer (*kšp, goēs, pharmakos*), Jer. 27:9; Rev. 21:8
154. sower (*speiron*), Matt. 13:3
155. spy (*rwgl, egkathetos*), Gen. 42:9; Luke 20:20
156. standard bearer (*dgwl*), Num. 2:2
157. steward, foreman (*epitropos*), Matt. 20:8
158. string player, musician (*nwgym*), Ps. 68:25
159. student (*tlmyd*), 1 Chron. 25:8
160. swimmer (*śwḥh*), Isa. 25:11
161. tanner (*burseus*), Acts 9:43
162. task master (*nwgś*), Exod. 5:10; Isa. 14:2
163. tax collector (*telōnēs*), Matt. 9:10

164. teacher (*didaskalos*), James 3:1
165. tent maker (*skēnopoios*), Acts 18:3
166. tetrarch (*tetraarchēs*), Matt. 14:1
167. tiller, plowman (*ḥwrš*), Ps. 129:3
168. traveler, wayfarer, caravaneer (*'wrḥ*), Gen. 37:25; 2 Sam. 12:4; Isa. 21:13
169. treasurer (*gzbr, gaza*), Ezra 1:8; Acts 8:27
170. tribal chief (*'lwp*), Gen. 36:15
171. trumpeter (*mḥṣrym, salpistēs*), 2 Chron. 5:13; Rev. 18:22
172. vine dresser (*kwrm, ampelourgos*), 2 Kings 25:12; Luke 13:7
173. wardrobe keeper (*šwmr hbgdym*), 2 Chron. 34:22
174. watchman (*ṣwph*), 2 Sam. 18:26
175. weaver, embroiderer (*'wrg*), Exod. 35:35
176. widow (*'lmnh, chēra*), 1 Kings 7:14; Matt. 23:14
177. wife (*'šh*), Prov. 3:10
178. wine (grape) treader (*dwrk*), Amos 9:13
179. winnower (*zwrh*), Ruth 3:2
180. witch (*mkšp*), Exod. 22:18
181. witness (*'d, martus*), Deut. 5:20; Acts 7:58
182. wizard (*yd'wny*), 2 Kings 21:6
183. woodsman (*ḥwṭb*), 2 Chron. 2:10
184. zealot (*zēlōtēs*), Luke 6:15

David's Mighty Men

2 Samuel 23:8–39	1 Chronicles 11:10–47

The Three:

  Josheb-Basshebeth
  Eleazar son of Dodai
  Shammah son of Agee

Not of the Three:

  Abishai son of Zeruiah
  Benaiah son of Jehoiada

The Thirty:

  Asahel brother of Joab
  Elhanan son of Dodo
  Shammah the Harodite
  Elika the Harodite
  Helez the Paltite
  Ira son of Ikkesh
  Abiezer from Anathoth
  Mebunnai the Hushathite
  Zalmon the Ahohite
  Maharai the Netophathite

The Three:

  Jashobeam the Hacmonite
  Eleazar son of Dodai
  —

Not of the Three:

  Abishai brother of Joab
  Benaiah son of Jehoiada

The Thirty:

  Asahel brother of Joab
  Elhanan son of Dodo
  Shammoth the Harorite
  Helez the Pelonite
  Ira son of Ikkesh
  Abiezer from Anathoth
  Sibbecai the Hushathite
  Ilai the Ahohite
  Maharai the Netophathite
  Heled son of Baanah

There were thirty-seven mighty men in all (2 Sam. 25:39).

171

2 Samuel 23:8–39	1 Chronicles 11:10–47
Heled son of Baanah	Ithai son of Ribai
Ithai son of Ribai	Benaiah the Pirathonite
Benaiah the Pirathonite	Hurai of Gaash
Hiddai of Gaash	Abiel the Arbathite
Abi-Albon the Arbathite	Azmaveth the Baharumite
Azmaveth the Barhumite	Eliahba the Shaalbonite
Eliahba the Shaalbonite	the sons of Hashem
the sons of Jashen	Jonathan son of Shagee
Jonathan son of Shammah	Ahiam son of Sacar
Ahiam son of Sharar	Eliphal son of Ur
Eliphelet son of Ahasbai	Hepher the Mekerathite
Eliam son of Ahithophel	Ahijah the Pelonite
Hezro the Carmelite	Hezro the Carmelite
Paarai the Arbite	Naarai son of Ezbai
Igal son of Nathan	Joel brother of Nathan
the son of Hagri	Mibhar son of Hagri
Zelek the Ammonite	Zelek the Ammonite
Naharai the Beerothite	Naharai the Berothite
Ira the Ithrite	Ira the Ithrite
Gareb the Ithrite	Gareb the Ithrite
Uriah the Hittite	Uriah the Hittite
	Zabad son of Ahlai
	Adina son of Shiza
	Hanan son of Maacah
	Joshaphat the Mithnite
	Uzzia the Ashterathite
	Shama and Jeiel sons of Hotham
	Jediael son of Shimri
	Joha brother of Jediael
	Eliel the Mahavite
	Jeribai son of Elnaam
	Joshaviah son of Elnaam
	Ithmah the Moabite
	Eliel
	Obed
	Jaasiel the Mezobaite

Deities, Foreign

OT Deities

1. Adrammelech, 2 Kings 17:31
2. Anammelech, 2 Kings 17:31
3. Ashima, 2 Kings 17:30; Amos 8:14
4. Ashtoreth (Astarte/Ishtar), Judg. 2:13; 10:6; 1 Sam. 7:3-4; 12:10; 31:10; 1 Kings 11:5, 33; 2 Kings 23:13
5. Baal, Zeph. 1:4 (and many other OT references)
6. Baal-Berith, Judg. 8:33; 9:4
7. Baal-Zebub, 2 Kings 1:2, 3, 6, 16
8. Bel, Isa. 46:1; Jer. 50:2; 51:44
9. Chemosh, Num. 21:29; Judg. 11:24; 1 Kings 11:7, 33; 2 Kings 23:13; Jer. 48:7, 13, 46
10. Dagon, Judg. 16:23; 1 Sam. 5:2-7; 1 Chron. 10:10
11. Kaiwan (Chiun), Amos 5:26
12. Marduk, Jer. 50:2
13. Molech (Malcom/Milcom), Lev. 18:21; 20:2, 3, 4, 5; 1 Kings 11:5, 7, 33; 2 Kings 23:10, 13; Jer. 32:35; Zeph. 1:5; cf. Acts 7:43
14. Nebo, Isa. 46:1
15. Nergal, 2 Kings 17:30
16. Nibhaz, 2 Kings 17:31
17. Nisroch, 2 Kings 19:37; Isa. 37:38
18. Queen of Heaven (Ashtoreth), Jer. 7:18; 44:17, 18, 19, 25
19. Raphan, Amos 5:26 (LXX; cf. Acts 7:43)

20. Succoth Benoth, 2 Kings 17:30
21. Tammuz (Dumuzi), Ezek. 8:14
22. Tartak, 2 Kings 17:31

NT Deities

1. Artemis (Diana), Acts 19:24, 27, 28, 34, 35
2. Castor and Pollux, Acts 28:11
3. Hermes (Mercury), Acts 14:12
4. "unknown gods," Acts 17:23
5. Zeus (Jupiter), Acts 14:12-13

Approximate Distances Between Cities Connected with the Ministry of Jesus

From Jerusalem to	Miles	Kilometers
1. Bethany	2	3.2
2. Bethlehem	6	9.6
3. Bethphage	1	1.6
4. Caesarea	57	91.2
5. Caesarea Philippi	105	168
6. Capernaum	85	136
7. Dead Sea	6	9.6
8. Emmaus	16	25.6
9. Jericho	15	24
10. Joppa	35	56
11. Jordan River	21	33.6
12. Mediterranean Sea	37	59.2
13. Nazareth	65	104
14. Salim	50	80
15. Samaria	36	57.6
16. Sea of Galilee	70	112

From Capernaum to	Miles	Kilometers
1. Bethsaida	6	9.6
2. Caesarea Philippi	27	45.2

From Capernaum to	Miles	Kilometers
3. Cana	16	25.6
4. Dalmanutha	6	9.6
5. Gennesaret	3	4.8
6. Nain	22	35.2
7. Nazareth	20	32
8. Tyre	35	56
9. Sidon	50	80
10. Sychar	55	88

Dimensions of the Seas	Miles	Kilometers
1. Sea of Galilee, width	7	11.2
2. Sea of Galilee, length	14	22.4
3. Sea of Galilee to the Dead Sea	65	104
4. Dead Sea, width	9.5	15.2
5. Dead Sea, length	48	76.8

Distances . . . Map

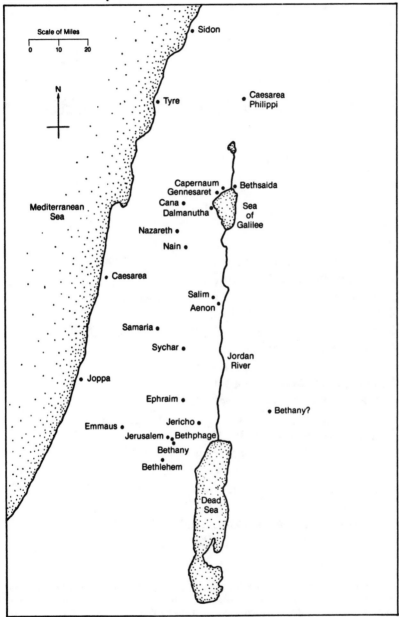

Dress and Ornamentation

OT Terms

1. sash, belt, especially of a priest (*'bnt*), Exod. 28:4
2. robe, garment (*'drt*), Jonah 3:6
3. waistcloth, undergarment (*'zwr*), 2 Kings 1:8
4. priestly garment (*'pwd*), Exod. 28:4
5. armlet, pace-chain (*'ṣ'dh*), 2 Sam. 1:10; cf. Num. 31:50
6. wool dyed red or purple (*'rgmn*), Num. 4:13
7. garment, clothes (*bgd*), 2 Kings 4:39
8. linen, finery (*bd*), 1 Sam. 2:18
9. mantle or wrap (*glwm*), Ezek. 27:24
10. papyrus garments or mirrors ? (*glywn*), Isa. 3:23
11. attire, ornament (*hdr*), Ps. 110:3
12. belt or sash (*ḥgwr*), 1 Sam. 18:4
13. loincloth or belt (*ḥgwrh*), Gen. 3:7
14. necklace of shells, ornaments (*ḥrwzym*), Song of Sol. 1:10
15. bag or purse (*ḥryt*), 2 Kings 5:23
16. breastplate, of a priest (*ḥšn*), Exod. 25:7
17. signet ring (*ḥwtmt*), Gen. 38:25

For the sake of accuracy and clarity the translation of these basic alphabetized Hebrew terms for dress and ornamentation in the OT is based on W. L. Holladay, *A Concise Hebrew and Aramaic Lexicon of the Old Testament* (Grand Rapids: Eerdmans, 1971). The several standard English versions translate or in some cases interpret the Hebrew terms in a variety of ways—occasionally distorting the meaning of the term due to the "Western" approach to ancient Near Eastern clothing.

18. ring, signet ring (*ṭb't*), Gen. 41:12
19. feminine ornament (*kwmz*), Exod. 35:22
20. clothes, ornaments (*kly*), Gen. 24:53; Deut. 22:5
21. turban (*krbl'*), Dan. 3:21
22. long, shirtlike garment (*ktwnt*), Gen. 37:3
23. high turban (*ktr*), Esther 1:11
24. garment, clothes (*lbwš*), Gen. 49:11
25. amulet (*lḥš*), Isa. 3:20
26. headband, of a priest (*mgb'h*), Exod. 28:40
27. garment (*md*), 1 Sam. 4:12
28. girdle (*mzḥ*), Isa. 23:10
29. finery, white festival clothing (*mḥlṣwt*), Zech. 3:4
30. mantle, wrap for women (*mṭpḥt*), Ruth 3:15
31. splendid garment (*mklwl*), Ezek. 27:24
32. linen trousers, breeches (*mknsym*), Exod. 28:42
33. outer garment (*mṭpt*), Isa. 3:22
34. sleeveless robe (*m'yl*), 1 Sam. 15:27
35. headband, turban (*mṣnpt*), Ezek. 21:31
36. silk, fine linen (*mšy*), Ezek. 16:10
37. ring (*nzm*), Gen. 24:22
38. diadem, headband (*nzr*), 2 Kings 11:12
39. earring (*nṭph*), Judg. 8:26
40. sandal (*n'l*), Josh. 9:5
41. boot, Assyrian (*s'wn*), Isa. 9:4
42. wook, skin, hide (*sp*), 2 Sam. 17:28
43. cloak or trousers (*srbl*), Dan. 3:21
44. earring, round ornament (*'gyl*), Num. 31:50
45. ornaments (*'dy*), 2 Sam. 1:24
46. crown, wreath (*'ṭrh*), 2 Sam. 12:30
47. headdress (*p'r*), Isa. 3:20
48. coat or trousers (*pṭyš*), Dan. 3:21
49. long tunic, tunic of colors ? (*ktwnt psym*), Gen. 37:23
50. fine linen (*ptylgyl*), Isa. 3:24
51. eyepaint (*pwk*), Jer. 4:30
52. fringe, tassel (*ṣyṣt*), Num. 15:38
53. bracelet (*ṣmyd*), Gen. 24:22
54. wool (*ṣmr*), 2 Kings 3:4
55. turban, mitre (*ṣnyp*), Isa. 62:3

56. ankle bracelets, chains (ṣ'dh), Isa. 3:20
57. shawl, veil (ṣ'yp), Gen. 24:65
58. breast-bands, woman's sash (qšwrym), Isa. 3:20
59. gold chain (rbyd), Gen. 41:42
60. garment, wrap (rdyd), Isa. 3:23
61. veil (r'lh), Isa. 3:19
62. embroidered garments (rgmh), Judg. 5:30
63. ornaments (śhrwnym), Judg. 8:21
64. mantle, wrapper (ślmh), 1 Kings 10:25
65. hairy garment (ś'r), Gen. 25:25
66. sackcloth (śq), 2 Sam. 21:10
67. headband (šbys), Isa. 3:18
68. bracelet, bangle (šr), Isa. 3:19
69. linen (šš), Gen. 41:42
70. fine leather (tḥš), Num. 4:25
71. checkered material ? (tšbṣ), Exod. 28:4

NT Terms

1. seamless garment (araphos), John 19:23
2. linen or fine linen (bussinos), Rev. 18:12
3. tunic or inner garment (chitōn), Matt. 10:10
4. scarlet robe (chlamus), Matt. 27:28
5. ring (daktulios), Luke 15:22
6. diadem, crown (diadēma), Rev. 12:3
7. braiding, of the hair (emplokē), 1 Peter 3:3
8. garment, clothing (enduma), Matt. 3:4
9. clothes or outer garment (ependutēs), John 21:7
10. mirror (esoptrou), 1 Cor. 13:12
11. cloak or coat (himation), Mark 2:21
12. clothing, fine clothing (himatismos), Luke 7:25
13. sandal, footwear (hupodēma), Matt. 3:11
14. veil, covering (kalumma), 2 Cor. 3:13
15. red or scarlet, of clothing (kokkinos), Matt. 27:28

For the sake of accuracy and clarity the translation of these basic alphabetized Greek terms for dress and ornamentation in the NT is based on F. W. Gingrich, *Shorter Lexicon of the Greek New Testament* (Chicago: University of Chicago Press, 1965). The several standard English versions translate or interpret the Greek terms in a variety of ways.

180

16. hem or tassle, of a garment (*kraspedon*), Matt. 23:5
17. sheepskin (*mēlōtē*), Heb. 11:37
18. cloak or mantle, veil (*peribolaion*), 1 Cor. 11:15; Heb. 1:12
19. wearing, of jewelry (*perithesis*), 1 Peter 3:3
20. cloak (*phailonēs*), 2 Tim. 4:13
21. phylactery, amulet (*phulaktērion*), Matt. 23:5
22. robe reaching to the feet (*podērēs*), Rev. 1:13
23. rod or staff (*rabdos*), Matt. 10:10
24. sackcloth (*sakkos*), Luke 10:13
25. sandal (*sandalion*), Acts 12:8
26. tunic, shroud for the dead (*sindōn*), Mark 14:51
27. wrap a baby in strips of cloth (*sparganoō*), Luke 2:7
28. robe of superior quality (*stolē*), Mark 12:38
29. belt, girdle, money belt (*zōnē*), Matt. 3:4

Fauna and Flora

OT Fauna

1. bull, stallion (*'byr*), Judg. 5:22
2. wild beasts, hyena, eagle-owl (*'wh*), Isa. 13:21, 22
3. jackal (*'y*), Jer. 50:39
4. falcon, black kite (*'yh*), Deut. 14:13
5. fallow deer (*'yl*), 1 Kings 4:23
6. plover or cormorant (*'np*), Lev. 11:19
7. gecko (*'nqh*), Lev. 11:30
8. snake, viper (*'p'h*), Isa. 30:6
9. young bird (*'prwh*), Deut. 22:6
10. wild goat (*'qw*), Deut. 14:5
11. locust (*'rbh*), Exod. 10:4
12. lion (*'ry*), Num. 23:24
13. hare (*'rnbt*), Lev. 11:6
14. she-ass (*'twn*), Gen. 12:16
15. beast (*bhmh*), 1 Sam. 17:44
16. behemoth, hippopotamus, crocodile ? (*bhmwt*), Job 40:15
17. young camel (*bkr*), Isa. 60:6

The English translation for these alphabetized Hebrew terms is based on W. L. Holladay, *A Concise Hebrew and Aramaic Lexicon of the Old Testament* (Grand Rapids: Eerdmans, 1971). As the list demonstrates, some Hebrew words have more than one meaning while the meanings of others are uncertain. The several standard English versions of the Bible reflect the problematic nature of Hebrew technical terminology in the variety of words used in the translation of the terms in question.

18. young camel (*bkrh*), Jer. 2:23
19. cows, cattle (*bqr*), Exod. 22:1
20. bird, goose, chicken ? (*brbr*), 1 Kings 4:23
21. serpent ? (*bšn*), Ps. 68:23
22. locust swarm (*gbh*), Isa. 33:4
23. locust swarm (*gwby*), Amos 7:1
24. kid (*gdy*), Gen. 27:9
25. turtledove, young bird (*gwzl*), Gen. 15:9
26. locust, caterpillar ? (*gzm*), Amos 4:9
27. camel (*gml*), Gen. 12:16
28. bird, kite (*d'h*), Lev. 11:14
29. bear (*dwb*), 2 Kings 2:24
30. bee (*dbwrh*), Deut. 1:44
31. fish (*dg*), Jonah 2:1
32. hoopoe bird (*dwkypt*), Lev. 11:19
33. bird of prey (*dyh*), Deut. 14:13
34. bison ? (*dyšwn*), Deut. 14:5
35. bird, swallow or dove ? (*drwr*), Ps. 84:3
36. wolf (*z'b*), Gen. 49:27
37. flies (*zbwb*), Isa. 7:18
38. gazelle (*zmr*), Deut. 14:5
39. rooster ? (*zrzyr*), Prov. 30:31
40. phoenix bird (*hwl*), Job 29:18
41. wild boar, swine (*hzyr*), Deut. 14:8
42. mole (*hwld*), Lev. 11:29
43. donkey (*hmwr*), Gen. 12:16
44. bird, stork or heron? (*hsydh*), Jer. 8:7
45. reptile (*hwmt*), Lev. 11:30
46. locust or cockroach ? (*hsyl*), 1 Kings 8:37
47. shrew (*hpprh*), Isa. 2:20
48. grasshopper (*hrgwl*), Lev. 11:22
49. ibis bird (*thwt*), Job 38:36
50. lamb (*tlh*), Isa. 40:11
51. dove (*ywnh*), Gen. 8:8
52. roebuck (*yhmwr*), Deut. 14:5
53. locust (*ylq*), Jer. 51:14
54. bird, ibis or owl ? (*ynšwp*), Lev. 11:17
55. ibex, mountain goat (*y'l*), Ps. 104:18

56. ostrich or owl ? (*y'nh*), Deut. 14:15
57. young ram (*kbś*), Exod. 12:5
58. screech owl (*kwś*), Lev. 11:17
59. lizard (*kwḥ*), Lev. 11:30
60. dog (*klb*), Judg. 7:5
61. gnats (*knm*), Exod. 8:16-18
62. young lion (*kpyr*), Judg. 14:5
63. young ram (*kr*), 2 Kings 3:4
64. female camel (*krkrh*), Isa. 66:20
65. lion, lioness (*lb', lb'h*), Ps. 57:4; Nahum 2:13
66. lioness (*lby'*), Gen. 49:9
67. leviathan, sea-monster (*lwytn*), Job 3:8
68. lizard, gecko ? (*lṭ'h*), Lev. 11:30
69. wood owl ? (*lylyt*), Isa. 34:14
70. lion (*lyš*), Isa. 30:6
71. fattened cattle (*mry'*), 1 Kings 1:9
72. snake, reptile (*nḥš*), Gen. 3:1
73. ant (*nmlh*), Prov. 6:6
74. leopard, panther (*nmr*), Jer. 5:6
75. falcon (*nṣ, nwṣh*), Lev. 11:14; Job 39:13
76. eagle, vulture (*nšr*), Exod. 19:4
77. horse (*sws*), Gen. 47:17
78. locust (*sl'm*), Lev. 11:22
79. thrush ? (*'gwl*), Jer. 8:7
80. calves (*'gl, 'glh*), 1 Kings 12:28
81. goat (*'z*), Gen. 27:9
82. black vulture ? (*'znyh*), Lev. 11:13
83. bat (*'ṭlp*), Lev. 11:19
84. birds of prey (*'yt*), Jer. 12:9
85. ass (*'yr*), Gen. 49:11
86. stallion, zebra (*'yr*), Gen. 32:16; Job 11:12
87. spider (*'kbyš*), Job 8:14
88. jerboa (*'kbr*), 1 Sam. 6:4
89. horned viper (*'kšwb*), Ps. 140:4
90. leech (*'lwqh*), Prov. 30:15
91. fawn, deer (*'wpr*), Song of Sol. 2:9
92. scorpion (*'qrb*), Deut. 8:15
93. swarm of insects (*'rwb*), Exod. 8:17

94. raven (*'wrb*), Gen. 8:7
95. moth (*'s*), Isa. 50:9
96. ram, he-goat (*'twd*), Gen. 31:10
97. young bull (*pr*), Gen. 32:15
98. zebra, wild ass, onager ? (*pr'*), Gen. 16:12
99. mule, she-mule (*prd, prdh*), 1 Kings 10:25; 1:33
100. bird, lammergeier ? (*prs*), Lev. 11:13
101. flea (*pr'wš*), 1 Sam. 24:14
102. cobra, asp (*ptn*), Deut. 32:33
103. sheep, small cattle (*sw'n*), Gen. 4:2
104. lizard (*ṣb*), Lev. 11:29
105. gazelle (*ṣb'*), 1 Chron. 12:8
106. hyena (*ṣbw'*), Jer. 12:9
107. gazelle (*ṣby*), 1 Kings 4:23
108. crickets (*ṣlṣl*), Isa. 18:1
109. bird (*ṣpwr*), Job 30:29
110. he-goat (*ṣpyr*), Dan. 8:5
111. venomous serpent (*ṣp'*), Isa. 14:29
112. serpent (*ṣp'wny*), Prov. 23:32
113. bird (*q't*), Deut. 14:17
114. ape (*qwp*), 1 Kings 10:22
115. hedgehog, owl ? (*qpwd*), Isa. 13:21; Zeph. 2:14
116. dart snake, owl ? (*qpwz*), Isa. 34:15
117. partridge (*qr'*), Jer. 17:11
118. kite (*r'h*), Deut. 14:13
119. wild ox (*r'm*), Ps. 22:21
120. sheep (*rḥl*), Isa. 53:7
121. carrion vulture (*rḥm*), Lev. 11:18
122. maggots (*rmh*), Job 7:5
123. mare (*rmkh*), Esther 8:10
124. small animals, reptiles (*rmś*), Gen. 1:24
125. female ostriches (*rnnym*), Job 39:13
126. lamb, kid (*śh*), Gen. 22:7
127. rooster, cock ? (*śkwy*), Job 38:36
128. quail (*ślw*), Exod. 16:13
129. gecko ? (*śmmyt*), Prov. 30:28
130. she-goat (*ś'yrh*), Lev. 4:28
131. fiery serpent (*śrp*), Num. 21:6

132. snail ? (*šblwl*), Ps. 58:8
133. fox (*šw'l*), Judg. 15:4
134. bull, ox, steer (*šwr*), Gen. 32:5
135. lion cub (*šhl*), Hos. 5:14
136. seagull, bat ? (*šḥp*), Lev. 11:16
137. ivory of elephants (*šnhbym*), 1 Kings 10:22
138. horned snake (*špypwn*), Gen. 49:17
139. coney (*špn*), Deut. 14:7
140. antelope, wild sheep ? (*t'w*), Deut. 14:5
141. maggot, worm (*twl'h*), Exod. 16:20
142. turtledove (*twr*), Gen. 15:9
143. owl, nighthawk ? (*tḥms*), Lev. 11:16
144. dolphin, porpoise ? (*tḥš*), Num. 4:6
145. he-goat (*tyš*), Prov. 30:31
146. poultry or baboons ? (*twkyym*), 1 Kings 10:22
147. jackal (*tn*), Lam. 4:3
148. sea monster, serpent (*tnyn*), Ps. 148:7; Exod. 7:9
149. lizard, chameleon ? (*tnšmt*), Lev. 11:30
150. barn owl ? (*tnšmt*), Lev. 11:18

OT Flora

1. reed, papyrus (*'bh*), Isa. 18:2
2. melon (*'bṭyḥ*), Num. 11:5
3. caper-berry (*'bywnh*), Eccles. 12:5
4. walnut tree (*'gwz*), Song of Sol. 6:11
5. reed, bulrush (*'gmwn*), Isa. 58:5
6. mallow (*'wrh*), 2 Kings 4:39
7. hyssop (*'zwb*), Exod. 12:22
8. bay tree ? (*'zrh*), Ps. 37:35
9. aloe tree (*'hlwt*), Ps. 45:8
10. reed (*'ḥw*), Job 8:11

The English translation of these alphabetized Hebrew terms is based on W. L. Holladay, *A Concise Hebrew and Aramaic Lexicon of the Old Testament* (Grand Rapids: Eerdmans, 1971). As in the case with the list of OT fauna, some Hebrew words have more than one meaning while the meanings of others are uncertain. The lists of fauna and flora demonstrate the richness of the Hebrew vocabulary for describing the natural environment. The several standard English versions of the Bible translate or interpret the terms in a variety of ways, reflecting the problematic nature of Hebrew technical terminology.

11. boxthorn (*'ṭd*), Judg. 9:14
12. great or stately tree (*'lh, 'lwn*), Gen. 13:18
13. almug wood (*'lmgym*), 1 Kings 10:11
14. cedar or fir tree (*'rz*), Ezra 3:7
15. laurel tree (*'wrn*), Isa. 44:14
16. tamarisk tree (*'šl*), Gen. 21:33
17. sour or wild grapes (*b'š*), Isa. 5:2
18. darnel (*b'šh*), Job 31:40
19. bdellium, gum-resin from a tree (*bdwlḥ*), Num. 11:7
20. pistachio nuts (*bṭnh*), Gen. 43:11
21. baka shrubs (*bk'*), 1 Chron. 14:14
22. onion (*bṣl*), Num. 11:5
23. grain, wheat (*br*), Gen. 41:35
24. juniper tree (*brwš*), 1 Kings 19:4
25. juniper or fir tree (*brwt*), Song of Sol. 1:17
26. thorns (*brqwn*), Judg. 8:7
27. balsam shrub (*bwśm*), Song of Sol. 5:1
28. coriander (*gd*), Num. 11:7
29. tumbleweed (*glgl*), Isa. 17:13
30. papyrus (*gwm'*), Isa. 35:7
31. vine (*gpn*), 2 Kings 4:39
32. gopher wood (*gwpr*), Gen. 6:14
33. grain, cereal (*dgn*), Deut. 7:13
34. mandrake tree (*dwd'ym*), Song of Sol. 7:13
35. sorghum (*dwḥn*), Ezek. 4:9
36. thistle (*drdr*), Hos. 10:8
37. new grass (*dš'*), Deut. 32:2
38. ebony (tree) (*hbnym*), Ezek. 27:15
39. myrtle (*hds*), Isa. 41:19
40. olive tree (*zyt*), Judg. 9:8
41. asphodel, crocus (*ḥbṣlt*), Isa. 35:1
42. brier (*ḥdq*), Mic. 7:4
43. thornbush, thistle (*ḥwḥ*), 2 Kings 14:9
44. wheat (*ḥth*), Exod. 9:32
45. galbanum (*ḥlbnh*), Exod. 30:34
46. grass or cattails (*ḥsyr*), 1 Kings 18:5; Isa. 35:7
47. leek (*ḥsyr*), Num. 11:5
48. vetch, wild artichoke ? (*ḥrwl*), Job 30:4

49. greens, vegetables (*yrq*), Prov. 15:17
50. green plant (*yrq*), Gen. 1:30
51. cummin (*kmwn*), Isa. 28:25
52. emmer-wheat (*ksmt*), Ezek. 4:9
53. henna (*kwpr*), Song of Sol. 1:14
54. saffron (*krkwm*), Song of Sol. 4:14
55. storax tree (*lbnh*), Hos. 4:13
56. myrrh (*lwṭ*), Gen. 37:25
57. wormwood (tree) (*l'nh*), Prov. 5:4
58. a salty plant (*mlwḥ*), Job 30:4
59. myrrh, resin (*mwr*), Exod. 30:23
60. bitter herbs (*mrwr*), Exod. 12:8
61. resin from a shrub ? (*nk'wt*), Gen. 37:25
62. a blossom (*nṣh*), Job 15:33
63. nard (*nrd*), Song of Sol. 1:12
64. camel-thorn (*n'ṣṣ*), Isa. 7:19
65. reed (*swp*), Exod. 2:3
66. burnet, thorny bush (*syrh*), Isa. 34:13
67. thorns (*slwn*), Ezek. 28:24
68. thorny shrub (*snh*), Deut. 33:16
69. stinging nettle (*srpd*), Isa. 55:13
70. lentils (*'dšym*), Gen. 25:34
71. tree (*'ṣ*), Deut. 22:6
72. thick oak (*'ṣ 'bwt*), Ezek. 6:13
73. poplar, willow (*'rbh*), Isa. 44:4
74. plane-tree (*'rmwn*), Ezek. 31:8
75. juniper tree (*'r'r*), Jer. 17:6
76. plants (*'śb*), Gen. 3:18
77. unripe figs (*pg*), Song of Sol. 2:13
78. broad beans or horse-beans (*pwl*), 2 Sam. 17:28; Ezek. 4:9
79. wild gourd (*p'wqwt*), 2 Kings 4:39
80. stalks of flax (*pšt*), Josh. 2:6
81. thorny shrub (*ṣ'lym*), Job 40:21
82. blossom, flower (*ṣyṣ, ṣyṣh*), Num. 17:5; Isa. 28:4
83. willow tree (*ṣpṣph*), Ezek. 17:5
84. resin, mastic tree (*ṣry*), Gen. 37:25
85. thorn bush (*qwṣ*), Gen. 3:18
86. castor-oil plant or a gourd (*qyqywn*), Jonah 4:6

87. weeds, nettles (*qmws*), Hos. 9:6
88. reed (*qnh*), 1 Kings 14:15
89. sweet cane (*qnh bwśm*), Exod. 30:23
90. oil grass (*qnh hṭwb*), Jer. 6:20
91. cinnamon (*qnmwn*), Song of Sol. 4:14
92. black cummin (*qṣh*), Isa. 28:25
93. cassia, cinnamon-flowers (*qṣy'h*), Ps. 45:8
94. cassia buds (*qṣy'h, qdh*), Ezek. 27:19
95. cucumber (*qś'h*), Num. 11:5
96. poisonous plant (*rw'š*), Deut. 29:18
97. pomegranate tree (*rmwn*), 1 Sam. 14:2
98. broom tree (*rwtm*), Ps. 120:4
99. shrub, bush (*śyh*), Job 30:4
100. thorn (*śk*), Num. 33:55
101. barley (*ś'wrh*), Exod. 9:31
102. grape vine (*śrqh*), Gen. 49:11
103. garlic (*šwmym*), Num. 11:5
104. lily, lotus flower (*šwšn*), 1 Kings 7:19, 26
105. acacia tree (*šṭh*), Exod. 25:5
106. briers (*šyt*), Isa. 5:6
107. thorn bush (*šmyr*), Isa. 5:6
108. almond tree (*šqd* or *lwz*), Gen. 30:37; Jer. 1:11
109. sycamore/fig tree (*šqmh*), 1 Kings 10:27
110. root (*šwrš*), Isa. 53:2
111. fig tree (*t'nh*), 2 Kings 18:31
112. cypress tree (*t'šwr*), Isa. 41:19
113. date palm (*tmr*), Exod. 15:27
114. apple tree (*tpwh*), Song of Sol. 2:3

NT Fauna

1. herd of swine (*agelē*), Matt. 8:30
2. eagle, vulture (*aetos*), Rev. 12:14
3. goatskin, sheepskin (*aigeios*), Heb. 11:37

The English translation of these alphabetized Greek terms for NT fauna is based on F. W. Gingrich, *Shorter Lexicon of the Greek New Testament* (Chicago: University of Chicago Press, 1965). The several standard modern English versions of the Bible render these terms with a variety of translations.

4. locust, grasshopper (*akris*), Matt. 3:4
5. rooster, cock (*alektōr*), Mark 14:30
6. fox (*alōpex*), Matt. 8:20
7. unblemished lamb, used of Christ (*amnos*), 1 Peter 1:19
8. lamb (*arēn*), Luke 10:3
9. sheep, lamb (*arnion*), Rev. 5:6
10. asp, Egyptian cobra (*aspis*), Rom. 3:13
11. frog (*batrachos*), Rev. 16:13
12. ox, cow, head of cattle (*bous*), Luke 13:15
13. heifer, young cow (*damalis*), James 3:7
14. viper, poisonous snake (*echidna*), Acts 28:3
15. kid or goat (*eriphion*), Matt. 25:33
16. kid or he-goat (*eriphos*), Luke 15:29
17. reptile (*herpeton*), Acts 10:12
18. horse, steed (*hippos*), Rev. 9:9
19. beast of burden, ass, ox, horse (*hupozugion*), Matt. 21:5
20. fish, little fish (*ichthudion*), Matt. 15:34
21. fish (*ichthus*), Matt. 7:10
22. camel (*kamēlos*), Matt. 23:24
23. sea monster, great fish (*kētos*), Matt. 12:40
24. gnat, mosquito (*kōnōps*), Matt. 23:24
25. raven, crow (*korax*), Luke 12:24
26. animal, pack animal, domesticated animal (*ktēnos*), Rev. 18:13
27. dog (*kumarion*), Mark 7:27
28. lion (*leōn*), 1 Peter 5:8
29. wolf (*lukos*), Matt. 10:16
30. pearl (*margaritēs*), Rev. 17:4
31. bees, inferred from honey (*meli*), Matt. 3:4
32. calf, young bull (*moschos*), Luke 15:23
33. the young of a bird (*nossion*), Matt. 23:37
34. the young of a bird, young doves (*nossos*), Luke 2:24
35. donkey (*onikos*), Matt. 18:6
36. male or female donkey, donkey's colt (*onos*), John 12:15
37. snake, serpent (*ophis*), Matt. 7:10
38. fish (*opsarion*), John 6:9
39. birds, fowl (*orneon*), Rev. 19:17
40. bird, cock, hen (*ornis*), Luke 13:34
41. leopard (*pardalis*), Rev. 13:2
42. pigeon, dove (*peristera*), Matt. 21:12

43. bird (*peteinon*), Matt. 13:4
44. colt of a horse, young donkey, animal (*pōlos*), Luke 19:30
45. lamb, sheep (*probation*), John 21:16
46. sheep (*probaton*), Matt. 12:11
47. fish (*prosphagion*), John 21:5
48. birds (*ptēnos*), 1 Cor. 15:39
49. moth (*sēs*), Matt. 6:19
50. worm (*skōlēx*), Mark 9:44
51. scorpion (*skoprios*), Luke 10:19
52. sponge (*spongos*), Matt. 27:48
53. sparrow (*strouthion*), Matt. 10:29
54. four-footed animal (*tetrapous*), Acts 10:12
55. wild animal, beast (*thērion*), Heb. 12:20
56. domesticated animal, sheep or goat (*thremma*), John 4:12
57. he-goat (*tragos*), Heb. 9:12
58. turtle-dove (*trugōn*), Luke 2:24

NT Flora

1. chaff (*achuron*), Matt. 3:12
2. wild olive tree (*agrielaios*), Rom. 11:17
3. thorn-plant (*akantha*), Mark 4:7
4. thorns (*akanthinos*), Mark 15:17
5. aloes, resin from the aloe tree (*aloē*), John 19:39
6. amomum, an Indian spice plant (*amōmon*), Rev. 18:13
7. grapevine (*ampelos*), Luke 22:18
8. dill plant (*anēthon*), Matt. 23:23
9. flower, blossom (*anthos*), 1 Peter 1:24
10. wormwood, bitter substance (*apsinthos*), Rev. 8:11
11. palm branch (*baion*) John 12:13
12. thorn bush (*batos*), Acts 7:30
13. herbs (*botanē*), Heb. 6:7
14. gall, poison (*cholē*), Matt. 27:34
15. grass, hay (*chortos*), Matt. 14:19

The English translation of these alphabetized Greek terms for NT flora is based on F. W. Gingrich, *Shorter Lexicon of the Greek New Testament* (Chicago: University of Chicago Press, 1965). The several standard modern English versions of the Bible render these terms with a variety of translations.

16. olive tree (*elaion*), Rev. 6:6
17. mint plant (*ēduosmon*), Matt. 23:23
18. forest (*hulē*), James 3:5
19. hyssop plant (*hussōpos*), John 19:29
20. reed (*kalamos*), Luke 7:24
21. cultivated olive tree (*kallielaios*), Rom. 11:24
22. fruit (*karpos*), Matt. 21:34
23. carob pods (*keration*), Luke 15:16
24. cinnamon (*kinnamōmon*), Rev. 18:13
25. seed, grain (*kokkos*), Mark 4:31
26. lily, flower (*krinon*), Luke 12:27
27. barley (*krithē*), Rev. 6:6
28. cummin (*kuminon*), Matt. 23:23
29. herbs, vegetables (*lachanon*), Matt. 13:32
30. frankincense, tree resin (*libanos*), Rev. 18:13
31. nard, spikenard (*nardos*), Mark 14:3
32. fruit (*opōra*), Rev. 18:14
33. rue, garden herbs (*pēganon*), Luke 11:42
34. palm tree (*phoinix*), John 12:13
35. foliage (*phullon*), Mark 11:13
36. pistachio tree (?) (*pistikos*), Mark 14:3
37. mustard plant (*sinapi*), Matt. 13:31
38. wheat, grain (*sitos*), Luke 16:7
39. myrrh, resin from the balsam bush (*smurna*), Matt. 2:11
40. seed (*sporos*), Luke 8:11
41. grapes (*straphulē*), Luke 6:44
42. mulberry tree (*sukaminos*), Luke 17:6
43. fig tree (*sukē*), Matt. 24:32
44. sycamore tree (*sukomorea*), Luke 19:4
45. citron wood, citron tree (*thuinos*), Rev. 18:12
46. incense (*thumiama*), Rev. 5:8
47. thistle (*tribolos*), Matt. 7:16
48. darnel (*zizanion*), Matt. 13:25

Foods

Seasonings

1. anise or dill (*anēthos*), Matt. 23:23
2. cinnamon (*qnmwn*), Song of Sol. 4:14
3. coriander seeds (*gd, korion*), Exod. 16:31
4. cummin (*kuminos*), Matt. 23:23
5. mint (*hēduosmos*), Matt. 23:23
6. mustard (*sinapeos*), Luke 13:19
7. salt (*mlḥ, halas*), Job 6:6; Matt. 5:13

Fruits

1. apple (*tpwḥ*), Song of Sol. 2:5
2. date (palm) (*tmr, phoinix*), Joel 1:12; John 12:13
3. fig (*t'nh, sukon*), Jer. 24:1; Matt. 7:16
4. grape (*'nb, straphulē*), Deut. 23:24; Matt. 7:16
5. mandrake (*dwd'ym*), Song of Sol. 7:13
6. melon (*'bṭyḥ*), Num. 11:5
7. olive/olive oil (*zyt, elaia*), Judg. 15:5; James 3:12
8. pomegranate (*rmwn*), Num. 13:23
9. raisin (*ṣmh*), 2 Sam. 16:1

Vegetables

1. bean (*pwl*), 2 Sam. 17:28
2. bitter herbs (*mrwrym*), Exod. 12:8

3. cucumber (*qš'h*), Num. 11:5
4. garlic (*šwmym*), Num. 11:5
5. herbs (*'śb*), Gen. 1:30
6. leek (*ḥsyr*), Num. 11:5
7. lentil (*'dšym*), 2 Sam. 17:28
8. onion (*bṣl*), Num. 11:5

Grains

1. barley (*śrh, krithinos*), Ruth 1:22; John 6:9
2. bread (*lhm, artos*), Gen. 3:19; John 6:5
3. flax (*pšth, linon*), Exod. 9:31; Matt. 12:20
4. flour (*qmḥ, semidalis*), Exod. 29:2; Rev. 18:13
5. millet or sorghum (*dḥn*), Ezek. 4:9
6. spelt or emmer wheat (*ksmt*), Isa. 28:25
7. wheat (*ḥth, sitos*), Gen. 30:14; Matt. 13:25

Meats

1. antelope (*t'w*), Isa. 51:20
2. chicken (*ornis, alektora*), Matt. 23:37; 26:34
3. dove, turtledove (*twr, peristera*), Gen. 15:9; Mark 11:15
4. fish (*dg, ichthus*), Num. 11:5; Matt. 15:34
5. gazelle (*ṣby*), Deut. 14:5
6. goat (*'z, eriphion*), Deut. 14:5; Luke 15:29
7. hart (*'yl*), Deut. 12:15
8. ibex (*dyšwm*), Deut. 14:5
9. mountain sheep (*zmr*), Deut. 14:5
10. ox (*šwr, bous*), Deut. 14:5; Luke 13:15
11. partridge (*qwr'*), 1 Sam. 26:20
12. pigeon (*ywnh*), Lev. 12:6
13. quail (*ślw*), Num. 11:32
14. roebuck (*yḥmwr*), Deut. 14:5
15. sheep (*kśb, probaton*), Deut. 14:5; Matt. 18:12
16. sparrow (*strouthia*), Matt. 10:29
17. venison (*ṣyd*), Deut. 14:5
18. wild goat (*'qw*), Deut. 14:5

Others

1. almonds (*sqd*), Gen. 43:11
2. bread and broth (*psōmion*), John 13:26
3. carob pods (*keration*), Luke 15:16
4. cheese (*gbynh*), Job 10:10
5. curds (*ḥm'h*), Judg. 5:25
6. eggs (*sh*), Deut. 22:6
7. honey (*dbs, meli*), Lev. 2:11; Matt. 3:4
8. locusts (*'rbh, akris*), Lev. 11:22; Matt. 3:4
9. manna (*mn*), Exod. 16:15
10. milk (*ḥlb*), Deut. 32:14
11. pistachio nuts (*bṭnh*), Gen. 43:11
12. vinegar (*ḥwmṣ, oxos*), Ruth 2:14; Matt. 27:48
13. water (*mym, hudōr*), Exod. 7:15; John 4:7
14. wine (*yyn, oinos*), Deut. 7:13; John 2:1-10; 1 Tim. 5:23

Unclean Foods

Leviticus 11:1–47	Deuteronomy 14:1–21
camel (*gml*)	camel (*gml*)
coney (*špn*)	rabbit (*'rnbt*)
rabbit (*'rnbt*)	coney (*špn*)
pig (*ḥzyr*)	pig (*ḥzyr*)
water creatures having no fins or scales	water creatures having no fins or scales
eagle (*nšr*)	eagle (*nšr*)
vulture (*prs*)	vulture (*prs*)
black vulture (*'znyh*)	black vulture (*'znyh*)
red kite (*d'h*)	red kite (*r'h*)
black kite (*'yh*)	black rite (*'yh*)
raven (*'wrb*)	falcon (*dyh*)
horned owl (*y'nh*)	raven (*'wrb*)

Although these foods were taboo for the Israelites they were undoubtedly eaten by other peoples. For convenience in comparison of the two passages, English translations of the Hebrew terms under "Unclean Foods" are based on the *NIV* and therefore may differ from similar terms listed under OT Fauna.

Leviticus 11:1–47	Deuteronomy 14:1–21
screech owl (*tḥms*)	horned owl (*y'nh*)
gull (*šḥp*)	screech owl (*tḥms*)
hawk (*nṣ*)	gull (*šḥp*)
little owl (*kws*)	hawk (*nṣ*)
cormorant (*šlk*)	little owl (*kws*)
great owl (*ynšwp*)	great owl (*ynšwp*)
white owl (*tnšmt*)	white owl (*tnšmt*)
desert owl (*q't*)	desert owl (*q't*)
osprey (*rḥm*)	osprey (*rḥm*)
stork (*hsydh*)	cormorant (*šlk*)
heron (*'nph*)	stork (*hsydh*)
hoopoe (*dwkypt*)	heron (*'nph*)
bat (*'ṭlp*)	hoopoe (*dwkypt*)
winged creatures with four unjointed legs	bat (*'ṭlp*)
weasel (*ḥwld*)	flying insects that swarm
rat (*'kbr*)	anything dead
great lizard (*ṣb*)	a goat in its mother's milk
gecko (*'nqh*)	
monitor lizard (*kwḥ*)	
wall lizard (*lṭ'h*)	
skink (*ḥwmṭ*)	
chameleon (*tnšmt*)	

Holy Days and Feasts of the Jews

1. Sabbath, the seventh day, Lev. 23:3
2. Passover/Unleavened Bread, the 14th day of the first month (Nisan)/eating of unleavened bread from the 15th-21st day of the first month, Lev. 23:4-8
3. Firstfruits, the day after the Sabbath following Passover, Lev. 23:9-14
4. Weeks or Pentecost, 50 days after Firstfruits, Lev. 23:15-22
5. Civil New Year or Trumpets, 1st day of the 7th month (Tishri), Lev. 23:23-25
6. Day of Atonement, 10th day of the 7th month, Lev. 23:26-32
7. Tabernacles, 15th-21st of the 7th month, Lev. 23:33-44
8. Sabbatical Year, the seventh year, Lev. 25:1-7
9. Year of Jubilee, every 50th year, Lev. 25:8-55
10. New Moon, the first day of every month, Num. 28:11-15
11. Purim, the 14th and 15th of the 12th month (Adar), Esther 9:18-32
12. Hanukkah or Dedication, 25th day of the 9th month (Kislev), 1 Macc. 4:51-59; 2 Macc. 10:6-8; cf. John 10:22

See "Jewish Calendar: Festivals," pp. 156-57

Jewels and
Precious Stones

1. adamant or corundum (*šmr*), Ezek. 3:9
2. agate (*kdkd*), Isa. 54:12
3. alabaster (*alabastron*), Matt. 26:7
4. amber (*ḥšml*), Ezek. 1:4
5. amethyst (*'ḥlm, amethustos*), Exod. 28:19; Rev. 21:20
6. basalt (available but not mentioned in the Bible)
7. bdellium ? (*bdwlḥ*), Gen. 2:12; Num. 11:7
8. beryl (*tršš, swhm* in Ezek. 28:13, *bērullos*), Exod. 28:20; Rev. 21:20
9. brass (*chalkos*), Matt. 10:9
10. bronze (*nḥsh*), Job 28:2
11. carbuncle (*brqt*), Exod. 28:17
12. carnelian (*'dm, sardion*), Ezek. 28:13; Rev. 21:20
13. chalcedony (*chalkēdōn*), Rev. 21:19
14. chrysolite (*tršš, chrusolithos*), Ezek. 1:16; Rev. 21:20
15. chrysoprase (*chrusoprasos*), Rev. 21:20
16. copper (*nḥwšt*), Ezra 8:27
17. coral (*rmwt, pnynym* in Lam. 4:7), Job 28:18
18. crystal (*gbš, qrḥ* in Ezek. 1:22, *krustallos*), Job 28:17; Rev. 22:1

The English translation of these Hebrew and Greek terms is based on W. L. Holladay, *A Concise Hebrew and Aramaic Lexicon of the Old Testament* (Grand Rapids: Eerdmans, 1971); and F. W. Gingrich, *Shorter Lexicon of the Greek New Testament* (Chicago: University of Chicago Press, 1965). Many of these identifications are only tentative. The Hebrew and Greek words often have uncertain meanings. This is reflected in the wide variety of terms found in the modern English versions of the Bible.

19. diamond ? (*yhlwm*), Exod. 28:18
20. emerald (*smaragdinos, smaragdos*), Rev. 4:3; 21:19
21. flint (*ḥlmš*), Deut. 8:15; Isa. 50:7
22. garnet (known in Egypt and used by the Greeks and Romans, but not mentioned in the Bible)
23. gold (*zhb, chrusion*), Exod. 3:22; Acts 3:6
24. green feldspar (*nwpk*), Exod. 28:13; Ezek. 28:13
25. hematite (known in Egypt, used by the Hebrews and Hittites, not mentioned in the Bible)
26. iron (*brzl, sidēreos*), Gen. 4:22; Acts 12:10
27. jacinth (*lšm, huakinthos*), Exod. 28:19; Rev. 21:20
28. jade ? (*yhlwm*), Ezek. 28:13; cf. #19
29. jasper (*yšp, iaspis*), Exod. 28:20; Rev. 4:3; 21:11
30. ligure (*šbw*), Exod. 28:19
31. limestone (known and used in Palestine), cf. Isa. 33:12
32. marble (*šš, marmaros*), Esther 1:6; Rev. 18:12
33. nephrite (known in Palestine, not mentioned in the Bible)
34. obsidian (known in Egypt, not mentioned in the Bible)
35. onyx (*šwhm, sardonux*), Exod. 25:7; Rev. 21:20
36. opal (known by the ancients but not mentioned in the Bible)
37. pearl (*margaritēs*), Matt. 7:6
38. ruby (a KJV mistranslation of *pnynym*), Prov. 3:15; 8:11; cf. #17
39. sapphire (*spr, sappheiros*), Exod. 24:10; Rev. 21:19
40. sardius, cf. #20 ?
41. sardonyx (*sardonux*), Rev. 21:20
42. silver (*ksp, arguros*), Exod. 25:3; Acts 17:29
43. soapstone (known in Palestine, not mentioned in the Bible)
44. topaz (*pṭd, topazion*), Exod. 28:17; Ezek. 28:13; Rev. 21:20
45. turquoise ? (*nwpk*), cf. #27

Judges in the Old Testament

1. Moses, Exod. 18:13
2. Judges appointed by Moses, Exod. 18:13-27
3. Judges, Josh. 8:33; 24:1
4. Othniel, Judg. 3:9-11
5. Ehud, Judg. 3:15-20
6. Shamgar, Judg. 3:31
7. Deborah, Judg. 4:4-5:31
8. Gideon, Judg. 6:7-8:35
9. Tola, Judg. 10:1-2
10. Jair, Judg. 10:3-5
11. Jephthah, Judg. 11:1-12:7
12. Ibzan, Judg. 12:8-10
13. Elon, Judg. 12:11-12
14. Abdon, Judg. 12:13-15
15. Samson, Judg. 13:2-16:31
16. Eli, 1 Sam. 4:18
17. Samuel, 1 Sam. 7:15
18. Samuel's sons, 1 Sam. 8:1
19. Chenaniah and his sons, 1 Chron. 26:29
20. Judges appointed by Jehoshaphat, 2 Chron. 19:5
21. Judges appointed by Ezra, Ezra 7:25

Kings and Queens

Kings (*mlk*) in the Bible

1. Amraphel, king of Shinar, Gen. 14:1
2. Arioch, king of Ellasar, Gen. 14:1
3. Kedorlaomer, king of Elam, Gen. 14:1
4. Tidal, king of Goiim, Gen. 14:1
5. Bera, king of Sodom, Gen. 14:2
6. Birsha, king of Gomorrah, Gen. 14:2
7. Shinab, king of Admah, Gen. 14:2
8. Shemeber, king of Zeboiim, Gen. 14:2
9. King of Bela, Gen. 14:2
10. Melchizedek, king of Salem, Gen. 14:18
11. Abimelech, king of Gerar, Gen. 20:2
12. Pharaoh, king of Egypt, Gen. 41:46; Exod. 1:8
13. King of Edom, Num. 20:14
14. King of Arad, Num. 21:1
15. Sihon, king of the Amorites, Num. 21:21
16. King of Moab, Num. 21:26
17. Og, king of Bashan, Num. 21:33
18. Evi, king of Midian, Num. 31:8
19. Rekem, king of Midian, Num. 31:8
20. Zur, king of Midian, Num. 31:8
21. Hur, king of Midian, Num. 31:8
22. Reba, king of Midian, Num. 31:8

23. Moses, king of Jeshurun, Deut. 33:5
24. Adoni-Zedek, king of Jerusalem, Josh. 10:3
25. Hoham, king of Hebron, Josh. 10:3
26. Piram, king of Jarmuth, Josh. 10:3
27. Japhia, king of Lachish, Josh. 10:3
28. Debir, king of Eglon, Josh. 10:3
29. Horam, king of Gezer, Josh. 10:33
30. Jobab, king of Madon, Josh. 11:1
31. 31 kings captured by Joshua, Josh. 12:9-24
32. Balak, king of Moab, Josh. 24:9
33. Cushan-Rishathaim, king of Aram Naharaim, Judg. 3:8
34. Eglon, king of Moab, Judg. 3:12
35. Jabin, king of Canaan, Judg. 4:2
36. Abimelech, king of Shechem, Judg. 9:6
37. King of Ammon, Judg. 11:13
38. King of Edom, Judg. 11:17
39. Agag, king of the Amalekites, 1 Sam. 15:8
40. Saul, king of Israel, 1 Sam. 15:35
41. Achish, king of Gath, 1 Sam. 21:10
42. David, king of Israel, 2 Sam. 2:4
43. Ish-Bosheth, king of Israel, 2 Sam. 2:10
44. Talmai, king of Geshur, 2 Sam. 3:3
45. Hiram, king of Tyre, 2 Sam. 5:11
46. Hadadezer, king of Zobah, 2 Sam. 8:3
47. Toi, king of Hamath, 2 Sam. 8:9
48. King of Maacah, 2 Sam. 10:6
49. Pharaoh, king of Egypt, 1 Kings 3:1
50. Solomon, king of Israel, 1 Kings 4:1
51. Shishak, king of Egypt, 1 Kings 11:40
52. Rehoboam, king of Judah, 1 Kings 12:27
53. Jeroboam, king of Israel, 1 Kings 13:4
54. Abijah, king of Judah, 1 Kings 15:1
55. Asa, king of Judah, 1 Kings 15:9
56. Nadab, king of Israel, 1 Kings 15:25
57. Baasha, king of Israel, 1 Kings 15:33
58. Elah, king of Israel, 1 Kings 16:8
59. Ben-Hadad, king of Syria, 1 Kings 15:20
60. Zimri, king of Israel, 1 Kings 16:15

61. Omri, king of Israel, 1 Kings 16:16
62. Ahab, king of Israel, 1 Kings 16:29
63. Ethbaal, king of the Sidonians, 1 Kings 16:31
64. Hazael, king of Syria, 1 Kings 19:15
65. Jehoshaphat, king of Judah, 1 Kings 22:10
66. Ahaziah, king of Israel, 1 Kings 22:51
67. Mesha, king of Moab, 2 Kings 3:4
68. Joram, king of Israel, 2 Kings 3:6
69. Joram, king of Judah, 2 Kings 8:16
70. Ahaziah, king of Judah, 2 Kings 8:25
71. Jehu, king of Israel, 2 Kings 9:2
72. Joash, king of Judah, 2 Kings 12:1
73. Jehoahaz, king of Israel, 2 Kings 13:1
74. Jehoash, king of Israel, 2 Kings 13:10
75. Amaziah, king of Judah, 2 Kings 14:1
76. Jeroboam II, king of Israel, 2 Kings 14:23
77. Azariah, king of Judah, 2 Kings 15:1
78. Zechariah, king of Israel, 2 Kings 15:8
79. Shallum, king of Israel, 2 Kings 15:13
80. Menahem, king of Israel, 2 Kings 15:17
81. Tiglath-Pileser, king of Assyria, 2 Kings 15:19
82. Pekahiah, king of Israel, 2 Kings 15:23
83. Pekah, king of Israel, 2 Kings 15:27
84. Jotham, king of Judah, 2 Kings 15:32
85. Ahaz, king of Judah, 2 Kings 16:1
86. Rezin, king of Aram, 2 Kings 16:5
87. Hoshea, king of Israel, 2 Kings 17:1
88. Shalmaneser, king of Assyria, 2 Kings 17:3
89. So, king of Egypt, 2 Kings 17:4
90. Hezekiah, king of Judah, 2 Kings 18:1
91. Sennacherib, king of Assyria, 2 Kings 18:13
92. Tirhakah, king of Ethiopia, 2 Kings 19:9
93. King of Hamath, 2 Kings 19:13
94. King of Arphad, 2 Kings 19:13
95. King of Sepharvaim, 2 Kings 19:13
96. Baladan, king of Babylon, 2 Kings 20:12
97. Manasseh, king of Judah, 2 Kings 21:1
98. Amon, king of Judah, 2 Kings 21:19

99. Josiah, king of Judah, 2 Kings 22:1
100. Necho, king of Egypt, 2 Kings 23:29
101. Jehoahaz, king of Judah, 2 Kings 23:31
102. Jehoiakim, king of Judah, 2 Kings 23:36
103. Nebuchadnezzar, king of Babylon, 2 Kings 24:1
104. Jehoiachin, king of Judah, 2 Kings 24:8
105. Zedekiah, king of Judah, 2 Kings 24:18
106. Evil-Merodach, king of Babylon, 2 Kings 25:27
107. Cyrus, king of Persia, Ezra 1:1
108. Esarhaddon, king of Assyria, Ezra 4:2
109. Darius the Mede, king of Persia, Ezra 4:5
110. Artaxerxes, king of Persia, Ezra 4:7
111. Xerxes, king of Persia, Esther 1:1
112. Sargon, king of Assyria, Isa. 20:1
113. Baalis, king of the Ammonites, Jer. 40:14
114. Pharaoh Hophra, king of Egypt, Jer. 44:30
115. Belshazzar, king of Babylon, Dan. 5:1
116. Darius, king of Persia, Hag. 1:1
117. Herod, Matt. 1:6
118. Caesar, John 19:15
119. Herod Agrippa, Acts 21:1
120. Agrippa, son of Herod Agrippa, Acts 25:13
121. Aretas, 2 Cor. 11:32
122. Jesus Christ, John 18:37; Rev. 15:3; 17:14

Queens (*mlkh*) in the Bible

1. Queen of Sheba, 1 Kings 10:1-13
2. Athaliah, 2 Kings 11:1-3
3. Queen Tahpenes, 1 Kings 11:19
4. Queen-mother Maacah, 1 Kings 15:13
5. Jezebel, 1 Kings 16:31
6. Queen of Artaxerxes, Neh. 2:6
7. Vashti, Esther 1:9-18
8. Esther, Esther 2:22; 5:2
9. "queen of heaven," Jer. 7:18
10. Queen-mother of Jehoiachin, Jer. 29:2
11. Queen-mother of Belshazzar, Dan. 5:10
12. Candace, Acts 8:27
13. Bernice, Acts 25:13, 23

The Kings of the United Monarchy

King	Father/Mother	Accession Age	Years of Reign	Death	Reference
1. Saul	Kish/?	30 (LXX)	40 (Acts 13:21)	suicide	1 Sam. 9-31; 1 Chron. 9-10
2. Ish-Bosheth	Saul/Ahinoam	40	2	murdered	2 Sam. 2:1-11; 4:1-12
3. David	Jesse/?	30	40	died	1 Sam. 16-2 Sam. 24; 1 Chron. 11-29
4. Solomon	David/Bathsheba	?	40	died	1 Kings 1-11; 2 Chron. 1-9

The Kings of Israel

King	Father/Mother	Accession Age	Years of Reign	Character	Death	Reference
1. Jeroboam	Nebat/Zeruah	?	22	evil	stricken by God	1 Kings 11–14; 2 Chron. 9–13
2. Nadab	Jeroboam/?	?	2	evil	murdered by Baasha	1 Kings 15:25–28
3. Baasha	Ahijah/?	?	24	evil	died	1 Kings 15–16; 2 Chron. 16
4. Elah	Baasha/?	?	2	evil	murdered by Zimri	1 Kings 16:6–14
5. Zimri	?/?	?	7 days	evil	suicide	1 Kings 16:9–20
6. Tibni	Ginath/?	?	?	evil	died	1 Kings 16:21–22
7. Omri	?/?	?	12	evil	died	1 Kings 16:15–28
8. Ahab	Omri/?	?	22	evil	in battle	1 Kings 16–22; 2 Chron. 18
9. Ahaziah	Ahab/?	?	2	evil	fell	2 Kings 1; 2 Chron. 20:35–37
10. Joram	Ahab/?	?	12	evil	murdered by Jehu	2 Kings 3–9; 2 Chron. 22
11. Jehu	Jehoshophat/?	?	28	evil	died	2 Kings 9–10; 2 Chron. 22
12. Jehoahaz	Jehu/?	?	17	evil	died	2 Kings 13:1–9
13. Jehoash	Jehoahaz/?	?	16	evil	died	2 Kings 13–14; 2 Chron. 25
14. Jeroboam II	Jehoash/?	?	41	evil	died	2 Kings 14:23–29
15. Zechariah	Jeroboam II/?	?	6 mos	evil	murdered by Shallum	2 Kings 14:29–15:12
16. Shallum	Jabesh/?	?	1 mo	evil	murdered by Menahem	2 Kings 15:10–15
17. Menahem	Gadi/?	?	10	evil	died	2 Kings 15:14–22
18. Pekahiah	Menahem/?	?	2	evil	murdered by Pekah	2 Kings 15:22–26
19. Pekah	Remaliah/?	?	20	evil	murdered by Hoshea	2 Kings 15:27–31; 2 Chron. 28
20. Hoshea	Elah/?	?	9	evil	deposed to Assyria	2 Kings 15–17

The Kings of Judah

King	Father/Mother	Accession Age	Years of Reign	Character	Death	Reference
1. Rehoboam	Solomon/Naamah	41	17	evil	died	1 Kings 11-14; 2 Chron. 9-12
2. Abijah	Rehoboam/Maacah	?	3	evil	died	1 Kings 14-15; 2 Chron. 13
3. Asa	Abijah/Maacah¹	?	41	good	died	1 Kings 15; 2 Chron. 14-16
4. Jehoshaphat	Asa/Azubah	35	25	good	died	1 Kings 22; 2 Chron. 17-20
5. Jehoram	Jehoshaphat/?	32	8	evil	stricken by God	2 Kings 8; 2 Chron. 21
6. Ahaziah	Jehoram/Athaliah	22	1	evil	murdered by Jehu	2 Kings 8-9; 2 Chron. 22
7. Athaliah	Ahab/Jezebel	?	6	evil	murdered by army	2 Kings 11; 2 Chron. 22-23
8. Joash	Ahaziah/Zibia	7	40	good	murdered by servants	2 Kings 11-12; 2 Chron. 22-24
9. Amaziah	Joash/Jehoaddin	25	29	good	murdered	2 Kings 14; 2 Chron. 25
10. Azariah (Uzziah)	Amaziah/Jecoliah	16	52	good	stricken by God/died	2 Kings 15; 2 Chron. 26
11. Jotham	Uzziah/Jerusha	25	16	good	died	2 Kings 15; 2 Chron. 27
12. Ahaz	Jotham/?	20	16	evil	died	2 Kings 16; 2 Chron. 28
13. Hezekiah	Ahaz/Abijah	25	29	good	died	2 Kings 18-20; 2 Chron. 29-32
14. Manasseh	Hezekiah/Hephzibah	12	55	evil	died	2 Kings 21; 2 Chron. 33
15. Amon	Manasseh/Meshullemeth	22	2	evil	murdered by servants	2 Kings 21; 2 Chron. 33
16. Josiah	Amon/Jedidah	8	31	good	wounded in battle	2 Kings 22-23; 2 Chron. 34-35
17. Jehoahaz	Josiah/Hamutal	23	3 mos	evil	deported to Egypt	2 Kings 23; 2 Chron. 36
18. Jehoiakim	Josiah/Zebidah	25	11	evil	died in siege	2 Kings 23-24; 2 Chron. 36
19. Jehoiachin	Jehoiakim/Nehushta	18	3 mos	evil	deported to Babylon	2 Kings 24; 2 Chron. 36
20. Zedekiah	Josiah/Hamutal	21	11	evil	deported to Babylon	2 Kings 24-25; 2 Chron. 36

1. The Hebrew is problematic here (literally, "his mother"). Either Abijah and Asa were brothers, or Abijah married a woman with the same name as that of his mother, or Maacah should be interpreted as the "grandmother" of Asa (so NIV).

Letter Carriers in the
New Testament

1. Romans, Phoebe, Rom. 16:1-2
2. 1 Corinthians, Stephanas, Fortunatus, Achaicus, and/or Titus, 1 Cor. 16:15-18; cf. 2 Cor. 2:12-13; 7:6-7
3. 2 Corinthians, Titus and "the brother," 2 Cor. 8:16-24
4. Galatians, ?
5. Ephesians, Tychicus, Eph. 6:21
6. Philippians, Epaphroditus, Phil. 2:25
7. Colossians, Tychicus, Col. 4:7-9
8. 1 Thessalonians, ?
9. 2 Thessalonians, ?
10. 1 Timothy, ?
11. 2 Timothy, ?
12. Titus, Zenas the lawyer and Apollos, Titus 3:13
13. Philemon, Onesimus, Philem. 10-13; cf. Col. 4:7-9
14. Hebrews, ?
15. James, (?), cf. Gal. 2:12
16. 1 Peter, Silas (?), 1 Peter 5:12-13
17. 2 Peter, ?
18. 1 John, ?
19. 2 John, ?
20. 3 John, Demetrius, 3 John 12
21. Jude, ?
22. Revelation, ?

Levirate Law

Levirate Marriage

The word "levirate" is derived from the Latin word *levir,* which means "husband's brother." A levirate marriage occurred when a man died without leaving an heir. The dead man's brother was expected to take his wife and marry her. The first son resulting from this marriage was considered a child of the deceased, thus continuing the family lineage and providing an heir for family properties and possessions. Levirate marriage was a custom common among the peoples of the ancient Near East.

Levirate Law in the OT

1. The levirate custom is indicated in Judah's response to Onan at the death of his brother Er (Gen. 38:8-10). Judah instructs Onan to fulfill the obligation of the brother-in-law (Heb. *ybm*).
2. The law of levirate marriage is stated in Deuteronomy 25:5-10. It provides for levirate marriage when the brothers are living together and one dies. The first son of the marriage is to carry the name of the deceased brother. The law also provides for the brother's refusal to perform the levirate duties. According to the law the widow is to take off one of the brother's sandals and spit in his face, in the presence of the elders.

209

3. In contrast, Leviticus 18:16 and 20:21 forbid a man to marry his brother's wife. These laws clearly contradict Deuteronomy 25:5-10 (unless Lev. 18:16 and 20:21 refer to a situation where the brother is yet living—though this is not specified).
4. The law of levirate marriage did not apply if a man had daughters, even if no male heir had been born. As in the case of Zelophehad's daughters (Num. 27:1-11), the surviving daughter(s) are to receive the deceased's inheritance. The text in Numbers gives no suport of levirate marriage, but states if a man dies childless his brothers are to receive his inheritance, and if he dies having no brothers the nearest relative is to receive his inheritance (Num. 27:8-11).

Levirate Law in the OT

5. In the story of Ruth (4:1-12) Naomi's closest relative refuses to "redeem" (*g'l*) Naomi's land and become her "kinsman-redeemer" (*go'ēl*). After the sandal ceremony (4:7-8), Boaz, who is next in line (4:4), becomes Naomi's "kinsman-redeemer." Boaz does not marry Naomi, however; he marries Ruth, perhaps because Naomi is past childbearing age. Obed, the son of Boaz and Ruth, is called the son of Naomi (4:17).

Levirate Law in the NT

6. Though it was probably not construed as a levirate marriage, John the Baptist condemns Herod Antipas for marrying the wife of his brother Philip while Philip was still alive (Matt. 14:3-4). John's condemnation was based upon the Levitical law (Lev. 18:16; 20:21).
7. The Sadducees use the levirate law to pose a hypothetical question to Jesus about the resurrection (Matt. 22:23-33).

The Levitical Sacrificial System

Offerings of Expiation

1. Sin Offering, Lev. 4:1-35; 6:24-30
2. Guilt Offering, Lev. 5:14-6:7

Offerings of Consecration

3. Burnt Offering, Lev. 1:3-17; 6:8-13
4. Grain Offering, Lev. 2; 6:14-23
5. Drink Offering, Num. 15:1-10

Offerings of Fellowship

6. Peace Offering, Lev. 3; 7:11-21
7. Wave Offering, Lev. 21; 23-24; Num. 13; 15; 21
8. Thank Offering, Lev. 7:12-15; 22:29
9. Votive Offering, Lev. 7:16-17; 22:17-20
10. Freewill Offering, Lev. 7:16; 22:18-23
11. Ordination Offering, Exod. 29:19-34; Lev. 8:22-32

The Megilloth

The Megilloth ("scrolls," "rolls") are five of the shorter books of the Old Testament which were read publicly during the annual festivals of the Jews. Below are the Megilloth and the feast at which the books were read:

1. Song of Solomon (Passover, Nisan 14)
2. Ruth (Pentecost, Sivan 6)
3. Lamentations (Day of Mourning for the Destruction of the Temple, Ab 9)
4. Ecclesiastes (Tabernacles, Tishri, 15-21)
5. Esther (Purim, Adar 14-15)

The Miracles of Jesus

1. Healing a leper, Matt. 8:2-3; Mark 1:40-42; Luke 5:12-13
2. Healing the centurion's servant, Matt. 8:5-13; Luke 7:1-10
3. Healing Peter's mother-in-law, Matt. 8:14-15; Mark 1:30-31; Luke 4:38-39
4. Calming the storm, Matt. 8:23-27; Mark 4:37-41; Luke 8:22-25
5. Healing the one/two Gadarenes, Matt. 8:28-34; Mark 5:1-13; Luke 8:27-33
6. Healing a paralyzed man, Matt. 9:2-7; Mark 2:3-12; Luke 5:18-25
7. Raising Jairus' daughter from the dead, Matt. 9:18-25; Mark 5:22-42; Luke 8:41-56
8. Healing a woman with a hemorrhage, Matt. 9:20-22; Mark 5:25-29; Luke 8:43-48
9. Healing two blind men, Matt. 9:27-31
10. Healing a dumb man, Matt. 9:32-33
11. Healing a man with a withered hand, Matt. 12:10-13; Mark 3:1-5; Luke 6:6-10
12. Healing a blind and dumb man, Matt. 12:22; Luke 11:14
13. Feeding the 5,000, Matt. 14:15-21; Mark 6:35-44; Luke 9:12-17; John 6:5-13
14. Walking on the water, Matt. 14:25; Mark 6:48-51; John 6:19-21
15. Healing the Canaanite woman's daughter, Matt. 15:21-28; Mark 7:24-30
16. Feeding the 4,000, Matt. 15:32-38; Mark 8:1-9

17. Healing a boy with epilepsy, Matt. 17:14-18; Mark 9:17-29; Luke 9:38-43
18. Finding of the coin in the fish's mouth, Matt. 17:24-27
19. Healing of Bartimaeus and another blind man, Matt. 20:29-34; Mark 10:46-52; Luke 18:35-43
20. The withered fig tree, Matt. 21:18-22; Mark 11:20-26
21. Healing a possessed man, Mark 1:23-26
22. Raising the widow of Nain's son from the dead, Luke 7:11-15
23. Healing a deaf and dumb man, Mark 7:31-37
24. Healing the blind man at Bethsaida, Mark 8:22-26
25. The catch of fish, Luke 5:1-11
26. Healing the woman bent double, Luke 13:11-13
27. Healing a man with dropsy, Luke 14:1-4
28. Healing the ten lepers, Luke 17:11-19
29. Healing Malchus' ear, Luke 22:50-51
30. Turning water to wine, John 2:1-11
31. Healing the official's son at Capernaum, John 4:46-54
32. Healing the man at the pool of Bethesda, John 5:1-9
33. The boat immediately reaching shore, John 6:21
34. Healing the man born blind, John 9
35. Raising Lazarus from the dead, John 11:1-44
36. A catch of fish, John 21:1-11

Mountains

Mountains play an important role in the biblical narrative. They are the site of revelation, preparation and prayer, important battles, and burial places. The word for mountain in the OT is *hr* or *hrr;* in the NT *oros.* See maps, pp. 217-220.

1. Sephar, Gen. 10:30
2. The mountain east of Bethel, Gen. 12:8
3. Seir, Gen. 14:6
4. Moriah, Gen. 22:2; cf. 22:14
5. Gilead, Gen. 31:21
6. Sinai, Exod. 19:11, or Horeb
7. Horeb, Exod. 33:6, or Sinai
8. Hor, Num. 20:22
9. Pisgath, Num. 21:20
10. Shepher, Num. 33:23
11. Mountain of the Amorites, Deut. 1:7
12. Hermon, Deut. 3:8; Sirion or Senir, Deut. 3:9; Siyon, Deut. 4:48
13. Gerizim, Deut. 11:29
14. Ebal, Deut. 11:29
15. Nebo, Deut. 32:49, in the Abarim Range
16. Paran, Deut. 33:2
17. The ancient mountains, Deut. 33:15
18. Halak, Josh. 11:17
19. The hill in the valley, Josh. 11:21

20. Ephron, Josh. 15:9
21. Jearim, Josh. 15:10, Kesalon
22. Baalah, Josh. 15:11
23. Bethel, Josh. 16:1
24. Ephraim, Josh. 17:15
25. Naphtali, Josh. 20:7
26. Judah, Josh. 20:7
27. Heres, Judg. 1:35
28. Lebanon, Judg. 3:3
29. Baal Hermon, Judg. 3:3
30. Tabor, Judg. 4:6
31. Moreh, Judg. 7:1
32. Zalmon, Judg. 9:48
33. Mountain of the Amalekites, Judg. 12:15
34. Gilboa, 1 Sam. 31:1
35. Olivet, 2 Sam. 15:30
36. Carmel, 2 Kings 2:25
37. Mount of Corruption, 2 Kings 23:13
38. Zemaraim, 2 Chron. 13:4
39. Bether, or rugged, Song of Sol. 2:17
40. Amana, Song of Sol. 4:8
41. Spice-laden mountains, Song of Sol. 8:14
42. Zaphon, Isa. 14:13
43. Holy mountain in Jerusalem, Isa. 27:13
44. Perazim, Isa. 28:21
45. Holy mountain of God, Ezek. 28:14
46. Mount Samaria, Amos, 4:1
47. Mountains of bronze, Zech. 6:1
48. Olives, Olivet, Zech. 14:4
49. Mountain of Jesus' temptation, Matt. 4:8
50. Mount of Jesus' sermon, Matt. 5:1
51. Mount where Jesus prayed, Matt. 14:23
52. Mount where Jesus healed, Matt. 15:29
53. Mount of Transfiguration, Matt. 17:1; Holy Mount, 2 Peter 1:18
54. The mountain in Galilee where Jesus commissioned the disciples, Matt. 28:16
55. A great mountain, Rev. 8:8
56. Zion, Rev. 14:1
57. Seven mountains, Rev. 17:9

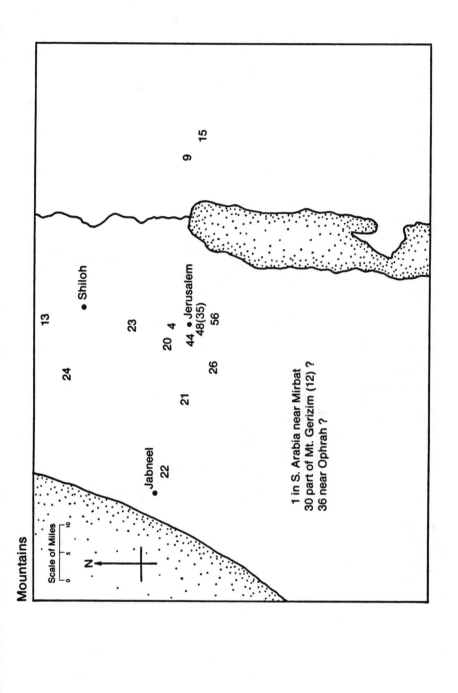

Mountains

Scale of Miles
0   5   10

N

Shiloh

13

24

23

20 4

44 ● Jerusalem
48(35)
56

21

26

22
Jabneel

9

15

1 in S. Arabia near Mirbat
30 part of Mt. Gerizim (12) ?
36 near Ophrah ?

Mountains

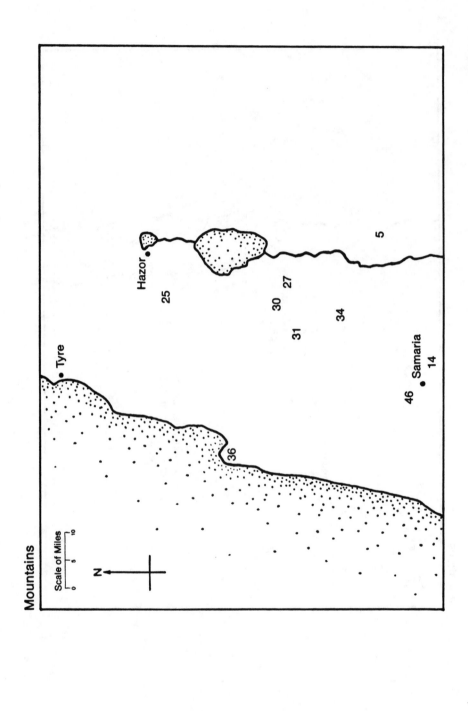

Scale of Miles
0   5   10

N

Tyre

Hazor

25

36

30   27

31

34

5

46   Samaria
14

Mountains

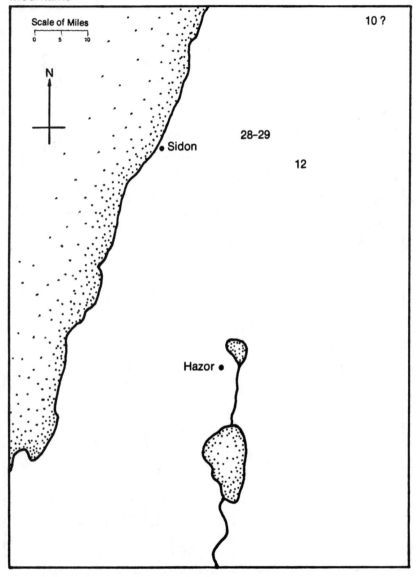

Mountains

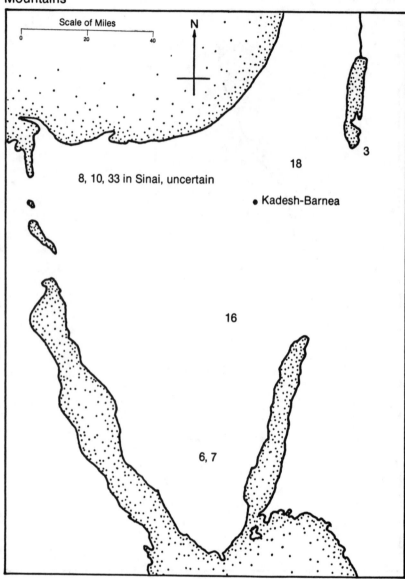

Scale of Miles
0   20   40

N

8, 10, 33 in Sinai, uncertain

18

3

• Kadesh-Barnea

16

6, 7

Music

Music in the OT

1. Jubal is called the first of all musicians, Gen. 4:21.
2. Music was a part of family gatherings and celebrations, Gen. 31:27; cf. Luke 15:25.
3. Music accompanied the labor of harvesting and well-digging, Isa. 16:10; Jer. 48:33; Num. 21:17.
4. Music was a part of military strategy and victory celebrations, Exod. 32:17-18; Josh. 6:4-20; Judg. 7:18-20; 11:34-35; 1 Sam. 18:6-7.
5. Dancing was often part of musical merrymaking, Exod. 15:20; 32:19; Judg. 11:34; 21:21; 1 Sam. 18:6; 21:11; 29:5; 30:16.
6. Music was a part of worship and the temple ministry, 1 Chron. 15:16; 23:5; 25:6-7; 2 Chron. 5:11-14; cf. Ezra 2:65 and Neh. 12:27-43.
7. Music was part of the court life of the kings, 1 Sam. 16:14-23; 2 Sam. 19:35; Eccles. 2:8; and also a part of the enthronement celebrations, 1 Kings 1:39-40; 2 Kings 11:14; 2 Chron. 13:14.
8. Music was associated with feasting and merrymaking, Isa. 5:12; 24:8-9; cf. Matt. 14:6.
9. Music expresses a wide range of human feelings; see the Book of Psalms.
10. Music was a vital part of mourning and lament, 2 Sam. 1:17-18; 2 Chron. 35:25; cf. Matt. 9:23.

11. Music was used for the restoration of prophetic gifts, 2 Kings 3:15; and to soothe troubled individuals, 1 Sam. 16:14-23.
12. Amos condemns idle music and feasting, Amos 6:5-6.
13. Singing and rejoicing are characteristic of the righteous man, Prov. 29:6.
14. Music will be a part of the "new" covenant, Jer. 31:7-13.

Musical Instruments in the OT

1. musical instruments (*zmr'*), Dan. 3:5
2. flute (*ḥlyl*), 1 Sam. 10:5
3. trumpet (*ḥṣṣrh*), 2 Kings 11:14
4. ram's horn (*ywbl*), Lev. 25:13
5. musical instruments (*kly*), Ps. 71:22
6. lyre (*knwr*), Gen. 4:21
7. stringed instruments (*mnym*), Ps. 150:4
8. sistrum or rattle (*mn'n'ym*), 2 Sam. 6:5
9. small bell (*mṣlh*), Zech. 14:20
10. cymbals (*mṣltym*), Ezra 3:10
11. flute or pipe (*mšrwqy*), Dan. 3:5
12. stringed instrument, harp ? (*nbl*), Ps. 33:2
13. string music (*ngynh*), Lam. 5:14
14. musical instrument (*swmpwnyh*), Dan. 3:5
15. flute (*'wgb*), Ps. 150:4
16. harp (*psnṭryn*), Dan. 3:7
17. bells (*p'mwn*), Exod. 28:33; 39:25-26
18. cymbals (*ṣlṣlym*), Ps. 150:5
19. lyre or lute (*qytrs*), Dan. 3:5
20. horn (*qrn*), Josh. 6:5
21. lyre (*śbk'*), Dan. 3:7
22. ram's horn (*šwpr*), 1 Kings 1:34
23. lyre with three strings (*šlyš*), 1 Sam. 18:6
24. tambourine, timbrel (*twp*), Gen. 31:27

The English translation of these alphabetized Hebrew terms is based on W. L. Holladay, *A Concise Hebrew and Aramaic Lexicon of the Old Testament* (Grand Rapids: Eerdmans, 1971).

Musical Notations of the Psalms

1. according to *'ylt hšḥr* ("the doe of the dawn"):

   22

2. for the flutes (*'l-hnḥylwt*):

   5 ·

3. according to *'l-tšḥt* ("do not destroy"):

   57
   58
   59
   75

4. with stringed instruments (*bngynwt*):

   4   61
   6   67
   54   76
   55

5. according to *gtyt* (an unknown musical term, suggested meanings: a) a Gathite instrument; b) "by the wine press" of the Feast of Tabernacles; c) of the New Year's festival):

   8
   81
   84

6. higgaion (*hgywn*, an interlude for resounding music?):

   9

7. a petition (*hzkyr*):

   38
   70

8. for or according to *ydwtwn* (?):

   39
   62
   77

The English translation of these alphabetized Hebrew musical notations is based on W. L. Holladay, *A Concise Hebrew and Aramaic Lexicon of the Old Testament* (Grand Rapids: Eerdmans, 1971).

9. according to *ywnt 'lml rḥwqym* ("a dove on distant oaks"):

56

10. for the choir director (*lmnṣḥ*):

4	13	31	45	54	61	69	84
5	14	36	46	55	62	70	85
6	18	39	47	56	64	75	88
8	19	40	49	57	65	76	109
9	20	41	51	58	66	77	139
11	21	42	52	59	67	80	140
12	22	44	53	60	68	81	

11. according to *mwt lbn* ("death of the son"):

9

12. psalm (*mzmwr*):

3	13	24	41	63	75	84	101
4	15	29	47	64	76	85	108
5	19	30	48	65	77	87	109
6	20	31	49	66	79	88	110
8	21	38	50	67	80	92	139
9	22	39	51	68	82	98	140
12	23	40	62	73	83	100	141
							143

13. according to *mḥlt* (according to one with a sickness or after a sad tone?):

53

14. according to *mḥlt l'nwt* (after a sad manner, to make humble?):

88

15. miktam (*mktm*, a mystery poem or song of expiation?):

16	58
56	59
57	60

16. maskil (*mśkyl*, an unknown musical term, suggested meanings: a) a cultic song; b) a passage for learning; c) a wisdom song put to music):

32	45	54	88
42	52	74	89
44	53	78	142

17. *selah* (*selāh*, an unknown musical term, suggested meanings: a) raising of the voice to a higher pitch; b) "forever"; c) a pause for a musical interlude; d) an acrostic indicating a change of voice or "da capo"):

3	32	50	61	77	88
4	39	52	62	81	89
7	44	54	66	82	140
9	46	55	67	83	143 (cf. Hab. 3:3, 9, 13)
20	47	57	68	84	
21	48	59	75	85	
24	49	60	76	87	

18. according to *'lmwt* (young women or to be sung by young women?):

46

19. shiggaion (*šgywn*, an unknown musical term):

7 (cf. Hab. 3:1)

20. to the tune of "lilies" (*šwšnym*):

45
69
80

21. a song (*šyr*):

30	66	75	87
46	67	76	88
48	68	83	108
65			

22. a song of ascents (*šyr hm'lwt*):

120	123	126	129	132
121	124	127	130	133
122	125	128	131	134

23. a wedding song (*šyr ydydwt*):

45

24. a song for the Sabbath day (*šyr lym hsbt*):

92

25. according to *šmynyt* ("on the eight-stringed instrument"?):

6
12

26. according to *ššn 'dwt* ("the lily of the covenant"):

60
80

27. a psalm of praise (*thlh*):

145

28. a prayer (*tplh*):

17	102
86	142
90	

Music in the NT

1. The Last Supper was concluded with the singing of a song (*humneō*) prior to the retreat to the Mt. of Olives, Matt. 26:30; Mark 14:26.
2. Mary sang a song after Elizabeth's greeting, Luke 1:46-56.
3. Zechariah prophesied in song after the announcement of John the Baptist's birth, Luke 1:67-79.
4. Paul and Silas were praying and singing songs (*humneō*) to God while in prison, Acts 16:25.

5. Paul quotes Ps. 18:49 in teaching that the singing of psalms (*psallō*) brings praise to God, Rom. 15:9.
6. Paul instructs the Corinthians to sing (*psallō*) with the spirit and the mind, 1 Cor. 14:15.
7. The hymn (*psalmos*) is part of structured worship according to Paul, 1 Cor. 14:26.
8. Paul exhorts the Ephesians to: "Speak to one another with psalms (*psalmos*), hymns (*humnos*) and spiritual songs (*ōdē pneumatikos*). Sing (*adō*) and make music (*psallō*) in your heart to the Lord, . . ." (Eph. 5:19; Col. 3:16, NIV).
9. The writer to the Hebrews quotes Ps. 22:22 in connection with the declarative nature of Jesus' ministry who sings (*humneō*) praises in the midst of the congregation, Heb. 2:12.
10. James commands those who are happy to sing (*psallō*), James 5:13.
11. The four living creatures and the twenty-four elders sing a new song (*adō . . . ōdē kainōs*) to the Lamb in John's revelation of Jesus Christ, Rev. 5:8.
12. The NT makes reference to musicians and several musical instruments including: the flute (*aulos*), 1 Cor. 14:7; the gong (*chalkos*), 1 Cor. 13:1; the harp (*kithara*), 1 Cor. 14:7; Rev. 5:8; 14:2; 15:2; and the harpist (*kitharodos*), Rev. 14:2; 18:22; the cymbal (*kumbalon*), 1 Cor. 13:1; the trumpet (*salpigx*), Matt. 24:31; 1 Cor. 14:8; 15:52; 1 Thess. 4:16; Heb. 8:2, 6, 13; 9:14; and the trumpeter (*salpizō/ salpistēs*), Matt. 6:2; 1 Cor. 15:52; Rev. 8:6, 7, 10, 12, 13; 9:1, 13; 10:17; 11:15; 18:22.

Nazarites

Teaching About Nazarites (Num. 6:1-21)

1. A Nazarite was one who made a special vow of separation unto God (6:1-2).
2. A Nazarite abstained from:

   a) drinking wine and fermented drinks (6:3-4).
   b) grape juice, grapes, grape seeds and skins, raisins (6:3-4).
   c) cutting the hair with a razor (6:5-8).
   d) contacting a dead body (6:6-12).

3. The Nazarite vow could be permanent or temporary (6:9-21; Judg. 13:5).
4. The Nazarite vow could be made by parents for a child or a person could take the Nazarite vow of his own volition (Judg. 13:1-7; 1 Sam. 1:9-11; Num. 6:1-2).
5. Special offerings were necessary when the Nazarite vow was ended (6:9-21).

Nazarites Elsewhere in the Bible

1. Samson, Judg. 13:1-7
2. Samuel, 1 Sam. 1:9-11
3. John the Baptist, Luke 1:15

228

Parables

1. Balaam's parable of the Moabites and Israelites, Num. 23:13-24
2. Jotham's parable of the trees who wanted a king, Judg. 9:7-15
3. Nathan's parable of a poor man's lamb, 2 Sam. 12:1-7
4. The woman of Tekoa's parable of the two sons, 2 Sam. 14:5-7
5. A prophet's son's parable to King Ahab about an escaped prisoner, 1 Kings 20:35-43
6. Jehoash's parable of the thistle and the cedar, 2 Kings 14:9
7. Isaiah's parable of the vineyard, Isa. 5:1-7
8. Ezekiel's parable of the two eagles and the vine, Ezek. 17:2-10
9. Ezekiel's parable of the lion's cubs, Ezek. 19:1-9
10. Ezekiel's parable of the vine planted by water, Ezek. 19:10-14
11. Ezekiel's parable of the boiling pot, Ezek. 24:3-5

The Parables of Jesus

1. A lamp under a bushel, Matt. 5:14-15; Mark 4:21-22; Luke 8:16; 11:33
2. Houses built upon rock and sand, Matt. 7:24-27; Luke 6:47-49
3. A new cloth on an old garment, Matt. 9:16; Mark 2:21; Luke 5:36
4. New wine in old wineskins, Matt. 9:17; Mark 2:22; Luke 5:37-38
5. The sower and the soils, Matt. 13:3-8; Mark 4:3-8; Luke 8:5-8
6. The tares, Matt. 13:24-30

7. The mustard seed, Matt. 13:31-32; Mark 4:30-32; Luke 13:18-19
8. Leaven, Matt. 13:33; Luke 13:20-21
9. Hidden treasure, Matt. 13:44
10. Pearl of great price, Matt. 13:45-46
11. The drag-net, Matt. 13:47-48
12. The lost sheep, Matt. 18:12-13; Luke 15:4-6
13. The unforgiving servant, Matt. 18:23-34
14. Workers in the vineyard, Matt. 20:1-16
15. The two sons, Matt. 21:28-31
16. The wicked tenants, Matt. 21:33-41; Mark 12:1-9; Luke 20:9-16
17. The wedding feast, Matt. 22:2-14
18. The fig tree, Matt. 24:32-33; Mark 13:28-29; Luke 21:29-32
19. The ten virgins, Matt. 25:1-13
20. The talents, Matt. 25:14-30; Luke 19:12-27
21. Sheep and goats, Matt. 25:31-46
22. Seedtime to harvest, Mark 4:26-29
23. The creditor and the debtors, Luke 7:41-43
24. The good Samaritan, Luke 10:30-37
25. A friend in need, Luke 11:5-8
26. The rich fool, Luke 12:16-21
27. The alert servants, Luke 12:35-40
28. The faithful steward, Luke 12:42-48
29. A fig tree without figs, Luke 13:6-9
30. Places of honor at the wedding feast, Luke 14:7-14
31. The great banquet, Luke 14:16-24
32. Counting the cost, Luke 14:28-33
33. The lost coin, Luke 15:8-10
34. The prodigal son, Luke 15:11-32
35. The dishonest steward, Luke 16:1-8
36. The rich man and Lazarus, Luke 16:19-31
37. The master and his servant, Luke 17:7-10
38. The persistent widow, Luke 18:2-5
39. The Pharisee and the tax collector, Luke 18:10-14

Paul's Missionary Journeys

First Missionary Journey

Companions
  Barnabas, John Mark

Date
  A.D. 46-48 or 47-49 (a time span of about 2 years)

Distance Traveled
  1200+ miles

Approximate Distances (miles)

Antioch Syria to Seleucia	15
Seleucia to Salamis	100
Salamis to Paphos	100
Paphos to Perga	175
Perga to Antioch Pisidia	100
Antioch Pisidia to Iconium	85
Iconium to Lystra	30
Lystra to Derbe	30
Derbe to Lystra	30
Lystra to Iconium	30
Iconium to Antioch Pisidia	85
Antioch Pisidia to Perga	100

Perga to Attalia	20
Attalia to Seleucia	320
Seleucia to Antioch Syria	15
	1,235

The Journey: Acts 13–14

1. Antioch (13:1-3)

    Saul and Barnabas were called out by the Holy Spirit during a time when five prophets and teachers were worshiping together. After prayer and fasting they laid hands on them and sent them out as missionaries.

2. Seleucia (13:4)

    They sailed from this port to Salamis on the island of Cyprus.

3. Salamis (13:5)

    Saul preached in the synagogues of Salamis. John Mark was with them.

4. Paphos (13:6-12)

    Saul and company traversed the island until they reached Paphos. Here they encountered Bar-Jesus/Elymas, a Jewish sorcerer and false prophet. Paul cursed him with temporary blindness because he was hindering their ministry. Sergius Paulus, Roman proconsul, was converted. Saul began to be called Paul.

5. Perga in Pamphylia (13:13)

    John Mark left Paul and Barnabas at this point and returned to Jerusalem.

6. Antioch Pisidia (13:14-52)

    Paul spoke in the synagogue for two Sabbaths. Many were converted but the Jews reacted with hate and envy and Paul was forced to leave the city. Paul rejected the Jews and directed his ministry to the Gentiles.

7. Iconium (14:1-5)

    Paul fled to Iconium and ministered there for "a long time." Finally, Paul was forced to flee the city because of threats against his life.

8. Lystra in Lycaonia (14:6-20)

   Paul healed a man lame from birth and the people of Lystra tried to worship Paul and Barnabas as the Greek gods Hermes and Zeus. Jews from Iconium persuaded those in Lystra to kill Paul; so they stoned him and dragged him out of the city. After a short time Paul got up and went back into the city. The next day they left for Derbe.

9. Derbe in Lycaonia (14:20-21)

   Paul preached in Derbe and converted a large number of disciples.

10. Lystra (14:21-23)

    Paul and Barnabas returned to the city, encouraging the believers, and appointing elders in the church.

11. Iconium (14:21-23)

    Paul and Barnabas returned to the city, encouraging the believers and appointing elders in the church.

12. Antioch Pisidia (14:21-23)

    Paul and Barnabas returned to the city, encouraging the believers and appointing elders in the church.

13. Perga (14:24-25)

    Paul and Barnabas "preached the word" in Perga and then left for Attalia.

14. Attalia (14:26)

    From Attalia they sailed to Syrian Antioch.

15. Antioch Syria (14:26-28)

    Paul and Barnabas returned to Antioch and reported their experiences to the church that had sent them out. They stayed with the disciples there for "a long time."

Paul's First Missionary Journey

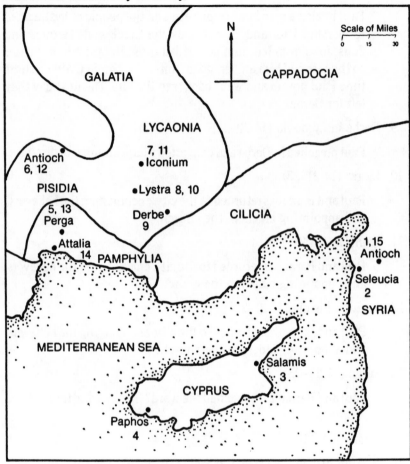

Second Missionary Journey

Companions

Silas, Timothy, Luke

Date

A.D. 49-52 or 50-53 (a time span of 2½-3 years)

Distance Traveled

2,700+ miles (1,290 sea and 1,410 land)

Approximate Distances (miles)

Antioch Syria to Cilician Gates	140
Cilician Gates to Derbe	100
Derbe to Lystra	30
Lystra to Iconium	30
Iconium to Antioch Pisidia	85
Phrygia and Galatia	200+
To Troas	200+
Troas to Samothrace	70
Samothrace to Neapolis	70
Neapolis to Philippi	10
Philippi to Amphipolis	30
Amphipolis to Apollonia	35
Apollonia to Thessalonica	40
Thessalonica to Berea	50
Berea to the coast	20
To Athens	250
Athens to Corinth	50
Corinth to Cenchrea	8
Cenchrea to Ephesus	250
Ephesus to Caesarea	650+
Caesarea to Jerusalem	65
Jerusalem to Antioch Syria	320+
	2,703+

The Journey: Acts 15–18

1. Antioch Syria (15:36-40)

    Paul and Barnabas disagreed over John Mark. Barnabas took John Mark to Cyprus. Paul chose Silas.

2. Syria and Cilicia (15:41)

    Paul strengthened the churches.

3. Derbe (16:1)

    Paul went to Derbe.

4. Lystra (16:1-3)

    Paul circumcised Timothy, and Timothy joined Paul and Silas on the journey.

5. "Town to town" (16:4-5)

    Though not named, Paul undoubtedly traveled through Iconium and Antioch Pisidia, as well as Derbe and Lystra, delivering the instructions from the Jerusalem Council to the churches.

6. Phrygia and Galatia (16:6)

    Paul, Silas, and Timothy traveled through Phrygia and Galatia preaching the word. They were prevented from entering Asia.

7. Mysia (16:7-8)

    At Mysia Paul and his party were prevented from entering the province of Bithynia by the Spirit of Jesus.

8. Troas (16:8-10)

    They passed by Mysia to Troas. In Troas Paul had a vision of a man calling him to Macedonia.

9. Samothrace (16:11)

    Paul and his party sailed from Troas to the island of Samothrace, spending the night there. Apparently Luke had joined Paul's group in Troas (note the "we" in 16:10).

10. Neapolis (16:11)

    From Samothrace they sailed to the port of Neapolis.

11. Philippi (16:12-40)

Paul and his party traveled from Neapolis to Philippi and stayed there "several days." During the stay Lydia was converted; Paul cast an evil spirit out of a slave girl which initiated a riot and landed Paul and Silas in prison. Paul and Silas were miraculously released from prison and the Philippian jailor was converted.

12. Thessalonica (17:1-9)

Passing through Amphipolis and Apollonia they came to Thessalonica. Some Jews and many Greeks were converted as Paul preached three Sabbaths in the synagogue. The Jews, however, caused trouble for Paul's converts and he fled the city by night.

13. Berea (17:10-14)

Paul preached in the synagogue in Berea, and many Jews and Greeks were converted. Jews from Thessalonica came to Berea and again stirred up the "mobs" against Paul. Paul was escorted to the coast by "brothers." Silas and Timothy remained in Berea.

14. Athens (17:15-34)

Paul sailed to Athens and "reasoned" with Jews and Greeks in the synagogue. Paul debated with philosophers at a meeting of the Areopagus, teaching the resurrection of Christ. A few Athenians were converted, including Dionysius and Damaris.

15. Corinth (18:1-17)

Paul met Aquila and Priscilla in Corinth and worked with them as a tentmaker. He preached in the synagogue in Corinth until the Jews opposed him. He then went next door to the house of Titius Justus. Crispus, the ruler of the synagogue, was converted by Paul. Silas and Timothy joined Paul in Corinth. The Jews brought charges against Paul but Gallio refused to hear the case. Paul stayed in Corinth for 1½ years.

16. Cenchrea (18:18)

In Cenchrea Paul shaved his head because of a vow he had taken.

17. Ephesus (18:19-21)

    Aquila and Priscilla sailed with Paul from Cenchrea to Ephesus. Paul preached in the synagogue in Ephesus. He promised to return if possible.

18. Caesarea (18:22)

    Paul sailed from Ephesus to Caesarea and greeted the church there. Aquila and Priscilla remained in Ephesus.

19. Antioch Syria (18:22)

    Paul then went to Antioch and informed the church there of his mission.

Paul's Second Missionary Journey

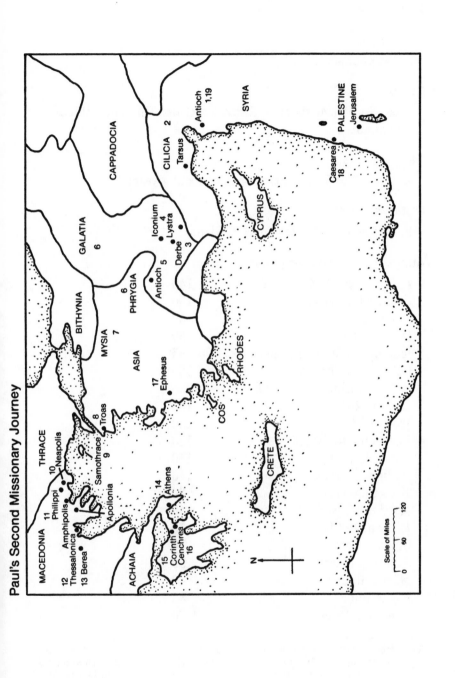

THRACE

MACEDONIA
11 Philippi
Neapolis 10
Amphipolis
12 Thessalonica
13 Berea
Apollonia
Samothrace 9
8 Troas

ACHAIA
15 Corinth
Cenchrea 16
Athens 14

BITHYNIA

MYSIA
7

ASIA
Ephesus 17

PHRYGIA
6
Antioch 5

GALATIA
6

CAPPADOCIA

Iconium
Lystra 4
Derbe 3

CILICIA 2
Tarsus

Antioch 1,19

SYRIA

PALESTINE
Jerusalem
Caesarea 18

CYPRUS

RHODES

COS

CRETE

N

Scale of Miles
0   60   120

Third Missionary Journey

Companions

Luke, Sopater, Aristarchus, Secundus, Gaius, Timothy, Tychicus, and Trophimus

Date

A.D. 53-57 or 54-58 (a time span of about 4 years)

Distance Traveled

2,500+ miles (1,190 sea and 1,325 land)

Approximate Distances (miles)

Antioch Syria to Cilician Gates	140
Cilician Gates to Derbe	100
Derbe to Lystra	30
Lystra to Iconium	30
Iconium to Antioch Pisidia	85
Galatia and Phrygia	200+
Antioch Pisidia to Ephesus	225
Ephesus to Troas	150
Troas to Macedonia	150
Macedonia to Greece	150+
Greece to Philippi	150+
Philippi to Troas	140
Troas to Assos	20
Assos to Mitylene	40
Mitylene to Chios	70
Chios to Samos	70
Samos to Miletus	50
Miletus to Cos	40
Cos to Rhodes	85
Rhodes to Patara	70

For the sake of completeness it is assumed: 1. Paul traveled through the Lycaonian cities on his way to Galatia and Phrygia, 2. Paul sailed to Macedonia from Troas. The distance of Paul's penetration into Greece can only be approximated. If Paul made a trip into North Galatia, that would add 500+ miles to the total for the third journey.

Patara to Tyre	400+
Tyre to Ptolemais	25
Ptolemais to Caesarea	30
Caesarea to Jerusalem	65
	2,515+

The Journey: Acts 18–21

1. Antioch Syria (18:23)

   Paul spent some time in Antioch.

2. Galatia and Phrygia (18:23)

   Paul traveled from place to place throughout the region.

3. Ephesus (19:1-41)

   Paul imparted the Holy Spirit to disciples in Ephesus who had been baptized only with John's baptism. Paul preached in the synagogue for three months and taught in the hall of Tyrannus for two years. Paul performed miracles which caused the sorcerers of the city to believe and to burn their scrolls. Paul's ministry hurt the silversmith trade at the Temple of Artemis to such a degree that there was a riot.

4. Macedonia (20:1-2)

   Paul traveled through Macedonia encouraging the disciples there.

5. Greece (20:2-3)

   Paul traveled into Greece.

6. Macedonia (20:4)

   Paul was forced to travel back through Macedonia because the Jews were plotting against him. He was accompanied by Sopater, Aristarchus, Secundus, Gaius, Timothy, Tychicus, and Trophimus.

7. Philippi (20:5-6)

   Paul's seven companions went on ahead of Paul to Troas. Paul and Luke (note "us" in v. 5) sailed from Philippi and rejoined the others five days later.

241

8. Troas (20:6-12)

Paul and the others stayed in Troas for seven days. Paul preached until midnight at the gathering on the first day of the week. Eutychus was raised from the dead after falling out of a window while Paul preached.

9. Assos (20:13)

Paul walked from Troas to Assos and boarded the ship in Assos.

10. Mitylene (20:14)

The group sailed from Assos to Mitylene.

11. Chios (20:15)

The next day they sailed from Mitylene to Chios.

12. Samos (20:15)

The following day saw them at the island of Samos.

13. Miletus (20:15-38)

From Samos the party sailed to Miletus, avoiding Ephesus because Paul was in a hurry to get to Jerusalem. While in Miletus Paul sent for the elders of the Ephesian church and bid them farewell.

14. Cos (21:1)
15. Rhodes (21:1)
16. Patara (21:1-3)

Paul and his companions changed ships in Patara. They sailed from Patara around the southern coast of Cyprus and on to Syria.

17. Tyre (21:3-6)

The ship unloaded its cargo in Tyre. Paul and his companions stayed with the disciples of Tyre for seven days.

18. Ptolemais (21:7)

The party greeted the brothers in Ptolemais and stayed with them for one day.

19. Caesarea (21:8-14)

Paul and his companions spent several days with Philip, one of the Seven. While in Caesarea Agabus the prophet came and predicted Paul's imprisonment in Jerusalem. Paul was not swayed; he intended to complete his mission.

20. Jerusalem (21:15-26)

Some of the disciples from Caesarea accompanied Paul's party to Jerusalem. They stayed with Mnason, a Cypriot and an early disciple. Paul reported the details of his ministry to James and the elders of the Jerusalem church. Paul "purified" himself and those with him at the request of James and the elders. Paul was subsequently arrested within seven days.

Paul's Third Missionary Journey

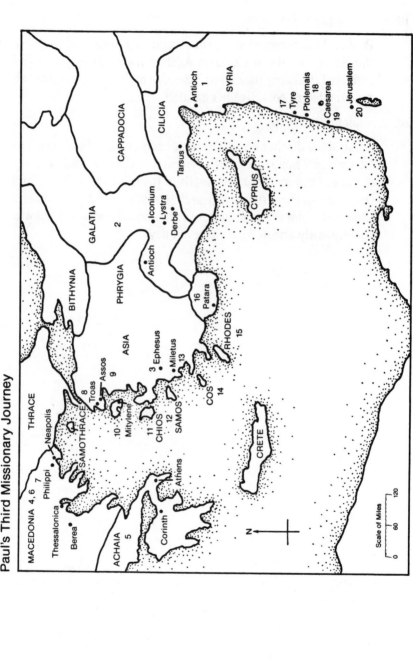

Journey to Rome

Companions

Luke, Aristarchus

Date

A.D. 59-62 or 60-63 (a time span of about 2½ years)

Distance Traveled

2,130+ miles (1,920 sea and 210 land)

Approximate Distances (miles)

Jerusalem to Caesarea	65
Caesarea to Sidon	70
Sidon to Myra	500
Myra to Cnidus	130
Cnidus to Salmone	130
Salmone to Fair Havens	80
Fair Havens to Phoenix	40
Phoenix to Cauda	50
Cauda to Malta	550+
Malta to Syracuse	85
Syracuse to Rhegium	85
Rhegium to Puteoli	200
Puteoli to Forum of Appius	100
Forum of Appius to Three Taverns	10
Three Taverns to Rome	35
	2,130+

The Journey: Acts 27-28

1. Jerusalem (21:27-23:22)

   Paul was arrested in Jerusalem because the Jews assumed he had taken a Gentile (Trophimus) into the temple area. Paul defended himself before the crowd. The next day he defended himself before the Sanhedrin. Paul's nephew informed Claudius Lysias, the Roman commander, of a plot to kill Paul. To protect his life Claudius Lysias sent Paul to Felix in Caesarea.

245

2. Caesarea (23:23-27:2)

Paul was put on trial before Felix and later before his successor Festus. King Agrippa also heard Paul's case. Rather than go back to Jerusalem to stand trial before the Jews, Paul appealed to Caesar. Paul was imprisoned in Caesarea for two years. Paul left from Caesarea for Rome with Luke, Aristarchus, and Julius, the Roman guard.

3. Sidon (27:3)

Julius allowed Paul to visit friends in Sidon.

4. Myra (27:4-6)

Paul's ship sailed north around Cyprus past the coasts of Cilicia and Pamphylia and landed at Myra. In Myra the party changed ships.

5. Cnidus (27:7)

The ship arrived off Cnidus after many days of slow travel.

6. Salmone (27:7)

Unfavorable winds necessitated a change of course. The ship sailed south around Crete.

7. Fair Havens (27:8-15)

Travel along the southern coast of Crete was slow. The ship anchored near the town of Lasea. On the advice of the ship's captain, Julius decided to winter at Phoenix. Shortly after the ship weighed anchor at Fair Havens a fierce wind ("Northeaster") took the ship off its course and carried it along.

8. Cauda (27:16-44)

The wind carried the ship past the island of Cauda off Crete. The sailors secured ropes around the ship to prevent it from breaking apart, and later they threw the cargo overboard. The ship was carried by the storm for 14 days and nights. The ship ran aground off Malta but all 276 on board reached land safely.

9. Malta (28:1-11)

The islanders showed unusual hospitality to the shipwrecked party. Paul was bitten by a viper but was unharmed. Publius, the ruler of the island, entertained the group for three days. Paul healed Publius' father and many others during the stay there. Paul's party wintered at Malta for three months. They left Malta on an Alexandrian ship bound for Syracuse.

10. Syracuse (28:12)

The ship lay over for three days in Syracuse.

11. Rhegium (28:13)
12. Puteoli (28:13-14)

Paul's party received a greeting from brothers in Puteoli and an invitation to stay for a week.

13. Forum of Appius (28:15)

Brothers from Rome came to meet Paul.

14. Three Taverns (28:15)

Brothers from Rome came to meet Paul.

15. Rome (28:16-31)

Paul was under "house arrest" for two years in Rome. Paul spoke to the Jewish leaders.

Paul's Journey to Rome

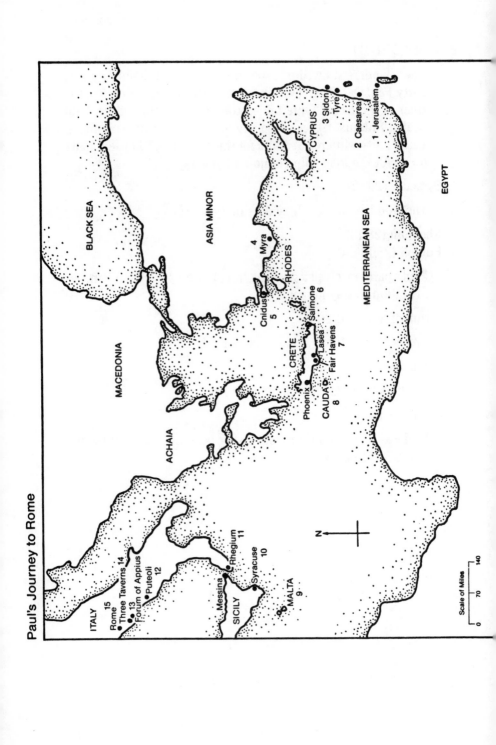

ITALY
Rome 15
Three Taverns 14
Forum of Appius 13
Puteoli 12
Rhegium 11
MESSINA
SICILY
Syracuse 10
MALTA 9

MACEDONIA

ACHAIA

BLACK SEA

ASIA MINOR

Myra 4

RHODES
Cnidus 5
Salmone 6
CRETE
Phoenix
Lasea
Fair Havens 7
CAUDA 8

CYPRUS
Sidon 3
Tyre
Caesarea 2
Jerusalem 1

MEDITERRANEAN SEA

EGYPT

N

Scale of Miles
0   70   140

People Associated with the Ministry of Paul

1. Achaicus, 1 Cor. 16:17
2. Agabus, Acts 11:28; 21:10
3. Agrippa, Acts 25:13, 22, 23, 24, 26; 26:1, 2, 7, 19, 27, 28, 32
4. Alexander, Acts 19:33
5. Alexander, 1 Tim. 1:20
6. Alexander the coppersmith, 2 Tim. 4:14
7. Ampliatus, Rom. 16:8
8. Ananias, Acts 9:10, 12, 13, 17; 22:12
9. Ananias the High Priest, Acts 23:2; 24:1
10. Andronicus, Rom. 16:7
11. Apelles, Rom. 16:10
12. Apollos, Acts 18:24; 19:1; 1 Cor. 1:12; 3:4, 5, 6, 22; 4:6; 16:12; Titus 3:13
13. Apphia, Philem. 2
14. Aquila, Acts 18:2, 18, 26; Rom. 16:3; 1 Cor. 16:19; 2 Tim. 4:19
15. Archippus, Col. 4:17; Philem. 2
16. Aristarchus, Acts 19:29; 20:4; 27:2; Col. 4:10; Philem. 24
17. Aristobulus, Rom. 16:10
18. Artemas, Titus 3:12
19. Asyncritus, Rom. 16:14
20. Bar-Jesus/Elymas, Acts 13:6-8
21. Barnabas, Acts 4:36; 9:27; 11:22, 25, 30; 12:25; 13:1, 2, 7, 43, 46, 50; 14:12, 14, 20; 15:2, 12, 22, 25, 35, 36, 37, 39; 1 Cor. 9:6; Gal. 2:1, 9, 13; Col. 4:10

22. Bernice, Acts 25:13, 23; 26:30
23. Caesar, Acts 17:7; 25:8, 11, 12, 21; 26:32; 27:24; 28:19
24. Carpus, 2 Tim. 4:13
25. Chloe, 1 Cor. 1:11
26. Claudia, 2 Tim. 4:21
27. Claudius Caesar, Acts 11:28; 18:2
28. Claudius Lysias, Acts 23:26
29. Clement, Phil. 4:3
30. Crescens, 2 Tim. 4:10
31. the cripple of Lystra, Acts 14:8-10
32. Crispus, Acts 18:8; 1 Cor. 1:14
33. Damaris, Acts 17:34
34. Demas, Col. 4:14; 2 Tim. 4:10; Philem. 24
35. Demetrius the silversmith, Acts 19:24, 38
36. Dionysius, Acts 17:34
37. Drusilla, Acts 24:24
38. Epaphras, Col. 1:7; 4:12; Philem. 23
39. Epaphroditus, Phil. 2:25; 4:18
40. Epenetus, Rom. 16:5
41. Erastus, Acts 19:22
42. Erastus, 2 Tim. 4:20
43. Erastus the treasurer of Corinth, Rom. 16:23
44. Eubulus, 2 Tim. 4:21
45. Eunice, 2 Tim. 1:5
46. Euodia, Phil. 4:2
47. Eutychus, Acts 20:9
48. Felix, Acts 23:24, 26; 24:3, 22, 24, 25, 27; 25:14
49. Fortunatus, 1 Cor. 16:17
50. Gaius, Acts 19:29
51. Gaius of Corinth, Rom. 16:23; 1 Cor. 1:14
52. Gaius of Derbe, Acts 20:4
53. Gallio, Acts 18:12, 14, 17
54. Gamaliel, Acts 22:3
55. Hermas, Rom. 16:14
56. Hermes, Rom. 16:14
57. Hermogenes, 2 Tim. 1:15
58. Herodion, Rom. 16:11
59. Hymenaeus, 1 Tim. 1:20; 2 Tim. 2:17

60. James (the brother of Jesus), Acts 15:13; 21:18; 1 Cor. 15:7; Gal. 1:19; 2:9, 12
61. Jesus/Justus, Col. 4:11
62. John the apostle, Gal. 2:9
63. John Mark, Acts 13:5, 13; 15:37, 39;   Col. 4:10; 2 Tim. 4:11; Philem. 24
64. Judas, Acts 9:11
65. Judas/Barsabas, Acts 15:22, 27, 32
66. Julia, Rom. 16:15
67. Julius, Acts 27:1-3
68. Junias, Rom. 16:7
69. Linus, 2 Tim. 4:21
70. Lois, 2 Tim. 1:5
71. Lucius, Rom. 16:21
72. Lucius of Cyrene, Acts 13:1
73. Luke, Col. 4:14; 2 Tim. 4:11; Philem. 24
74. Lydia, Acts 16:14, 40
75. Manaen, Acts 13:1
76. Mary, Rom. 16:6
77. Mnason, Acts 21:16
78. Narcissus, Rom. 16:11
79. Nereus, Rom. 16:15
80. Nereus' sister, Rom. 16:15
81. Nympha, Col. 4:15
82. Olympas, Rom. 16:15
83. Onesimus, Col. 4:9; Philem. 10
84. Onesiphorus, 2 Tim. 1:16; 4:19
85. Patrobas, Rom. 16:14
86. Paul's nephew, Acts 23:16
87. Persis, Rom. 16:12
88. Peter, Acts 15:7; Gal. 1:18; 2:7, 8, 11, 14
89. Philemon, Philem. 1
90. Philetus, 2 Tim. 2:17
91. Philip, Acts 21:8
92. Philip's four daughter's, Acts 21:9
93. the Philippian jailor, Acts 16:29ff.
94. Philologus, Rom. 16:15
95. Phlegon, Rom. 16:14

96. Phoebe, Rom. 16:1
97. Phygellus, 2 Tim. 1:15
98. Porcius Festus, Acts 24:27; 25:1, 4, 9, 12, 13, 14, 22, 24; 26:24, 25, 32
99. Priscilla, Acts 18:2, 18, 26; Rom. 16:3; 1 Cor. 16:19; 2 Tim. 4:19
100. Publius, Acts 28:7-8
101. Pudens, 2 Tim. 4:21
102. Quartus, Rom. 16:23
103. Rufus, Rom. 16:13
104. Rufus' mother, Rom. 16:13
105. Secundus, Acts 20:4
106. Sergius Paulus, Acts 13:7
107. Silas, Acts 15:22, 27, 32, 34, 40; 16:19, 25, 29; 17:4, 10, 14, 15; 18:5; 2 Cor. 1:19; 1 Thess. 1:1; 2 Thess. 1:1
108. Simeon called Niger, Acts 13:1
109. a slave girl, Acts 16:16-18
110. Sopater, Acts 20:4
111. Sosipater, Rom. 16:21
112. Sosthenes, Acts 18:17
113. Sosthenes, 1 Cor. 1:1
114. Stachys, Rom. 16:9
115. Stephanas, 1 Cor. 1:16; 16:15, 17
116. Stephen, Acts 11:19; 22:20
117. Syntyche, Phil. 4:2
118. Tertius, Rom. 16:22
119. Tertullus, Acts 24:1-2
120. Timothy, Acts 16:1; 17:14, 15; 18:5; 19:22; 20:4; Rom. 16:21; 1 Cor. 4:17; 16:10; 2 Cor. 1:1, 19; Phil. 1:1; 2:19; Col. 1:1; 1 Thess. 1:1; 3:2, 6; 2 Thess. 1:1; 1 Tim. 1:2, 18; 6:20; 2 Tim. 1:2; Philem. 1; Heb. 13:23
121. Titius Justus, Acts 18:7
122. Titus, 2 Cor. 2:13; 7:6, 13, 14; 8:6, 16, 23; 12:18; Gal. 2:1, 3; 2 Tim. 4:10; Titus 1:4
123. Trophimus, Acts 20:4; 21:29; 2 Tim. 4:20
124. Tryphena, Rom. 16:12
125. Tryphosa, Rom. 16:12
126. Tychicus, Acts 20:4; Eph. 6:21; Col. 4:7; 2 Tim. 4:12; Titus 3:12
127. Tyrannus, Acts 19:9
128. Urbanus, Rom. 16:9
129. Zenas, Titus 3:13

Prophets and Prophetesses

Prophets (*nby'*) in the OT

1. Abraham, Gen. 20:7
2. Aaron, Exod. 7:1
3. 70 elders, Num. 11:25
4. Eldad, Num. 11:27
5. Medad, Num. 11:27
6. A prophet like me [Moses], Deut. 18:15
7. Moses, Deut. 34:10
8. A prophet, Judg. 6:8
9. Samuel, 1 Sam. 3:20
10. A company of prophets, 1 Sam. 10:5
11. Saul, 1 Sam. 10:11-12
12. Saul's messengers, 1 Sam. 19:20
13. Gad, 1 Sam. 22:5
14. Nathan, 1 Kings 1:8
15. Ahijah, 1 Kings 11:29
16. A prophet, 1 Kings 13:11-29
17. An old prophet, 1 Kings 13:11-29
18. Jehu, 1 Kings 16:7
19. 100 prophets, 1 Kings 18:4
20. Elijah, 1 Kings 18:36
21. A prophet, 1 Kings 20:13 (cf. 20:35-43)
22. Micaiah, 1 Kings 22:8

23. Elisha, 2 Kings 6:12
24. Jonah, 2 Kings 14:25
25. Isaiah, 2 Kings 19:2
26. Shemaiah, 2 Chron. 12:15
27. Iddo, 2 Chron. 13:22
28. Azariah, 2 Chron. 15:1-8
29. Oded, 2 Chron. 15:8
30. Hanani, 2 Chron. 16:7-10
31. 400 prophets, 2 Chron. 18:5
32. Jahaziel son of Zechariah, 2 Chron. 20:14-17
33. Eliezer son of Dodavahu, 2 Chron. 20:37
34. Zechariah son of Jehoiada, 2 Chron. 24:20-22
35. Jeremiah, 2 Chron. 36:12
36. Uriah son of Shemaiah, Jer. 26:20-24
37. Hananiah, Jer. 28:15
38. Ezekiel, Ezek. 1:1
39. Daniel, Dan. 1:6
40. Hosea, Hos. 1:1
41. Joel, Joel 1:1
42. Amos, Amos 1:1
43. Obadiah, Obad. 1:1
44. Micah, Mic. 1:1
45. Nahum, Nah. 1:1
46. Habakkuk, Hab. 1:1
47. Zephaniah, Zeph. 1:1
48. Haggai, Hag. 1:1
49. Zechariah, Zech. 1:1
50. Malachi, Mal. 1:1

Prophetesses (nby'h) in the OT

1. Miriam sister of Aaron, Exod. 15:20
2. Deborah wife of Lapidoth, Judg. 4:4
3. Huldah wife of Shallum, 2 Kings 22:14
4. Noadiah, Neh. 6:14
5. Unnamed prophetess, Isa. 8:3

Prophets (*prophētēs*) in the NT

1. Jesus, Matt. 21:11
2. John the Baptist, Luke 7:26-28
3. David, Acts 2:29-30
4. Agabus, Acts 11:28
5. Barnabas, Acts 13:1
6. Lucius of Cyrene, Acts 13:1
7. Manaen, Acts 13:1
8. Saul (Paul), Acts 13:1
9. Simeon called Niger, Acts 13:1
10. Bar-Jesus/Elymas, Acts 13:6
11. Judas, Acts 15:32
12. Silas, Acts 15:32
13. Enoch, Jude 14
14. False prophet, Rev. 19:20

Prophetesses (*prophētis*) in the NT

1. Anna, Luke 2:36
2. Four daughters of Philip, Acts 21:9
3. Jezebel, Rev. 2:20

OT Prophets Named in the NT

1. Jeremiah, Matt. 2:17
2. Isaiah, Matt. 8:17
3. Jonah, Matt. 12:39
4. Elijah, Matt. 16:14
5. Zechariah, Matt. 23:35
6. Daniel, Matt. 24:15
7. Elisha, Luke 4:27
8. Joel, Acts 2:16
9. Moses, Acts 7:37
10. Aaron, Acts 7:40
11. Samuel, Acts 13:20
12. Hosea, Rom. 9:25
13. Balaam, 2 Peter 2:15-16

Quotations of and Allusions to the Apocrypha in the NT

Book	No. of References	NT References
1. 1 Esdras	1	
1:32 (LXX)		Matt. 1:11
2. 2 Esdras	0	
3. Tobit	8	
4:6 (LXX)		John 3:21
5:15		Matt. 20:2
7:17		Matt. 11:25
11:9		Luke 15:20
13:7, 11		Rev. 15:3
13:18		Rev. 19:1
14:4		Matt. 23:38
14:5		Luke 21:24
4. Judith	3	
11:19		Matt. 9:36; Mark 6:34
16:17		James 5:3
5. Additions to Esther	0	
6. The Wisdom of Solomon	26	
2:11		Rom. 9:31
2:18-20		Matt. 27:43

Based on the indexes of K. Aland et al., eds., *The Greek New Testament* (New York: United Bible Societies, 1968).

Book	No. of References	NT References
2:23		1 Cor. 11:7
3:8		1 Cor. 6:2
4:10		Heb. 11:5
5:5		Acts 20:32; 26:18
5:15		1 John 2:17
5:18		Eph. 6:14; 1 Thess. 5:8
5:22		Luke 21:25
6:18		John 14:15
7:1		Acts 10:26
7:7		Eph. 1:17
9:1		John 1:3
9:16		John 3:12
12:12		Rom. 9:20
12:13-14		Acts 5:39
14:3		1 Peter 1:17
15:3		John 17:3
15:7		Rom. 9:21
16:9		Rev. 9:3
16:13		Matt. 16:18
16:22		Rev. 8:7
18:1		Acts 9:7; 22:9
7. Ecclesiasticus	34	
1:8		Rev. 4:2, 9, 10; 5:1, 7, 13; 6:16; 7:10, 15; 19:4; 21:5
1:10		1 Cor. 2:9
5:3		1 Thess. 4:6
5:11		James 1:6
5:13		James 1:19
11:19		Luke 12:19-20
15:11-13		James 1:13
16:14		Rom. 2:6
23:1		Matt. 6:13
23:4		1 Peter 1:17
25:23		Heb. 12:12
27:6		Matt. 7:16
28:2		Matt. 6:12
28:18		Luke 21:24

Book	No. of References	NT References
29:11		Matt. 6:20; Luke 18:22
33:1		Matt. 6:13
35:19		Matt. 16:27
37:28		1 Cor. 6:12
38:18		2 Cor. 7:10
44:16		Heb. 11:5
44:21		Gal. 3:8; Heb. 6:14; 11:12
48:10		Luke 1:17
8. Baruch	2	
4:7		1 Cor. 10:20
4:35		Rev. 18:2
9. The Song of the Three Children	0	
10. Susanna	1	(Theodotion) Matt. 27:24
11. Bel and the Dragon	0	
12. The Prayer of Manasseh	0	
13. 1 Maccabees	6	
1:54		Matt. 24:15; Mark 13:14
2:60		2 Tim. 4:17
3:45, 51		Luke 21:24
4:59		John 10:22
6:7		Matt. 24:15
14. 2 Maccabees	5	
3:26		Luke 24:4
6:18–7:42		Heb. 11:35
13:4		1 Tim. 6:15; Rev. 17:14; 19:16
Total	87	

Quotations of and
Allusions to the
Pseudepigrapha in the NT

Book	No. of References	NT References
1. The Book of Jubilees	0	
2. The Letter of Aristeas	0	
3. The Life of Adam and Eve	0	
4. The Martyrdom of Isaiah	1	
5:11-14		Heb. 11:37
5. 1 Enoch	14	
1:2		1 Peter 1:12
1:9		Jude 14-15
9:4		Rev. 15:3; 17:14; 19:16
14:22		Rev. 5:11
25:5		Rev. 15:3
27:3		Rev. 15:3
46:3		Col. 2:3
51:2		Luke 21:28
60:8		Jude 14
63:10		Luke 16:9
69:27		John 5:22
70:1-4		Heb. 11:5

Based on the indexes of K. Aland et al., eds., *The Greek New Testament* (New York: United Bible Societies, 1968).

Book	No. of References	NT References
6. The Testament of the Twelve	0	
7. The Sibylline Oracles	0	
8. The Assumption of Moses	1	
—[1]		Jude 9
9. 2 Enoch	0	
10. 2 Baruch	0	
11. 3 Baruch	0	
12. 4 Ezra	0	
13. The Psalms of Solomon	6	
5:4		Luke 11:21–22
5:9–11 (LXX)		Matt. 6:26
7:6		John 1:14
17:23–24		Rev. 2:26–27
17:34(31)		Rev. 21:24, 26
14. 3 Maccabees	6	
2:5		Rev. 14:10; 20:10; 21:8
5:35		1 Tim. 6:15; Rev. 17:14; 19:16
15. 4 Maccabees	2	
2:5		Rom. 7:7
7:19		Matt. 22:32
16. Pirke Aboth	0	
17. The Story of Ahikar	0	
18. The Zadokite Work	0	
Total	30	

1. *The Assumption of Moses,* as it presently exists, is a combination of two written sources. We can give no explicit reference here because this combined work does not contain the actual material found in Jude 9.

Riddles

1. God spoke to Moses face to face, not in riddles, Num. 12:8.
2. Samson told a riddle about a lion and some honey, Judg. 14:12-20.
3. The Queen of Sheba tested Solomon with riddles (usually translated "hard questions"), 1 Kings 10:1.
4. The psalmists mention the word "riddle" (*hydh*) twice, Ps. 49:4; 78:2.
5. One of the purposes of Proverbs is to gain an understanding of proverbs, parables, and riddles, Prov. 1:6.
6. God directed Ezekiel to tell a riddle, Ezek. 17:2.
7. In Daniel, Antiochus Epiphanes is described as one who understands riddles, Dan. 8:23.
8. Habakkuk taunts the rich with a riddle, Hab. 2:6.
9. The only true riddle in the NT is Rev. 13:18.

Rivers

Several terms used in the Bible are translated by the English word "river." In the OT the terms include: *nhr* (Gen. 2:10), *nhl* (Deut. 2:37), *y'r* (Gen. 41:1), *ywbl* (Jer. 17:8), *'pyqym* (Ezek. 6:3), *plgym* (Job 29:6). The translation *river* is often misleading, since the terms are used to refer to rivers, brooks, streams, canals, ravines, valleys, wadis, etc. *Potamos* is used in the LXX and the NT for the preceding terms.

1. River of Eden, Gen. 2:10
2. Pishon, Gen. 2:11
3. Gihon, Gen. 2:13
4. Tigris (Hiddekel), Gen. 2:14
5. Euphrates, Gen. 2:14
6. River of Egypt (Nile), Gen. 15:18
7. Arnon, Deut. 2:24
8. Jabbok, Deut. 2:37
9. Kanah, Josh. 16:8
10. Kishon, Judg. 4:13
11. Abana, 2 Kings 5:12
12. Pharpar, 2 Kings 5:12
13. Gozan (or the Habor River), 2 Kings 17:6
14. Ahava, Ezra 8:21
15. Rivers of God, Ps. 65:9
16. Rivers of Babylon, Ps. 137:1
17. Rivers of Egypt, Isa. 7:18

18. Rivers of Ethiopia, Isa. 18:1
19. Kebar, Ezek. 1:1
20. River of the Temple, Ezek. 47:1-2
21. Ulai, Dan. 8:2
22. Jordan, Mark 1:5
23. River outside Philippi, Acts 16:13
24. River of Life, Rev. 22:1; cf. John 7:38

Rivers

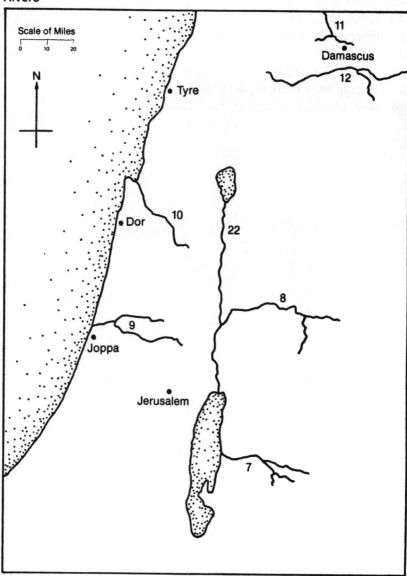

Rivers

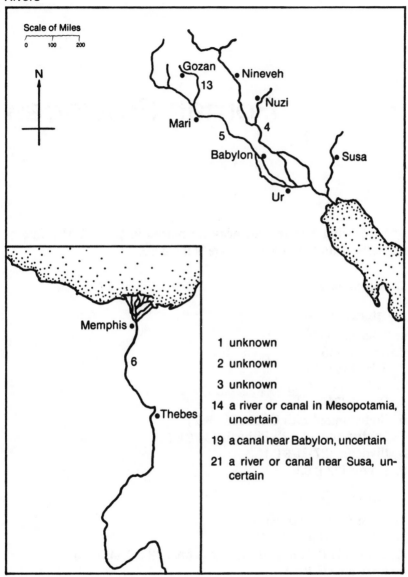

Scale of Miles

0   100   200

N

Gozan

13

Nineveh

Nuzi

Mari

4

5

Babylon

Susa

Ur

Memphis

6

Thebes

1 unknown

2 unknown

3 unknown

14 a river or canal in Mesopotamia, uncertain

19 a canal near Babylon, uncertain

21 a river or canal near Susa, uncertain

265

Roman Provinces

The following Roman provinces are named in the NT. The date of admission into the Roman Empire is included.

Classifications

Senatorial Provinces

1. Macedonia (146 B.C.)
2. Achaia (146 B.C.)
3. Asia (133 B.C.)
4. Bithynia (74 B.C.)
5. Cyrene (74 B.C.)
6. Crete, united with Cyrene (67 B.C.)
7. Pontus, united with Bithynia (64 B.C.)
8. Illyricum (27-11 B.C.)
9. Cyprus (22 B.C.)

Imperial Provinces

1st Class (ruled by consuls)
1. Syria (64 B.C.)
2. Cilicia (64 B.C., united with Syria from 22 B.C.-A.D. 72)
3. Illyricum (11 B.C.)
4. Dalmatia (A.D. 9)

Dates for the Roman provinces based on B. Reicke, *The New Testament Era*, trans. D. E. Green (Philadelphia: Fortress, 1968).

2nd Class (ruled by praetors)
1. Pamphylia (part of Cilicia from 102-44 B.C., united with Asia from 44 B.C.-A.D. 43, and united with Lycia after A.D. 43)
2. Egypt (30 B.C.)
3. Galatia (25 B.C.-A.D. 72; after A.D. 72 it was united with Cappadocia and Armenia Minor and made a 1st Class province)
4. Lycia (A.D. 43-69)

3rd Class (ruled by procurators)
1. Judea (A.D. 6-41, 44-70, part of Syria from 63-40 B.C.)
2. Cappadocia (A.D. 17-72, after A.D. 72 it was united with Galatia and Armenia Minor and made a 1st Class province)

Provinces and Tetrarchies of Palestine

1. Judea
2. Samaria
3. Galilee
4. Iturea
5. Abilene
6. Syria

7. Trachonitis
8. Batanea
9. Decapolis
10. Perea
11. Idumea
12. Nabatea

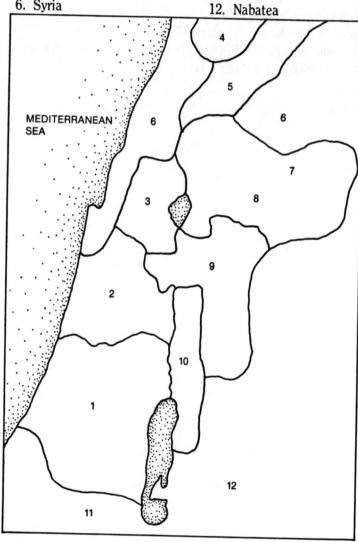

Provinces of Asia Minor

1. Asia
2. Bithynia and Pontus
3. Galatia
4. Armenia Minor
5. Armenia
6. Syria

7. Commagene
8. Cilicia
9. Cappadocia
10. Cilicia Trachea
11. Pamphylia
12. Lycia

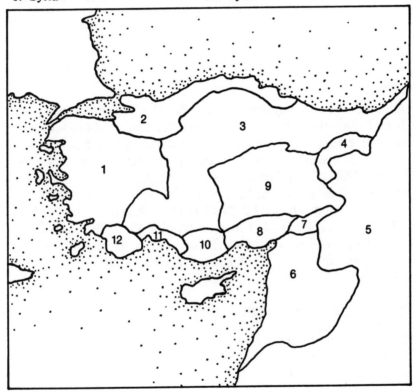

Spiritual Gifts

Although not expressly designated "gifts," there are many instances in the OT where the Spirit of God came upon certain individuals (usually a prophet, a king, or a leader) to provide divine enablement for specific tasks (e.g., leadership, decision making, prophesying, military ability, artistic ability). The OT passages where the Spirit of God provided divine enablement for specific tasks or ministries are listed here: Exod. 28:3; 31:3; 35:31; Num. 11:25; 24:2; 27:18; Deut. 34:9; Judg. 3:10; 6:34; 11:29; 13:25; 14:6, 14, 19; 15:14; 1 Sam. 10:10; 11:6; 16:13; 19:20, 23; 2 Sam. 23:2; 1 Kings 18:12; 2 Kings 2:15-16; 1 Chron. 12:18; 2 Chron. 15:1; 24:20; Isa. 48:16; 61:1; 63:14; Ezek. 2:2; 3:12, 14, 24; 8:3; 11:1, 5, 24; 37:1; 43:5.

The Gifts (*charismata*) in Rom. 12:6-8

1. prophesying (*prophēteian*)
2. serving (*diakonian*)
3. teaching (*didaskōn*)
4. encouraging (*parakalōn*)
5. contributing (*metadidous*)
6. leadership (*proistamenos*)
7. showing mercy (*eleōn*)

The Spiritual Gifts (*pneumatikōn*) in 1 Cor. 12:7-11

1. the message of wisdom (*logos sophias*)
2. the message of knowledge (*logos gnōseōs*)

3. faith (*pistis*)
4. gifts of healing (*charismata iamatōn*)
5. miraculous powers (*energēmata dunameōn*)
6. prophecy (*prophēteia*)
7. distinguishing between spirits (*diakriseis pneumatōn*)
8. speaking in different tongues (*genē glōssōn*)
9. interpreting tongues (*hermēneia glōssōn*)

The Gifts in Eph. 4:11–13

1. apostles (*apostolous*)
2. prophets (*prophētas*)
3. evangelists (*euangelistas*)
4. pastors, teachers (*poimenas kai didaskalous*)

The Gifts (*charisma*) in 1 Peter 4:10–11

1. speaking (*lalei*)
2. serving (*diakonei*)

The Tabernacle (Exodus 25–38)

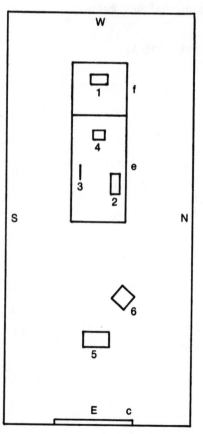

Furniture

1. ark of the covenant
2. table of shewbread
3. golden lampstand
4. altar of incense
5. altar of burnt offering
6. basin

Furniture (Exod. 37–38)

1. the ark (*'rwn*), 37:1-9, 2½ cubits (3¾') by 1½ cubits (2¼') by 1½ cubits (2¼')
   the mercy seat/cover (*kpwrt*), 37:6, 2½ cubits (3¾') by 1½ cubits (2¼')
   the poles (*bdym*), 37:4
2. the table (*šlhn*), 37:10-16, 2 cubits (3') by 1 cubit (1½') by 1½ cubits (2¼')
   poles (*bdym*), 37:15
   plates (*qᶜrh*), 37:16
   ladles (*kp*), 37:16
   bowls (*mnqyt*), 37:16
   pitchers (*qśwh*), 37:16
3. the lampstand (*mnwrh*), 37:17-24
   lamps (*nyr*), 37:23
   snuffers (*mlqhym*), 37:23
   trays (*mhth*), 37:23
4. the altar of incense (*mzbh qtwrt*), 37:25-29, 1 cubit (1½') by 1 cubit (1½') by 2 cubits (3')
   poles (*bydm*), 37:28
5. the altar of burnt offering (*mzbh ᶜwlh*), 38:1-7, 5 cubits (7½') by 5 cubits (7½') by 3 cubits (4½')
   pots (*syr*), 38:3
   shovels (*yᶜh*), 38:3
   bowls (*mzrq*), 38:3
   forks (*mzlg*), 38:3
   firepans (*mhth*), 38:3
6. the basin (*kywr*), 38:8
   stand (*kn*), 38:8

Dimensions of the Tabernacle

a. courtyard: 100 cubits (150') by 50 cubits (75')
b. curtains: 5 cubits high (7½')
c. entrance curtain: 20 cubits (30') by 5 cubits (7½')
d. tabernacle proper: 30 cubits (45') by 10 cubits (15')

273

e. the holy place: 20 cubits (30′) by 10 cubits (15′) by 10 cubits (15′)

f. the most holy place: 10 cubits (15′) by 10 cubits (15′) by 10 cubits (15′)

g. tabernacle curtains: 10 curtains, 28 cubits (42′) by 4 cubits (6′); 11 curtains, 30 cubits (45′) by 4 cubits (6′)

h. tabernacle frames: 48 frames, 10 cubits (15′) by 1½ cubits (2¼′)

Time

The Jews divided the day into 12 equal parts, beginning at 6:00 A.M. and ending at 6:00 P.M. Apparently the Babylonians were the first to adopt this division of time. According to Herodotus (ii, 109) the Greeks adopted this practice from the Babylonians. It is possible the Jews adopted the custom while in captivity in Babylon. The term for *hour* (Aram. *sha'ah*) occurs in Daniel 3:6 and 5:5. In the NT the third, sixth, and ninth hours (Grk. *hōra*) are frequently mentioned (cf. John 11:9).

The Jewish Day

6:00 A.M.	sunrise, end of fourth watch, Mark 16:2
7:00	first hour
8:00	second hour
9:00	third hour, first hour of prayer, Acts 2:15
10:00	fourth hour
11:00	fifth hour
12:00	sixth hour, noon, Matt. 20:5
1:00 P.M.	seventh hour, John 4:52
2:00	eighth hour

The NT reflects the Roman system of four night watches, rather than the Jewish system of three night watches. The first watch for the Jews was 6:00 to 10:00 P.M. (cf. Lam 2:19), the second watch from 10:00 P.M. to 2:00 A.M. (cf. Judg. 7:19), and the third watch from 2:00 to 6:00 A.M. (cf. Exod. 14:24). See further, J. Finegan, *Handbook of Biblical Chronology* (Princeton: Princeton University Press, 1964).

3:00	ninth hour, Matt. 27:45, hour of prayer, Acts 3:1
4:00	tenth hour, John 1:39
5:00	eleventh hour, Matt. 20:6
6:00	sunset, beginning of first watch
7:00	
8:00	
9:00	end of first watch, beginning of second watch, Luke 12:38
10:00	
11:00	
12:00	midnight, Acts 16:25, end of second watch, beginning of third watch, Luke 12:38
1:00 A.M.	
2:00	
3:00	end of third watch, beginning of fourth watch, Matt. 14:25, Mark 6:48, cockcrow, Matt. 26:75, Mark 13:35
4:00	
5:00	

Weights and Measures

Old Testament

Weights

Hebrew	English	Equivalence	U.S. Avoirdupois	Metric
grh	gerah		8.81 grains	.6 grams
bqʻ	beka	10 gerahs	88.14 grains	6.0 grams
šql	shekel	2 bekas	176.29 grains	11.0 grams
mnh	mina	50 shekels	1.10 pounds	500.0 grams
kkr	talent	60 minas	66.00 pounds	30.0 kilograms

The royal (heavy) shekel weighed .5 oz. or 13 grams. The double-standard (heavy) talent weighed 135 lbs. or 60 kg.

gerah (*grh*; Assyr. *giru*): ¹⁄₂₀ of a shekel (Exod. 30:13; Ezek. 45:12).

beka (*bqʻ*): used in the weighing of gold (Gen. 24:22) and for paying the poll-tax (Exod. 38:26).

shekel (*šql*; Akkad. *šiqlu*; Aram. and Ugar. *ṯql*): the basic weight of all Semitic metrologies. Royal shekel (2 Sam. 14:26); common shekel (1 Sam. 17:5; 2 Kings 7:1; Ezek. 4:10); temple shekel (Exod. 30:13; Lev. 5:15) was equivalent to a beka or ½ shekel (later it equaled ⅓ shekel, cf. Neh. 10:32).

mina (*mnh*; Akkad. *manu*): common in the weighing of gold, silver, etc. (1 Kings 10:17; Ezra 2:69; Neh. 7:71; cf. Gen. 23:15; Exod. 30:24). The common mina was equivalent to 50 shekels. The mina in Ezek. 45:12 is equivalent to 60 shekels.

talent (*kkr*): the heaviest unit of weight. Used especially in the weighing of metals (Zech. 5:7; 2 Sam. 12:30; 1 Kings 20:39; 1 Chron. 29:7; Exod. 38:29, cf. 1 Kings 10:14; 2 Kings 18:14).

pim (*pm*; 1 Sam. 13:21): a weight, apparently ⅔ of a shekel.

peres (*prs*; Dan. 5:25, 28): a subdivision of the shekel used in Babylon. Perhaps ½ of a shekel (?).

qesitah (*qśyth*; Gen. 33:19; Josh. 24:32; Job 42:11): an unknown weight.

Dry Measures

Hebrew	English	Equivalence	U.S. Measures	Metric
lg	log		.32 quart	.30 liter
qb	qab (kab)	4 logs	1.35 quarts	1.20 liters
'mr	omer	7 logs	2.30 quarts	2.20 liters
ṣ'h	measure (seah)	6 qabs	1.00 peck	7.30 liters
'ph	ephah	3 measures	.75 bushel	22.00 liters
ltk	lethech	5 ephahs	3.75 bushels	110.00 liters
ḥmr	homer	2 lethechs	7.50 bushels	220.00 liters

The *śrn* (¹⁄₁₀ of an ephah) is equivalent to the omer.

The *ḥmr* is a dry and a liquid measure and is equivalent to the cor.

log (*lg*): a measure of oil. It occurs only in Lev. 14:10.

qab (*qb*): occurs only in 2 Kings 6:25.

omer ('*mr*): occurs only in Exod. 16:16, 18, 22, 32, 33, 36. The omer is ¹⁄₁₀ of an ephah.

tenth-part ('*śrn*): a measure for flour equivalent to the omer (Exod. 39:40; Num. 15:4; 28:5).

seah (*ṣ'h*; Akkad. *sutu*): a measure for grain and flour (Gen. 18:6; 1 Kings 18:32).

ephah ('*ph*): a measure for grains (Lev. 19:36; Judg. 6:19; Amos 8:5; Prov. 20:10).

lethech (*ltk*): used only in Hosea 3:2 as a measure for barley equivalent to ½ homer.

homer (*ḥmr*; Akkad. *imēr*): commonly called "a donkey load." Used as a measure for grains (Lev. 27:16; Ezek. 45:13) and quails (Num. 11:32).

shalish (*šlš*; Ps. 80:5; Isa. 40:12): literally "a third." The exact capacity of this measure is unknown.

artaba (Grk. *artabe*; Bel and Dragon 3): a measure for grain equal to 1.8 bushels.

Liquid Measures

Hebrew	English	Equivalence	U.S. Measures	Metric
lg	log		.67 pint	.30 liter
qb	qab	4 logs	1.35 quarts	1.20 liters
hn	hin	3 qabs	1.01 gallons	3.60 liters
bt	bath	6 hins	6.07 gallons	22.10 liters
kr	cor/measure	10 baths	60.74 gallons	220.10 liters

The *kr* is a liquid and a dry measure and is equivalent to the *ḥmr.*

log (*lg*): a measure of oil. It occurs only in Lev. 14:10.

qab (*qb*): occurs only in 2 Kings 6:25.

hin (*hn*; Egyp. *hnw*): used for the measure of wine (Lev. 23:13); water (Ezek. 4:11); oil (Exod. 29:40).

bath (*bt*): a common liquid measure and the liquid equivalent of the ephah (Ezek. 45:11, 14; 1 Kings 7:26; Isa. 5:10).

cor (*kr*; Akkad. *gur*): a large measure equal to the homer (Ezek. 45:14; 1 Kings 4:22; 2 Chron. 2:10), used to measure wheat and barley and oil.

Measures of Length

Hebrew	English	Equivalence	U.S. Measures	Metric
ṣbʻ	finger		.73 inch	19.00 mm.
tph	handbreadth	4 fingers	2.90 inches	76.00 mm.
zrt	span	3 handbreadths	8.75 inches	230.00 mm.
gmd	gomed	⅔ cubit	12.00 inches	300.00 mm.
'mh	cubit	2 spans	17.50 inches	445.00 mm.
qnh	reed	6 cubits	105.00 inches	2,670.00 mm.

The "long cubit" of Ezekiel (40:5; 43:13) is equal to seven handbreadths (20.40 in.).

finger or digit (*ṣbʻ*): the smallest division of a cubit (Jer. 52:21).

handbreadth or palm (*tph*): the width of the hand at the base of the four fingers (1 Kings 7:26; Exod. 25:25; Ezek. 40:5).

span (*zrt*): Exod. 28:16; 1 Sam. 17:4; Ezek. 43:13.

gomed (*gmd*): occurs only in Judg. 3:16, where it measures a weapon.

cubit (*'mh*; Akkad. *ammātu*): the distance from the elbow to the finger tip (Deut. 3:11; 1 Sam. 17:4; Esther 5:14; Gen. 7:20).

long cubit: equivalent to seven handbreadths (Ezek. 40:5; 43:13).

reed (*qnh*): a length of six cubits (Ezek. 40:5).

Biblical Data

Measure of Area

Hebrew	English	Equivalence	U.S. Measures
ṣmd[1]	acre		?

[1]The *ṣmd* was the area a pair of yoked animals could plow in a day. In Babylonia this was computed as 6,480 square cubits (⅖ of an acre). During the Roman period this was equivalent to the Latin *jugum* (28,800 square feet or ⅝ acre). Another method of determining area was to estimate the amount of seed required to sow it (cf. Lev. 27:16; 1 Kings 18:32).

New Testament

Weights

Greek	English	Equivalence	U.S. Avoirdupois	Metric
litra	pound	Latin libra	.72 pounds	327 grams
mina	pound	Hebrew mina	1.10 pounds	500 grams
talenton	talent	Hebrew talent	66.0 pounds	30 kilograms

litra: John 12:3; 19:39. The term is used in reference to precious oil. It may be a weight or a measure of capacity here. The *litra* was probably the Roman pound of 11.5 ounces or 327 grams.

mina: Luke 19:13-25. The term apparently refers to a sum of money and not a weight.

talenton: Rev. 16:21. There is no consensus on the weight of the NT talent; estimates range from 45 to 90 pounds.

Dry Measures

Greek	English	Equivalence	U.S. Measures	Metric
xestēs	pot	Latin sextarius	.96 pint	.44 liter
choinix	quart		.98 quart	.91 liter
modios	bushel	Latin modius/ 16 sextarii	7.68 quarts	8.70 liters
saton	measure	1.5 modii/ Hebrew seah	11.52 quarts	13.00 liters
koros	measure	10 metrētēs/ Hebrew cov	103.00 gallons	395.00 liters

pot (*xestēs;* Mark 7:4, 8): The *xestēs* was a dry and a liquid measure.

quart (*choinix;* Rev. 6:6): According to Herodotus (vii. 187), it was the daily ration of grain for a soldier in Xerxes' army.

bushel (*modios*): Matt. 5:15; Mark 4:21; Luke 11:33.

measure (*saton;* Matt. 13:33; Luke 13:21): Cf. Josephus, *Ant.* ix. 4.5.

measure (*koros;* Luke 16:7): The *koros* was a dry and a liquid measure. According to Josephus (*Ant.* xv. 9.2), the *koros* was equivalent to 157 gallons or 525 litres. Apparently Josephus mistook the *medimnos* for the *metrētēs* (cf. Ezek. 45:11, where the *batos* is rated as 1/10 of a *koros*).

Liquid Measures

Greek	English	Equivalence	U.S. Measures	Metric
xestēs	pot	Latin sextarius	1.17 pints	.54 liter
batos	measure	Hebrew bath	6.07 gallons	22.10 liters
metrētēs	measure/ firkin		10.30 gallons	39.50 liters

pot (*xestēs;* Mark 7:4, 8): a dry and a liquid measure

measure (*batos;* Luke 21:6): a measure for oil. According to Josephus (*Ant.* viii. 2.9), the *batos* is nearly equivalent to the *metrētēs* (72 sextarii) or between 8-9 gallons

measure (*metrētēs;* John 2:6): a measure for liquids.

Biblical Data

Measures of Length

Greek	English	U.S. Measures	Metric
pēchus	cubit	21.60 inches	550.00 millimeters
orguia	fathom	72.44 inches	1.85 meters
stadion	furlong/ stadium	606.00 feet	185.00 meters
milion	mile	4,824.00 feet	1,478.00 meters

During the rule of the Roman Empire the Jewish cubit measured slightly longer than the cubit of the OT (17.5 in.). A Sabbath day's journey was fixed at 2,000 cubits.

cubit (*pēchus*): during Roman times the Jewish cubit measured 21.6 inches (John 21:8; Rev. 21:17; Matt. 6:27; Luke 12:25).

fathom (*orguia*): the length of outstretched arms, about six feet (Acts 27:28).

furlong (*stadion*): according to tradition the race course at Olympia was one stade long, hence the use of the word *stadium* for an arena (1 Cor. 9:24; cf. Luke 24:13; John 6:19; 11:18; Rev. 14:20).

mile (*milion*): the Roman mile was equivalent to eight stadia or 1,618 yards or 1,478 meters.

Measure of Area

No measures of area are used in the NT. The Roman unit of measure was the acre (*jugerum*) and was based upon the amount of land a yoke of oxen could plow in one day. This was calculated at 2 square furrows (*actus*) or 120 by 240 feet, about 3,200 square yards or 28,800 square feet. (See also Hebrew Measure of Area above).

Other sources will vary slightly from the above figures for OT and NT weights and measures as there is no absolute fixation of equivalents for many of the biblical weights and measures. These lists represent a compilation of data from several sources, including W. F. Arndt and F. W. Gingrich, *A Greek-English Lexicon of the New Testament* (Chicago: University of Chicago Press, 1957); W. L. Holloday, *A Concise Hebrew and Aramaic Lexicon of the Old Testament* (Grand Rapids: Eerdmans, 1971); F. B. Huey, "Weights and Measures," in *Zondervan Pictorial Encyclopedia of the Bible*, ed. M. C. Tenney (Grand Rapids: Zondervan, 1975); *Josephus* (The Loeb Classical Library), trans. H. St. J. Thackeray and R. Marcus (Cambridge, MA: Harvard University Press, 1950), 9 vols.; A. R. S. Kennedy, "Weights and Measures," in *Hastings Dictionary of the Bible*, ed. J. Hastings (Edinburgh: T. and T. Clark, 1900); R. B. Y. Scott, "Weights and Measures of the Bible," *Biblical Archaeologist* XXII/2 (1959); J. Walton, *Chronological Charts of the Old Testament* (Grand Rapids: Zondervan, 1978); D. J. Wiseman and D. H. Wheaton, "Weights and Measures," in *The New Bible Dictionary*, ed. J. D. Douglas (Grand Rapids: Eerdmans, 1965).

Women

Well-known Women of the OT

1. Abigail, 1 Sam. 25:3-42; 2 Sam. 2:2; 3:3
2. Athaliah, 2 Kings 8:26; 11:1-20; 2 Chron. 22:2-12; 23:12-21
3. Bathsheba, 2 Sam. 11:3; 12:24; 1 Kings 1:11-31
4. Beloved, Song of Sol. 1:8
5. Deborah, Judg. 4-5
6. Delilah, Judg. 16
7. Dinah, Gen. 34
8. Esther, Esther 2:7
9. Eve, Gen. 3:20; 4:1
10. Ezekiel's wife, Ezek. 24:15-27
11. Gomer, Hos. 1:3
12. Hagar, Gen. 16; 21
13. Hannah, 1 Sam. 1-2
14. Huldah, 2 Kings 22:14
15. Jael, Judg. 4:17
16. Jezebel, 1 Kings 16:31; 18:4, 13; 19:1-2; 21; 2 Kings 9
17. Job's wife, Job 2:9
18. Jochebed, Exod. 2; 6:20
19. Leah, Gen. 29:16-32; 30:9-20; 31:4, 14; 33:1-7
20. Lot's daughters, Gen. 19:30-38
21. Lot's wife, Gen. 19:26

22. Michal, 1 Sam. 14:49; 18:20, 27-28; 19:11-17; 25:44; 2 Sam. 3:13-14; 6:16-23
23. Miriam, Exod. 15:20-21; Num. 12:1-15; Deut. 24:9
24. Naomi, Ruth 1:2
25. Potiphar's wife, Gen. 39
26. Queen of Sheba, 1 Kings 10; 2 Chron. 9
27. Rachel, Gen. 29; 30; 31:4-35; 33:1-7; 46:19-25; 48:7
28. Rahab, Josh. 2:1-3; 6:17-25
29. Rebekah, Gen. 22:23; 24:15-67; 25:20-28; 26:7-35; 27:5-46; 28:5; 49:31
30. Ruth, Ruth 1:4
31. Sarah, Gen. 11-12; 16-17; 18; 20-21; 23; 24:36; 25:10; 49:31
32. Tamar, Gen. 38
33. Tamar, 2 Sam. 13
34. Vashti, Esther 1-2
35. Widow of Zarephath, 1 Kings 17:7-24
36. Witch of Endor, 1 Sam. 28:7-8
37. Woman of Shunem, 2 Kings 4
38. Zelophehad's daughters, Num. 27; 36
39. Zipporah, Exod. 2:21

Women in the NT

1. Anna, Luke 2:36
2. Apphia, Philem. 2
3. Bernice, Acts 25:13
4. Chloe, 1 Cor. 1:11
5. Claudia, 2 Tim. 4:21
6. Damaris, Acts 17:34
7. Daughters of Jerusalem, Luke 23:27-28
8. Dorcas, Acts 9:36
9. Drusilla, Acts 24:24
10. Elect lady, 2 John 1 (a lady or a church ?)
11. Elizabeth, Luke 1:40
12. Eunice, 2 Tim. 1:5
13. Euodia, Phil. 4:2
14. Herodias, Matt. 14:3
15. Herodias' daughter, Matt. 14:6

16. Jairus' daughter, Mark 5:22-23
17. Jesus' sisters, Matt. 13:56
18. Jezebel, Rev. 2:20
19. Joanna, Luke 8:3
20. Julia, Rom. 16:15
21. Lois, 2 Tim. 1:5
22. Lydia, Acts 16:14, 40
23. Martha of Bethany, John 11:1
24. Mary, the mother of James and John, Mark 16:1
25. Mary, the mother of Jesus, Matt. 13:55
26. Mary, the mother of John Mark, Acts 12:12
27. Mary, wife of Clopas, John 19:25
28. Mary of Bethany, John 11:1
29. Mary of Rome, Rom. 16:6
30. Mary Magdalene, Luke 8:2
31. Nereus' sister, Rom. 16:15
32. Nympha, Col. 4:15
33. Other women, Luke 8:3
34. Persis, Rom. 16:12
35. Peter's mother-in-law, Luke 4:38-39
36. Philip's daughters, Acts 21:9
37. Phoebe, Rom. 16:1
38. Priscilla, Acts 18:2
39. Rhoda, Acts 12:13
40. Rufus' mother, Rom. 16:13
41. Salome, Mark 16:1
42. Samaritan woman, John 4:7
43. Sapphira, Acts 5:1
44. Servant girl, Matt. 26:69
45. Servant girl, Matt. 26:71
46. Sinful woman, Luke 7:37-38
47. Slave girl, Acts 16:16-18
48. Susanna, Luke 8:3
49. Syntyche, Phil. 4:2
50. Syrian Phoenician woman, Mark 7:24-30
51. Tryphena, Rom. 16:12
52. Tryphosa, Rom. 16:12
53. Widow of Nain, Luke 7:11-17

54. Widow who gave two coins, Mark 12:41-44
55. Widows, Acts 6:1
56. Wife of Peter, 1 Cor. 9:5
57. Wives of the apostles, 1 Cor. 9:5
58. Wives of the Lord's brothers, 1 Cor. 9:5
59. Woman caught in adultery, John 8:3
60. Woman in the crowd, Luke 11:27-28
61. Woman who was crippled, Luke 13:11
62. Woman with a hemorrhage, Mark 5:25-29
63. Women, Acts 1:14
64. Women, Acts 17:4
65. Women, Acts 17:12

Women Associated with Christ's Ministry

1. Mary, the mother of Jesus, Matt. 1:18
2. Jesus' sisters, Matt. 13:56
3. Syrian Phoenician woman, Mark 7:24-30
4. Salome, Mark 15:40
5. Jairus' daughter, Mark 5:22-23
6. Widow who gave two coins, Mark 12:41-44
7. Woman with a hemorrhage, Mark 5:25-29
8. Elizabeth, Luke 1:39-40
9. Anna, Luke 2:36
10. Mary, the mother of James the younger and Joses, Mark 15:40
11. Peter's mother-in-law, Luke 4:38-39
12. Widow of Nain, Luke 7:11-17
13. Sinful woman, Luke 7:37-38
14. Mary Magdalene, Luke 8:2
15. Joanna, Luke 8:3
16. Susanna, Luke 8:3
17. Other women, Luke 8:3
18. Woman in the crowd, Luke 11:27-28
19. Crippled woman, Luke 13:11
20. "Daughters of Jerusalem," Luke 23:27-28
21. Samaritan woman, John 4:7
22. Adulteress, John 8:3
23. Martha of Bethany, John 11:1

24. Mary of Bethany, John 11:1
25. Mary, the wife of Clopas, John 19:25

Women Associated with Paul's Ministry

1. Apphia, Philem. 2
2. Bernice, Acts 25:13, 23; 26:30
3. Chloe, 1 Cor. 1:11
4. Claudia, 2 Tim. 4:21
5. Damaris, Acts 17:34
6. Drusilla, Acts 24:24
7. Eunice, 2 Tim. 1:5
8. Euodia, Phil. 4:2
9. Julia, Rom. 16:15
10. Lois, 2 Tim. 1:5
11. Lydia, Acts 16:14, 40
12. Mary, Rom. 16:6
13. Nereus' sister, Rom. 16:15
14. Nympha, Col. 4:15
15. Persis, Rom. 16:12
16. Philip's daughters, Acts 21:9
17. Phoebe, Rom. 16:1
18. Priscilla, Acts 18:2, 18, 26; Rom. 16:3; 1 Cor. 16:19; 2 Tim. 4:19
19. Rufus' mother, Rom. 16:13
20. Slave girl, Acts 16:16–18
21. Syntyche, Phil. 4:2
22. Tryphena, Rom. 16:12
23. Tryphosa, Rom. 16:12